The librarian's guide to
Microcomputers for information management

The librarian's guide to
Microcomputers for information management

PAUL F. BURTON
and
J. HOWARD PETRIE

 Van Nostrand Reinhold (UK) Co. Ltd

First published in 1984 as *Introducing Microcomputers:
a guide for librarians* by
Van Nostrand Reinhold (UK) Co. Ltd
Molly Millars Lane, Wokingham,
Berkshire, England

Reprinted 1985
This edition 1986

Typeset in Plantin 10 on 12pt by
Columns of Reading

Printed in Great Britain by
The Thetford Press Ltd, Thetford, Norfolk

Library of Congress Cataloging-in-Publication Data

Burton, Paul F.
   The librarian's guide to microcomputers for
information management.

   Bibliography: p.
   Includes index.
   1. Libraries—Automation.   2. Library science—
Data processing.   3. Microcomputers—Library
applications.   I. Petrie, J. Howard.   II. Title.
Z678.9.B86   1986   025.3′028′5   86–19072
ISBN 0–442–31770–0

British Library Cataloguing in Publication Data

Burton, Paul F.
   The librarian's guide to microcomputers
for information management.

   I. Microcomputers—Library applications
   I. Title   II. Petrie, J. Howard
   III. Burton, Paul F. Introducing
microcomputers

025′.0028′5416   Z678.9
ISBN 0–442–31770–0

Contents

Preface

When we prepared *Introducing Microcomputers: a guide for librarians* we were conscious that the speed with which microcomputer technology was changing meant that a new edition would be needed within a few years (on the assumption that the book was successful in the first place!). It was well received, but such has been the pace of development in this area that a new edition proved necessary after two years, if the book was to continue to be of value to practising librarians and students. We have, therefore, made many changes, although the overall pattern of the previous edition has been maintained.

The chapters on hardware have been revised to reflect the many changes in that area, and some emphasis has been given to the optical disk, since it is the authors' view that this technology represents a major step forward in microcomputer-based information storage and retrieval. Subsequent chapters on applications have also been extensively revised to include new software and applications, including the 'new generation' of integrated microcomputer software for library applications. Similarly, the appendices on software and the bibliography have been completely updated. We have also tried to take into account the constructive comments made in some of the reviews of the book.

It is our hope, therefore, that this book will continue to be of value to the librarian and the student, and also perhaps to the computer specialist interested in library and information applications. It has remained our intention, as was suggested in the earlier book, 'to provide a single source of information on the process of automating with a microcomputer'.

ACKNOWLEDGEMENTS

We are again grateful to all those who have contributed in one way or another to the making of this book, by asking questions, describing

1

applications or commenting in general on the use of microcomputers in library and information work. Any errors and omissions, however, remain our responsibility.

Once again, our thanks go to Lindesay and Mandy for their patience during the writing of this edition. JHP would also like to thank Wendy Shoulder, who typed his chapters.

Preface to the first edition

It hardly needs to be said that the microcomputer is now a fact of life, but its impact upon the world of information retrieval and libraries generally has been less marked than in many other areas. One reason for this is an apparent uncertainty among librarians about just what the microcomputer is capable of in a library context. In the early days of microcomputing (i.e. towards the end of the 1970s!) there was some reason to be doubtful about the potential for library applications: storage was limited and suitable software was in even shorter supply.

These problems have now been overcome, but the interested librarian (and there are many) is faced with a plethora of articles and conference papers which are scattered throughout the professional journals. There is a need for a book which brings together this wealth of information, in order to provide a single source of information on the process of automating with a microcomputer.

The authors hope that this book will satisfy that need, for it considers the requirements of information retrieval and other library routines, and suggests how these can be operated on a microcomputer. Particular emphasis has been placed on software, because without software a computer is simply a collection of electronic circuits: without the right kind of software, attempts at automation are doomed from the start. In addition to the discussions of suitable programs for each application, there is an appendix listing details of library-specific software.

The book is intended for the practising librarian and the student, and it is hoped that it will serve as both textbook and reference work. Each chapter is, as far as possible, self-contained, and so it is possible to study either a single application or the entire subject. The core of the book (Chapters 4 to 6) provides guidelines for specific applications, while Chapters 8 and 9 look at the equally vital topics of software and hardware selection, with a discussion of the necessary management principles following in Chapter 10.

The authors feel that, while it is perfectly feasible to use a microcomputer without any idea of what makes it 'tick', a knowledge of the basic technology will help to get the best from both software and hardware. To draw an analogy, it is perfectly possible to drive from A to B without knowing how the internal combustion engine works. However, unless the driver is prepared to call in a mechanic, it is useful to know how to top up the oil or the radiator (and why), and some knowledge will also make it easier to detect faults and to discuss them sensibly when a mechanic does have to be called in. By the same token, knowing the basics of microcomputers technology will help the librarian to appreciate why the computer does what it does with bibliographic records, for example, and so an introduction to the technology is provided in Chapters 1 to 3.

With such a work as this, in order to ensure clarity without excessive detail, it is inevitable that certain complex concepts have to be simplified. There are numerous works on software and hardware which treat the subject in more depth. Similarly, the reader can be referred to a number of dictionaries of the new technology for any unfamiliar terms.

Illustrative examples are provided, whenever possible, of actual practice in libraries, since one of the most useful ways of successfully implementing a microcomputer is to consider the experiences of others. Those who have had the courage to describe their problems and successes are listed in the Bibliography.

1
Electronics for microcomputers

1.1 MILLIONS OF MICROCOMPUTERS

There are millions of microcomputers in homes in North America, Western Europe and elsewhere. The cheapest of these machines costs under $100 and they can be bought in stores, supermarkets and by mail-order. The number and sizes of microcomputer magazines have rocketed: *Byte* which is perhaps the leader, regularly tops 500 pages per issue.

The list of available software and the bibliography at the end of this book show that information retrieval and library applications are not being left behind. However, it is likely that a machine will have a cost of at least ten times that of a $100 personal computer if it is to be of real use to a library or information service.

It is difficult to define, therefore, how a microcomputer differs from its larger relations, the minicomputer and the even larger mainframe machine. They are certainly at the cheap end of the market and their availability has been brought about by the development of integrated circuits. These have been used to produce a range of electronic devices or 'chips' at low cost which can be put together to make computers at the extremely low prices we see today.

The development of integrated circuits has led to the birth of large numbers of new companies and the success of the microcomputer led even the giant IBM to begin to produce its own machines, a move which did much to make the microcomputer industry come of age.

Microcomputers are not the answer to all our computer problems, although they are taking on many more tasks today than would have been thought possible even five years ago. For very small organizations, they may serve most of the immediate needs, but for larger ones they may not be the answer, or may only be of use in quite limited circumstances. Larger computers have also benefited from developments in microelectronics and there is often a range of hardware and software solutions to a particular need.

The storage and retrieval of information are of interest to us all and are not the sole domains of librarians or information specialists. The microcomputer has given us the chance to improve the control of information in libraries, information services and a wide range of occupations. For instance, real estate agents can retrieve more extract details of property for sale and networks of car dealers can locate vehicles more in line with a customer's requirements using information retrieval techniques.

The content of this book will, it is hoped, provide insight into how microcomputers work (Chapter 1–3), their application to information retrieval and other library automation problems (Chapters 4–7), acquisition of hardware and software (Chapters 8 and 9) and, once obtained, how to make them work successfully (Chapter 10). First of all, we shall look at the electronics that is the basis of all computers.

1.2   FROM VALVES TO SEMICONDUCTORS

Early computers were built with valves or tubes, just as old-fashioned radios were. They were extremely large, consumed large amounts of electricity and were unreliable. The invention of the transistor changed both computers and other electronic machines, since here was a device that was smaller, more reliable and consumed less electricity than the valve.

Valves work by passing electric currents through a vacuum between electrodes: transistors are built from materials called semiconductors, which have properties which make them neither good conductors nor good insulators. Silicon and germanium crystals are most frequently used to make transistor devices.

The trick comes in altering the properties of the semiconductor by introducing a very small amount of an impurity. The process is called *doping* and it interferes with the conducting properties of the semiconductor. There are two basic ways of doing this. One is called n-type which is formed by adding an impurity which produces an excess of electrons (these are the basis of the conduction of electricity). The other (p-type) produces a deficiency of electrons. By putting the two together, a p–n junction is formed which can form the basis of a device called a *diode* which will conduct a greater current in one direction than in the other (see Fig. 1.1).

By putting three pieces of doped semiconductor together, transistors are formed which can be made to have various electrical properties. For instance, the n–p–n transistor, formed by sandwiching a piece of p–type semiconductor between two pieces of n–type, can be made to amplify a current (see Fig. 1.2). This particular property is used, for instance, in audio amplifiers, and the transistor effect is also used in computers.

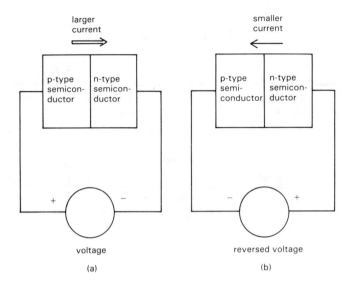

Figure 1.1 A diode formed from a p–n junction conducts a greater current in one direction (a) than in the other (b).

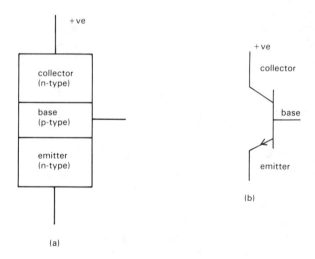

Figure 1.2 Arrangement of semiconductor materials in an n–p–n transistor (a) and its symbol used in diagrams (b).

1.3   INTEGRATED CIRCUITS

The first transistors were individual devices with wires joining them to other electronic components such as resistors, capacitors and other transistors. It became clear that the production of electronic circuits could be made more efficient if transistors, other devices and the circuits connecting them could be built up together (integration). At first, electronic devices with only a few circuits could be fabricated this way but the numbers increased as techniques became more advanced. Today it is possible to build a whole computer on a single chip of silicon crystal. A photolithographic process selectively dopes minute areas of the silicon and so builds up circuits. The chips are very small and the whole process must be very accurately controlled.

1.4   MANUFACTURE OF INTEGRATED CIRCUITS

Most of the integrated circuits in use today employ silicon as the basic semiconducting material. Sand is the raw material used in the production of modern integrated circuits and the process begins by heating the purified material until it becomes molten. A small single crystal of silicon is then dipped into the molten silicon and, as the crystal is withdrawn, it begins to grow as molten silicon attaches itself to the crystal. This process, which is known as *seeding*, creates a large crystal with the same atomic arrangement as the original, small seed crystal. The enlarged crystal is then sliced into individual discs or wafers which, after polishing, are about a quarter of a millimetre thick. Each wafer is large enough to produce around a hundred integrated circuits.

The aim of the manufacturing process is to build up a series of selectively doped areas of silicon which are connected together by metal wiring. The surface of the wafer is first oxidized to form silicon dioxide and is then coated with a layer of a light-sensitive material called a *photoresist*. The treated wafer is then exposed to ultraviolet light which is shone onto its surface through a mask, thus exposing only part of the photoresist (see Fig. 1.3). The process can be likened to the way in which photographic negatives are turned into prints in a darkroom. Fig. 1.4 shows how the mask is used to create an identical pattern in the photoresist. The ultraviolet light hardens the photoresist and the unexposed material is chemically washed away (see Fig. 1.5). The wafer is then etched with acid which removes the silicon dioxide but leaves the pure silicon untouched (Fig. 1.6) and then the remaining photoresist is removed (Fig. 1.7). The dopant is then introduced into the pure silicon. Fig. 1.8 shows the dopant diffusing into the silicon where the surface is exposed, thus reflecting the design of the mask. It is not possible to lay down all the circuits at once and hence the process is repeated a number of times. The silicon dioxide layer is refreshed as shown in Fig. 1.9 before re-starting the operation.

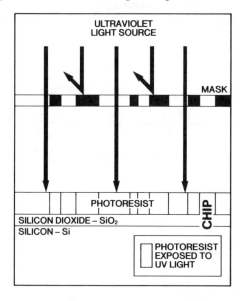

Figure 1.3   Chip surface covered with photoresist and exposed to ultraviolet light.
(Reproduced courtesy of IBM.)

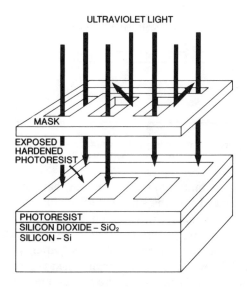

Figure 1.4   Photoresist exposure pattern governed by pattern of mask.
(Reproduced courtesy of IBM.)

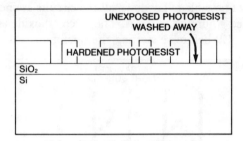

Figure 1.5   Unexposed photoresist washed away. (Reproduced courtesy of IBM.)

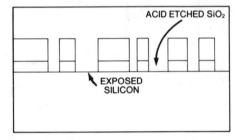

Figure 1.6   Exposed silicon dioxide acid-etched away. (Reproduced courtesy of IBM.)

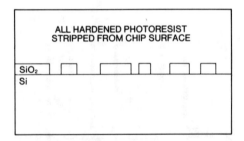

Figure 1.7   Hardened photoresist stripped from surface — chip ready to receive dopant.
(Reproduced courtesy of IBM.)

Once the devices are built into the silicon, they have to be wired together. Contact holes are etched into the surface and an aluminium–copper alloy is sprayed on. A photoetching process then removes the unwanted alloy, leaving the required wiring pattern (see Fig. 1.10). A typical wafer may be subjected to ten or more sequences of work patterns and all must be precisely aligned. The finished wafer is then sealed and connectors made to the outside world. After testing, wafers are broken into separate *chips* which are embedded into a substrate containing pin connectors to allow easy connection to other devices.

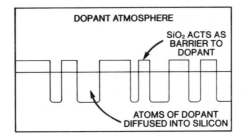

Figure 1.8   Introduction of dopant into silicon. (Reproduced courtesy of IBM.)

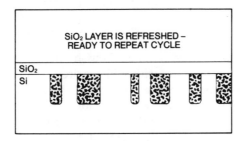

Figure 1.9   Silicon dioxide layer refreshed. Chip is ready to be retreated.
(Reproduced courtesy of IBM.)

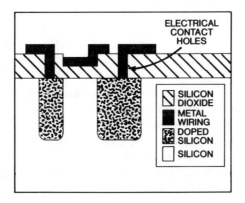

Figure 1.10   Addition of connectors and wiring to create a finished transistor.
(Reproduced courtesy of IBM.)

11

1.5 SCALE OF INTEGRATION

There are integrated circuits to perform many different tasks, such as storing or processing data. Single chip computers, in which all the various functions are integrated, are also available. The number of circuits which can be stored in a single chip has increased rapidly over the last few years, so much so that there are now a number of degrees of integration:

SSI — small scale integration (tens of transistors on a single chip)
MSI — medium scale integration (hundreds of transistors)
LSI — large scale integration (thousands of transistors)
VLSI— very large scale integration (hundreds of thousands of transistors)
ULSI— ultra-large scale integration (millions of transistors).

Devices which contain several hundred thousand transistors on one chip are in regular production and ones with millions are available.

Some chips are termed 'general-purpose' in that they can be used in a wide range of applications (for example storage devices) but others are specially built, as controlling devices for washing machines, for example. There are also chips which are general-purpose but which can be customized to a particular application. Most microcomputer designers would try to use general-purpose chips to reduce costs: volume production leads to very low prices. Indeed, the cost of the chips represents only a small fraction of the total cost of a microcomputer.

1.6 BINARY DIGITS

At the heart of every computer is a large number of electronic circuits that manipulate electric currents and voltages. Very early on, it was realized that electric power was easy to regard as a two-state system; for example, a light is either on or off, a voltage might be present or not. If, by convention, one of these states represents a *zero* and the other a *one*, there begins to be the basis of a number processing system. Fig. 1.11 illustrates the principle.

The decimal system is used as the basis of the normal counting system; it is convenient because we have ten fingers. Ones and zeros on their own can form a counting system just as the digits zero to nine do in the decimal system; it is just a different convention. (If mathematics is your weak point don't give up — understanding is reasonably easy.) The binary equivalents of the decimal numbers one to ten are shown in Fig. 1.12. Starting from zero, decimal zero and one are the same as binary. However, decimal two becomes binary 10 (not ten). This is because in binary we are dealing with a base of two, and not ten as in decimal.

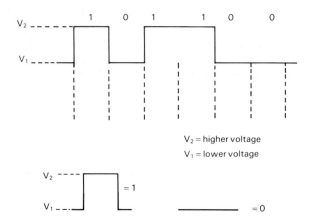

V₂ = higher voltage
V₁ = lower voltage

Figure 1.11   Convention for representing binary numbers with voltages.

Binary	Decimal
0	0
1	1
10	2
11	3
100	4
101	5
110	6
111	7
1000	8
1001	9
1010	10

Figure 1.12   Decimal numbers from 0 to 10 and binary equivalents.

Each *B*inary dig*IT* is known as a *bit* and eight bits together provide a range of numbers between zero (00000000) and 255 (11111111). Such a group of eight bits is often referred to as a *byte*. This is significant in computing, as will be explained below.

Conversion of binary to decimal is easy when it is remembered that each binary digit represents a power of 2. But first look at decimal numbers. The number 134 is:

$$1 \times 10^2 + 3 \times 10^1 + 4 \times 10^0$$
i.e. $100 + 30 + 4 = 134$

Similarly, the 8-bit binary number (10000110) is:

1	0	0	0	0	1	1	0	
(1×2^7) +	(0×2^6) +	(0×2^5) +	(0×2^4) +	(0×2^3) +	(1×2^2) +	(1×2^1) +	(0×2^0)	
128 +	0 +	0 +	0 +	0 +	4 +	2 +	0	= 134

13

The transmission of ones and zeros through electronic circuits is often achieved by means of voltage pulses. These can be produced by a generator that produces a sudden change in voltage for a specified length of time. A series of pulses representing the number 134 would be as shown in Fig. 1.13, where the presence of a pulse is, by convention, a one, and the absence of a pulse, a zero. These pulses may, for instance, be sent down a single wire one after another (*serially*) or simultaneously down eight wires side-by-side (*in parallel*).

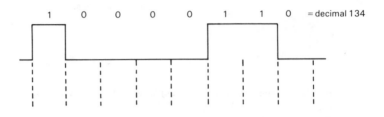

Figure 1.13   Representation of the decimal number 134 by binary pulses.

1.7   REPRESENTATION OF DATA

In the early days, computers were used by mathematicians to process numbers. It was necessary to store different sorts of numbers, but it was found useful to store letters and symbols as well, so conventions for storing different types of data were devised.

Each symbol or character was given an equivalent number, and early conventions developed into the ASCII (American Standard Code for Information Interchange) code. Here the significance of the byte comes in, as the following examples show:

	8 bits = 1 byte
The letter A is represented by 01000001	= 65
The letter B is represented by 01000010	= 66
The symbol % is represented by 00100101	= 37

The size of the byte provides 256 possibilities (0–255) so that this number of symbols can be stored, which is sufficient for most applications. Sometimes, however, this is not enough and extra symbols, e.g. for a non-Roman alphabet, can be stored by a more complex arrangement of multiple bytes.

1.8 COMPUTER DEVICES

It is not hard to imagine that computers have complex transistor circuitry; one has only to look at an audio amplifier which also has electronic circuits to manipulate voltages and currents, but for a different purpose. However, the individual circuits are themselves quite simple. A common operation in computing is to add two numbers together and a simple circuit can be built to carry this out. As an example, take the decimal numbers *one* and *two* and add them together.

in decimal 2 + 1 = 3
in binary 10 + 01 = 11

An adding device can be constructed with input and output (result) lines as shown in Fig. 1.14. The two numbers to be added together are sent as pulses along wires into the adding device. Pairs of digits from the two numbers are added together in separate circuits and a 'one' can be carried from a less significant to a more significant pair. The result is sent out by the adding device along the output lines.

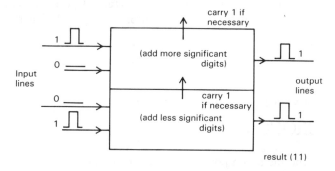

Figure 1.14   An adding device to add together two (two-digit) binary numbers.

Adders are built into chips, along with devices to perform all the operations needed in a computer. It is not really necessary to know how these are arranged in order to understand how a computer operates. For this level of detail the reader should turn to a basic book on computer hardware. The whole computer is built of many circuits, each performing different functions and integrated on chips of silicon.

In Chapter 2 the essential building blocks of a computer system and how they are put together will be described.

2
Microcomputers: the building blocks

Most manufacturers of microcomputers used integrated circuits fabricated by specialist manufacturers. Even IBM uses the products of other companies, such as the Intel Corporation, for its machines. There are single chips available which perform all the necessary operations of a micro-computer, sometimes called a computer-on-a-chip. However, in micro-computers used for serious business and general purpose operations, a number of individual chips, each performing a special function, are combined.

2.1 ARRANGEMENT OF CHIPS IN A MICROCOMPUTER

An outline of the main components of a microcomputer is shown in Fig. 2.1. The processing of data is carried out by a *central processing unit* (CPU) which is sometimes called a *microprocessor unit* (MPU). Adding devices, similar to the one shown in Fig. 1.14, are part of the MPU. Instructions and data are read in by the MPU and processed data come out. The operation of the MPU is determined by a set of *machine instructions* (ADD is one); there are usually around a hundred of them. Processing is carried out according to a *program* which is a sequence of machine instructions designed to carry out a particular task.

The program is stored in *memory* and the immediate memory which feeds the MPU is of two basic types (see Fig. 2.1):

(a) ROM (read only memory);
(b) RAM (random access memory or read/write memory).

The microcomputer also has, among other things, a clock device which synchronizes all the various high speed operations, so that they do not get

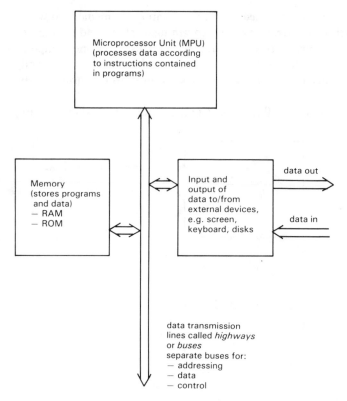

Figure 2.1   The main components of a microcomputer.

out of step. It has, in addition, interface chips that are used to connect the microcomputer to other devices such as *printers* and *visual display terminals*.

Buses Transmission of data between individual chips is carried out by means of a number of buses. A bus is a group of lines joining together individual electronic components and they are often of three types:

(a) address bus: for the direction of data to and from individual locations;
(b) data bus: for transmission of data (most frequently from MPU to memory and vice versa);
(c) control bus: for controlling the operation of the various devices that make up the microprocessor.

In some microcomputers one bus can carry different traffic, e.g. both data and address signals, without getting them mixed up. The term 'bus' is used because it is a common highway to which individual devices of the microcomputer connect and data are moved around them as if by bus.

The *address* bus: the MPU receives program instructions and data from the memory and transmits results back to it. In this case the address bus is used by the MPU to select particular locations in memory to which data are to be written and from which program instructions and data are to be read.

The *data* bus carries data and instructions from one component of the microcomputer to another. A usual route is between the MPU and memory.

The *control* bus carries the signals required to organize the operation of the microcomputer.

An outline of the flow of instructions and data is shown in Fig. 2.2.

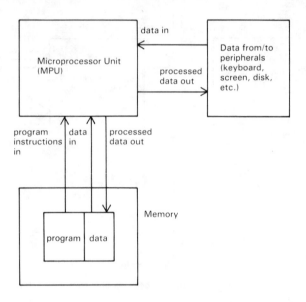

Figure 2.2   Flow of program instructions and data in a microcomputer.

2.1.1   Categorization of microprocessor units

Microprocessors are often referred to as 8-bit, 16-bit etc. This refers to the size of a normal machine instruction that the MPU can process. The size occupied by such an instruction is often referred to as the word length. For example the Motorola MC68000 16-bit microprocessor has a word length of 16 bits, although the microprocessor can deal with 'long words' of 32 bits. The instruction to add together two numbers in the MC68000 is stored in a 16-bit word, as shown in Fig. 2.3. The 4 bits on the left contain the instruction number, which is binary 1101 for the ADD instruction. The rest of the word contains details of where to find the data and other details of how to execute the instruction. This explanation is very oversimplified and the reader interested in further detail is advised to consult a book on computer hardware. A large word size provides room to store larger numbers, giving scope for more instructions, and a larger range of addresses and other instruction information. It is therefore associated with more powerful microprocessors. The size of the word often coincides with the size of the data bus. Normally an 8-bit MPU will have an 8-bit data bus but this is not necessarily the case. The 16-bit Intel 8088 MPU has an 8-bit data bus so that it can fit in with other chips made for 8-bit machines. In theory, therefore, it takes longer to process data with the 8088 than it would do with a 16-bit data bus as is found in the Intel 8086. Fig. 2.4 shows the transmission of data along an 8-bit data bus from memory to MPU.

Many 8-bit MPUs have a 16-bit address bus which allows the MPU to address 64 K different storage locations. Sixteen bits gives 2^{16} possibilities, i.e. 65536 (1 K is 2^{10} or 1024).

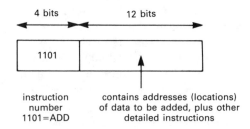

Figure 2.3 Format of the ADD instruction stored in a 16-bit word (Motorola MC 68000 microcomputer).

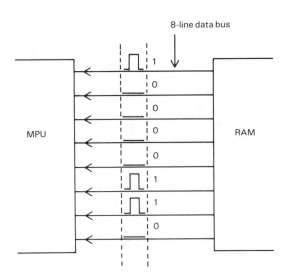

Figure 2.4 Transfer of data from RAM memory to the microprocessor unit along an 8-bit data bus. Example shows binary 10000110 (134) transmitted from RAM to MPU.

The size of the microcomputer is not the only factor to determine its power. The speed of operation, that is, the time taken to process an instruction, is important. Some microprocessors are designed to operate with a *co-processor*. They are built to carry out particular tasks, such as handling arithmetic operations or the processing needed to display information graphically, and hence relieve the main processor of this burden. Another important factor is the size of the address bus which will determine the size of memory which can be addressed, although the ability to specify in a program a memory size larger than is actually physically available (*virtual memory*) is now possible in some microprocessors. A number of microprocessors provide the required hardware arrangement to support several users and/or several programs operating simultaneously. It is difficult, therefore, to compare the power of processors on just a few factors. Perhaps the most critical point will be how the system builder has put the chips together into a working machine.

One of the first MPUs was the Intel 4004 which was introduced in 1971 and had a 4-bit data bus. However, until the development of the 8-bit MPU the general-purpose microcomputer was not feasible. The Intel 8080 was the device which really made things happen, the 8085 being the current version of it. Other manufacturers have included Motorola (MC6800) and MOS Technology (6500/2), but probably the most successful 8-bit chip has been the Zilog Z-80. Many microcomputers are now available with 16-bit MPUs. The Intel 8086 will support a 20-bit address bus and a 16-bit data bus, but 16 bits of the address bus are shared with the data bus. Thus this chip can address 2^{20} or 1 048 576 locations (1 megabyte) and process a simple instruction of 16 bits. The Intel 8086/8088 MPUs are said to be compatible with the earlier 8080/8085 chips so that programs developed on 8-bit machines can be run on 16-bit machines. Intel has also introduced more powerful MPUs, such as the 80286, as used in the IBM PC AT microcomputer, and which can address over 16 million locations.

Zilog manufactures the Z-8000 series which is again compatible with Z-80/Intel 8080/5. The Motorola MC68000 has a 24-bit address bus which can address over 16 million locations. This microprocessor, introduced in 1979, was the first of a family of 16-bit offerings from Motorola. The MC68008 has an 8-bit data bus and 20-bit address bus, and the MC68010 introduces virtual memory features into the 68000 design.

A wide range of microcomputers employing 16-bit MPUs is now available. By far the most popular is the IBM range of machines which uses the Intel 8088 or 80286 MPUs. In addition, a number of companies manufacture IBM compatible machines. The Motorola 68000 is also a leading 16-bit MPU, being used in the Apple Macintosh, Atari 1040ST and a range of other equipment.

With 16-bit machines firmly established in the marketplace, 32-bit MPUs are increasingly becoming available. Notable ones include the National Semiconductor 32000 series, the Motorola 68020 and the Intel 80386. There are other trends in chip technology which could become significant. Inmos has devised what it calls a *transputer*, a device to process instructions in a parallel fashion, so as to provide increased computing power. Another development is the *reduced instruction set computer* (RISC) which provides extra power through simplification of the microprocessor by reducing the number of different machine instructions available. The power of the microcomputer is growing to an extent that it is difficult to define such a machine, except on the basis of cost. The arrival of the 32-bit machine makes the definition even more difficult.

A technical survey of MPUs is given in Osborne's microprocessor handbooks [1,2].

2.1.2   Central memory

The MPU can operate very quickly: a simple addition operation can be executed in less than a microsecond. In order, therefore, for the MPU to operate efficiently, it needs to be able to read instructions and data from memory quickly, and to write processed data just as quickly back into memory. If this can be done, the MPU will not be waiting for data and instructions to process, but will be operating at maximum efficiency. Bearing in mind that the MPU operates sequentially, i.e. it processes instructions one at a time, it needs a 'fast' storage device to back it up. The two major devices, ROM and RAM, are both integrated circuits. Both devices are directly addressable in that the MPU can get almost immediate access to any byte. Fig. 2.5 shows how this is carried out.

Data which are to be permanently stored in directly addressable, fast-access storage can be placed in ROM. Data are written into ROM by special equipment and, once done, they are stored permanently, i.e. they remain even when the machine is switched off. ROMs are often used for storing programs that will not need to be changed and that need to be used frequently. Operating systems (see Chapter 3) are sometimes placed in ROM on cheaper machines that do not have disk drives or in machines which have a larger address space (see p.22 for an explanation of address space). The major advantage is that a program in ROM is always ready for use, with the disadvantage that the memory space cannot be used for anything else should this be required without changing the ROM. Variants of ROMs include PROMs (programmable read-only memories) and EPROMs (erasable PROMs) which offer some flexibility over ROMs but do not get over the problem of the MPU not being able to write data to them. In some machines, ROMs can be easily exchanged, allowing new programs to be loaded when required.

Random access memory (RAM) is the most important type of central memory in general-purpose microcomputers. The operation of reading data from RAM is essentially the same as reading from ROM. The main

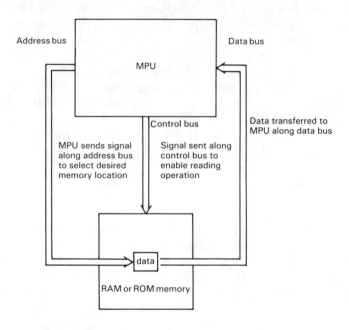

Figure 2.5   Retrieval of data from memory and transfer to MPU.

differences are that RAM can be written to by the MPU, and when the power is switched off the data are lost. The number of bits of data which can be stored on a single RAM is expanding. Currently RAMs up to 256 K bits are readily available, and 1 megabit (Mbit) RAMs are on the market. A number of RAMs are used together to increase storage capacity: several megabytes is not uncommon in some 16-bit machines. The manufacture of these high-density chips is problematical and sometimes partially occupied chips are used: these are higher capacity devices that are used at a lower capacity because some of the storage locations are not correctly formed.

The range of storage locations that an MPU can address is sometimes called the *address space*. A 16-bit address bus can address 64 K memory locations (bytes) and so many 8-bit microcomputers with a 16-bit address bus have this amount of storage available. It is possible to address more than 64 K by switching between different groups of 64 K using a technique called *bank-switching*. Most 16-bit machines have raised this storage limitation quite significantly.

The address space can be made up of different physical devices as, for instance, shown in Fig. 2.6 in which part is ROM and part RAM.

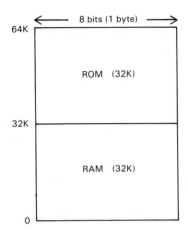

Figure 2.6   Different physical devices in address space.

2.1.3   The 'stored program' concept

A computer program is a set of instructions to the microcomputer designed to carry out a desired operation. Without a program, or *software* as it is also known, the microcomputer is useless. The operation of a program will be dealt with in this section and an explanation of programming languages will be given in Chapter 3. Programs are usually written in so-called *high-level languages*, which are fairly easily manipulated by human beings. The *machine language* understood by the MPU is essentially different and much more restrictive. High-level languages, such as BASIC, must be translated into machine language by the computer before a program can be executed.

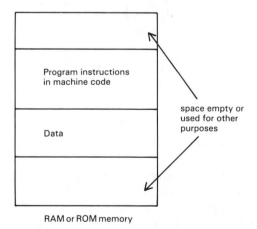

Figure 2.7   Storage of program and data in RAM or ROM memory.

The translated program, of machine instructions and data, is stored in RAM or ROM (see Fig. 2.7). The hundred or so different machine instructions will be sufficient to carry out the full range of microcomputer operations, including:

(a) data transfer (e.g. moving data from one location to another);
(b) data manipulation (adding, Boolean logic, etc.);
(c) transfer of control (e.g. branching to another instruction);
(d) input/output (e.g. bringing data from external devices);
(e) machine control.

Each instruction type has a unique number and a sample program in machine language is described later in this chapter. Figure 2.3 shows an example of an ADD instruction in the MC68000.

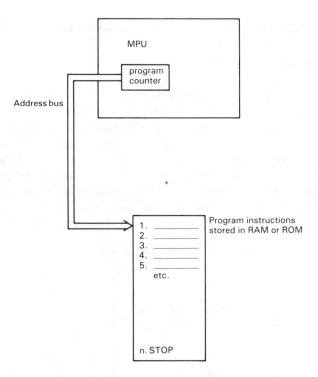

Figure 2.8 Program instructions and program counter.

The *execution* of a program is controlled by a *program counter* (PC) which points at the start of execution to the first instruction (see Fig. 2.8). Instructions are processed one after another, and after the execution of one instruction by the MPU, the PC points to the following one unless the previous one involved a branch to a different part of the program. Instructions from the program are processed until the program is interrupted or the 'stop' instruction is reached. The data to be processed are usually stored in a different part of the memory to the program.

The microprocessor operates in three steps:

(a) fetch the instruction from memory;
(b) decode the instruction;
(c) execute the instruction.

Signals are placed on the various buses to fetch the instruction. Decoding is carried out in the MPU and execution employs the necessary circuits within the MPU to carry out the instruction, together with any reading and writing of data. The procedure followed in order to carry out a simple instruction is shown in Fig. 2.9, in which the program counter (PC) is pointing to the first instruction (Instr. 1). The first operation is to fetch this instruction from memory and store it in the MPU. It is shown in the top box of the MPU in Fig. 2.9. The instruction is then decoded and executed. In this particular case, Inst. 1 is an instruction to read data from memory into the

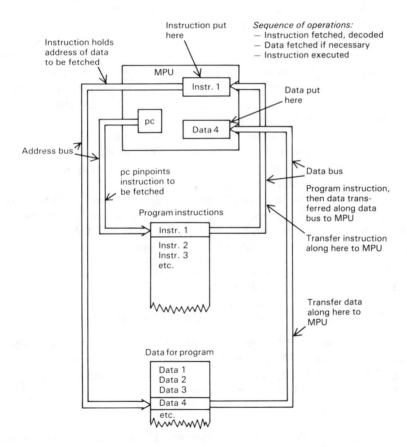

Figure 2.9 Processing of a simple (one-byte) instruction.

MPU. The instruction contains the memory address of the required data. The MPU sends out this address along the address bus to locate the required data which are then transferred (DATA 4 in Fig. 2.9) along the data bus into the MPU. Subsequent instructions would be likely to process DATA 4 in some way.

2.1.4 Assembly languages

An assembly language is a symbolic version of a machine language. In such a program, the word ADD rather than the numerical equivalent would be used. Programs are sometimes written in the machine language; if this is necessary, the symbolic or assembly language version is normally used because programs can be written more quickly. Assembly languages are used when a high-level language would place too many restrictions on the programmer and/or the language would not be able to express what was required. For instance, it might be required to write a program which occupied the smallest possible amount of memory or which operated with the minimum number of machine instructions. Use of the machine language gives the programmer more control over these factors than would a high-level language, even though the program would probably take longer to write. Assembly languages are normally only used by programming experts, but an example will be given as an aid to understanding how a microcomputer operates.

An 8-bit MPU, such as the Motorola MC6800, has a number of storage locations called *registers* in the MPU itself. The MC6800 has two registers into which data are loaded from memory: they are called A and B. Larger MPUs have more storage registers than this.

The following simple assembly language program loads a number (25) into A and a second number (35) into B. It then adds the two together and stores the result in a location called TEMP, which is in RAM. The program comprises four mnemonic instructions as follows:

```
LDA  A  #25      (this means load 25 into A)
LDA  B  #35      (load 35 into B)
ABA              (add contents of B into A)
STA  A  TEMP     (store contents of A in TEMP)
```

The instructions are translated into machine instructions by an *assembler* and are stored in RAM. The program is then ready to execute as shown in Fig. 2.10. The numbers in the boxes are the translated instructions and data. The assembly language instruction:

```
LDA  A  #25
```

is stored in the RAM as two 8-bit numbers, 134 and 25. The MPU knows that 134 means 'load into accumulator A': it also knows that the next box of

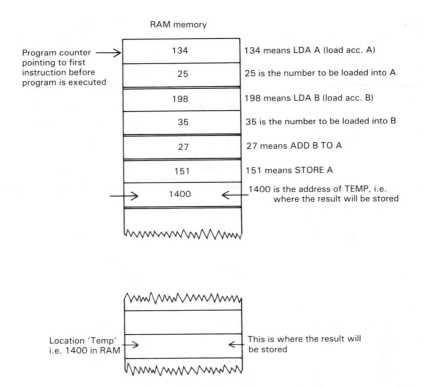

Figure 2.10 Machine instructions for program to add two numbers.

8 bits (one byte) contains the data to be loaded into accumulator A. A similar consideration applies for the second instruction. 198 means 'load into accumulator B' and the content of the next byte (35) is loaded. The MPU similarly knows that 27 means 'add accumulator B into accumulator A'. This instruction occupies only 8 bits as there are no data to fetch from memory. A 2-byte instruction such as 'LDA A #25' will involve two fetches from memory with this 8-bit MPU. A 16-bit MPU would probably cut this down to one.

An assembly language usually allows the programmer to use symbolic names for storage locations. The location 'TEMP' in the program is an example. The assembler assigns a unique location for TEMP; in Fig. 2.10 it is shown as location 1400.

It is reasonable to ask at this stage how adding together, or comparing the sizes of two numbers can be relevant to, say, an information retrieval system. Such a system would probably be programmed in a high-level language, such as COBOL or BASIC. Statements such as:

IF KEYWORDA = KEYWORDB THEN DO. . .ETC.

might be used to compare two strings of characters, for example, a search term input at a terminal and a word in a bibliographic record. An information retrieval system would comprise thousands of instructions like the one above and all the statements would be translated into machine instructions by a special program called a *compiler*. A single high-level language statement would generate a number of machine instructions, the exact number varying from one high-level language statement to another. In the sample statement just shown, it is very likely that one of the machine instructions generated by the compiler would be to compare two numbers to see whether they were equal. It was shown in Chapter 1 how individual characters are stored as numbers, so an English word can be regarded as a string of numbers. All high-level language program statements are reduced to a series of simple machine instructions in a similar way. They need to be, in order for the microprocessor to be able to obey them.

2.2   MAGNETIC STORAGE DEVICES

Something more than RAMs or ROMs is required for the permanent storage of significant quantities of data. The main task of both these devices is to service the MPU and they can store only limited amounts of the data required for immediate or frequent processing. Magnetic disks and tapes are the main media for storing data permanently, although bubble memories are also used and optical storage devices are now becoming increasingly available (see section 2.3).

The MPU can process a single instruction in less than a microsecond. It takes significantly longer to read data from disk or tape into RAM, and hence some strategy is needed to manage data or programs so that those most likely to be needed are most readily available. There are techniques which can be used to handle files of data to speed up access and these are described in Chapter 3.

Important criteria for judging the performance of storage devices include:

(a) the total storage capacity;
(b) the cost per byte stored;
(c) the time required to access data and the transfer rate into the microcomputer;
(d) the ability to exchange the storage medium.

It is fairly obvious that the ideal medium should have a large capacity, be inexpensive, be able to retrieve data and transfer them to the central memory quickly and be flexibly designed so that one storage device can be removed from the unit and replaced by another.

Data coming from peripheral devices, such as magnetic tapes or disks, can be fed via the MPU into the RAM memory as shown in Fig. 2.11. There is, however, a method that bypasses the MPU and feeds data directly

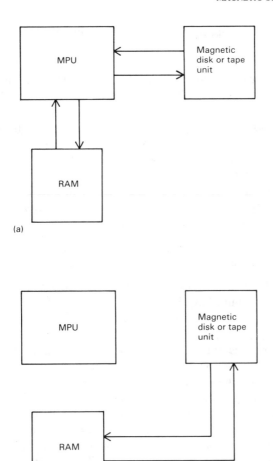

Figure 2.11   Transfer of data from/to magnetic disk or tape unit and RAM.
(a) Transfer via MPU; (b) transfer by direct memory access.

into the RAM. This usually involves another chip but has the advantage of freeing the MPU from this task. The technique is called *direct memory access*.

Magnetic tape devices on microcomputers are usually of the cassette tape variety and are often found on cheaper models. Standard audio cassette recorders can be used and are inexpensive. Reel-to-reel recorders are available and their performance is very much better, but they are expensive and are rarely used with microcomputers.

The time to transfer data from a magnetic tape to a microcomputer depends on the time to locate the required data on the tape and the actual speed of transfer once located. This can be several seconds or, more likely, minutes, depending on where the data are on the tape. The speed of operation and the capacity of reel-to-reel drives are much greater than cassette tapes.

Sinclair Research formerly manufactured its 'microdrive' for the QL machine with a capacity approaching 100 Kbytes which is comparable with that of a cassette tape, but it is much faster in operation. The cartridges used by the drive are also exchangeable.

Magnetic disks are, without doubt, the most important medium for bulk data storage in microcomputers. A magnetic disk is a film of magnetic material on a disk substrate. The whole disk is rotated and read/write heads are used to read data from the disk and to write data onto it. The magnetic material is essentially the same as that used for magnetic tapes but the set-up of the device enables data to be accessed much more quickly (in the order of milliseconds). There are two main types:

(a) floppy disks (so-called because the disk can be bent);
(b) hard disks (so-called because the disks cannot be bent).

Without the floppy disk, sometimes known as a *diskette*, data processing on microcomputers would have been severely retarded.

Floppy disks come in different diameters: 8″, 5¼″ and the more recent 3½″. The original floppy disks were 8″ and *single sided*, i.e. data were recorded on one side only. Disk drives are now available which will record data on both sides at twice the original density (*double density*) and with double track recording, giving twice the data per track. One 5¼″ disk can thus hold up to several million characters. The cost of floppy disk drives depends on the capacity but several hundred dollars per unit is typical.

In the sub-5¼″ drive market, the 3½″ disk has been widely adopted. Present capacities can be above one megabyte and the disks have a rigid plastic cover and hence cannot strictly be called 'floppy'.

It remains to be seen just where the market will go as the full impact of the sub-5¼″ disks is not yet clear. The big advantage of 8″ disks remains the standardization. The plethora of disk formats for 5¼″ drives makes it difficult to transfer disks from one machine to another.

Rigid, or hard disks have been an essential part of large computers for a long time and, more recently, have been adapted for use with micro-computers. A disk is made up of a series of individual rigid disks, arranged one above another, and spinning about a vertical axis. Some disk drives allow this arrangement of disks or *disk pack* to be removed or exchanged for another. A series of magnetic reading heads, which is usually movable and arranged like a comb, is used to read and write data (see Fig. 2.12).

IBM invented a disk drive, known as the *Winchester*, in which the whole disk pack was hermetically sealed, and this design has become the basis for the Winchester disks available on microcomputers. Most Winchester disks cannot be removed from the drive, but ones that can are becoming available. The design of the Winchester has produced a less expensive product, with a lighter read/write head travelling closer to the surface of the

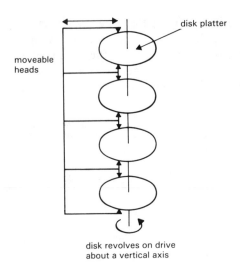

Figure 2.12   Outline of the operation of a disk drive.

disk. These disk drives have been incorporated into microcomputers at astonishingly low prices. Available sizes are 14″, 8″, 5¼″ and 3½″, and capacities can be over 100 Mbytes, although 10 to 40 Mbytes is the range of capacities most commonly seen. Microcomputers with Winchester disks are now widely available for considerably less than $5000.

The large capacity of Winchesters is problematical when backing-up files. They can be copied to floppy disks but it is likely that several floppy disks would need to be used as their capacity is so much smaller. Some Winchesters have a built-in magnetic tape unit called a *streamer* to which the whole disk can be copied. Another alternative is to have a second Winchester drive. The answer will depend on the application and the budget available. Generally speaking, it is valuable to have both floppy and Winchester disks and a comparison of their attributes is given in Fig. 2.13.

In order to arrange data on a disk, the surface is divided up into a number of *tracks*, each being that part of the disk which the head can read

Floppy disks	Winchester disks
Comparatively high disk failure rate	Comparatively low disk failure rate
Lower disk capacity	Higher disk capacity
Lower total cost for drive	Higher total cost for drive
Disk exchangeable	Disk usually not exchangeable
Backup easy to another floppy disk	Backup to floppy clumsy, to another Winchester is expensive, to video tape is error prone, to tape streamer
Lower data access speed and transfer speed	Higher data access speed and transfer speed

Figure 2.13   Comparison of the attributes of floppy disk and Winchester disk magnetic storage media.

without moving. Disks with more than one 'platter' can use the concept of a cylinder for organizing data. This is a device for reading or writing a group of tracks together, so as to maximize the speed at which data can be transferred. A cylinder comprises the tracks which can be written without moving the heads (see Fig. 2.14).

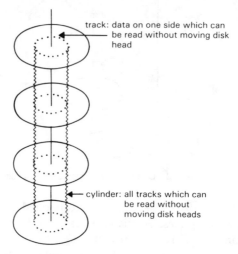

track: data on one side which can be read without moving disk head

cylinder: all tracks which can be read without moving disk heads

Figure 2.14 Tracks and cylinders on rigid (hard) disks.

There are two methods of *sectoring* floppy disks: *hard* sectors and *soft* sectors. Hard sectors use physical holes in the disk itself to mark the beginning of each sector. Soft sectored disks have just one hole in the disk to mark the beginning of the first sector. The remaining sectors are specified by software. The latter method is most frequently used (see Fig. 2.15). A device called a *RAM disk* is sometimes used; this is made from RAM memory but has a similar capacity to a floppy disk. It is not a substitute for a floppy disk drive because the data are not retained after the machine is switched off.

Magnetic bubble memory may increasingly become a competitor to floppy disk drives. A bubble is a minute cylindrical magnetic *domain* (basically a small magnet) held in a thin film of magnetic material. Bubbles can be moved and the presence or absence of a bubble is used to represent a one or a zero. Bubbles are created from electrical signals by a bubble generator within the memory (writing) and can be reconverted to electrical signals by a bubble detector (reading). A magnetic field propels the bubbles in the right direction through the film. The data bubbles circulate past the pick-up point in order to be read. Thus bubble memories are serial storage devices akin to disk memories. However, in the disk, the stored bits are stationary (relative to the medium) and the whole medium moves: in the bubble memory, the medium is stationary and the bits move. Bubble memories

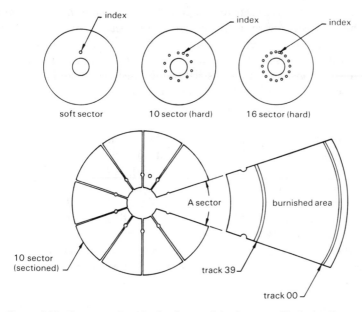

Figure 2.15 Sectors and tracks for floppy disks (courtesy Verbatim Corporation).

have some advantages over other memories. They are non-volatile, i.e. the magnetic domains are not lost when the power is switched off (unlike RAM). They have no electromechanical parts, are compact and use very little power (unlike disks). With the present state of the art, their capacities are already several million bits per device.

2.3 VIDEO DISKS, COMPACT DISKS AND DIGITAL OPTICAL DISKS

A range of peripherals, which use optical processes to store and retrieve data, is becoming available at prices which make it practicable to link these devices to microcomputers. Most of them use a spinning disk and hence the mode of operation is not unlike that of a magnetic disk, although there are some fundamental differences. There are also other formats, notably optical tape and optical card systems, the latter storing several megabytes of data on a card no bigger than a credit card. Their arrival presents some exciting possibilities to use microcomputers in ways which were not possible before.

Optical disks can be broadly grouped into three categories:

(a) video disks,
(b) compact disks,
(c) digital optical disks.

Video disks were introduced to compete with videotape in the consumer market, but they were never a serious competitor because of the inability to record as required. However, because it is possible to quickly locate individual video frames on a disk, the equipment is being used in a range of interactive situations, such as industrial training, education and at points of sale in retail stores. Although the storage mechanism is best suited to images, a technique has also been developed to store digital data on the video disk.

Compact disks (CD) were developed jointly by Philips and Sony for the storage and playback of audio material and have proved to be extremely successful in this respect. Recently a version of the CD (the CD-ROM) was introduced which stores digital data.

Digital optical disks are mass storage peripherals designed especially for connection to computers. They offer some distinct advantages over magnetic storage devices.

In practice, all three of the above categories of optical disk can be connected to a microcomputer, functioning as direct access mass storage peripherals.

2.3.1 Video disks

The permanent storage of moving visual images and accompanying recorded sound on disk has been a goal of researchers for many years. Early systems used a process similar to that employed for the recording of gramophone records. However, the use of lasers to record video information on a disk and playback afterwards has provided the most satisfactory solution.

The production of video disks is somewhat similar to the production of audio disks. Once a master disk is produced, copies can be made inexpensively by a stamping process. A copy is placed onto a turntable and read by a read head, again in a similar way to the audio disk. There are, however, some important differences, as will be outlined below.

Hendley's [3] comprehensive survey of optical disks notes that there are two methods of recording which seem to be viable today, i.e. capacitive and optical. In the former, a signal recorded on a circular disk is read by measuring the change in capacitance between an electrode and the surface of the disk. The Video High Density (VHD) system, developed by the Victor Company of Japan, uses the capacitance effect. However, the optical video disk seems to be the system with the most potential. The data (images etc.) to be transferred onto a master disk are first encoded on videotape. The data then modulates a laser beam, which is focused onto a master disk coated with a thin film of material which is sensitive to light (photoresist). After recording, the exposed areas of photoresist are etched away to leave the data encoded in the surface of the disk. A metal coating is then applied to the master and a number of sub-masters are produced from which copies are taken.

Data are read from the disk by means of a low-power laser beam, which is shone onto the disk and the modulated reflected light reads back the contents into a detector.

A number of companies manufacture optical video disk systems, but perhaps the best known is the Laservision system. It employs a 12″ diameter disk and the data are encoded in the surface of the disk in a series of small, variable-length holes in the disk surface (pits). The video disk can hold up to 54 000 television frames on one side of a disk, together with sound and control data. Two methods of recording, Constant Angular Velocity (CAV) and Constant Linear Velocity (CLV), are employed. In the former, the disk always spins at the same angular velocity and hence the density of storage is lower on the outer than on the inner parts of the disk. The speed of rotation is chosen to enable a single TV frame to be read many times, in order to give a 'freeze frame' image on a TV screen.

The other method of recording, Constant Linear Velocity (CLV), allows more data to be stored on the outer parts of the disk and the drive spins faster when this part of the disk is being read. This mode is superior to CAV for the continuous viewing of sequentially organized images, e.g. a film or movie, because more images can be stored on the disk. Stills and sound can also be recorded.

The video disk player can locate an individual frame on a disk in a matter of seconds. It is this possibility which brings in the microcomputer as a controlling device. Each of the 54 000 frames is numbered and the microcomputer can be used to store indexes to the content of the disk. Images can be of textual material as well as diagrams, still photographs and movies. For instance, if still photographs were stored, each could be described using a variety of indexing terms, such as name of photographer, date, description of scene. Using an information retrieval system, the descriptions of the photographs could be searched, and the corresponding image(s) located on the disk and displayed. Video disk players can contain in-built microcomputers to provide the access to individual frames. However, more sophistication is likely to be achieved by attaching the video disk player to a separate general-purpose microcomputer, with the display of frames under the control of the latter, rather than the player itself. The potential for use of the video disk in computer-assisted-learning has already been recognized and the microcomputer is beginning to play an increasingly important role in the operation of sophisticated image retrieval and presentation systems. However, the number of interactive videos available for educational purposes is not large as the cost of production is still quite high. Nevertheless, the potential for the future is evident and the impact on library services could be important.

Although the video disk was devised primarily for the storage of visual images and sound, it has been adapted to store digital data. It can then act as a read-only mass storage device. At the present time, the LaserData system can store up to 800 megabytes of data. When connected to an IBM PC through a LaserData controller, a standard industrial video disk player can offer access times of only a few seconds to images and sound on the same disk as well as data.

2.3.2 Compact disks

The compact disk (CD) was designed to provide high fidelity sound in the home, using a digital recording technique. Since its introduction, the CD has become popular at an extremely rapid rate and playing equipment and disks are widely available, from a number of manufacturers.

The use of a digital recording technique meant that it was relatively easy to modify the hardware to store computer data, and hence use the compact disk as a mass storage peripheral with microcomputers. This version of the compact disk is called a compact disk read-only memory (CD-ROM).

The compact disk is mass-produced in a similar way to a video disk. There are three stages to the manufacturing process: pre-mastering, mastering and replication (see Fig. 2.16). In the pre-mastering process, the

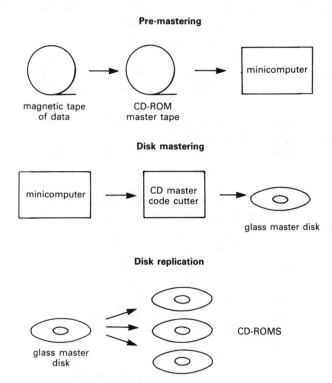

Figure 2.16   CD-ROM production process (courtesy Sony Corporation).

data base is converted to a CD-ROM master tape. This is then fed into a minicomputer which drives the mastering process. The minicomputer controls a CD master code cutter which produces a glass master disk. The disk is covered with photoresist and a laser beam in the code cutter is shone onto it to create a pattern according to the data to be encoded. After treatment by an etching process, the photoresist exposes a series of pits (holes) and lands (no holes) which correspond to the stored data.

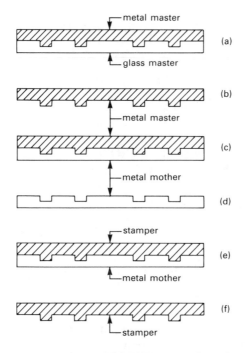

Figure 2.17 Production of CD-ROM stamper from glass master
(courtesy Sony Corporation).

The glass master is subjected to a complex duplication process in order to produce a 'stamper'. Fig. 2.17 shows the successive steps. A metal master is first made from the glass master (a, b). The metal master is then used to produce a metal mother (c, d) and finally the stamper is made from the metal mother (e, f). The CD-ROMs themselves are produced from the stamper by an injection moulding process, using a transparent poly-carbonate resin. Each CD-ROM copy is subjected to a final treatment with the addition of reflective and protective layers (Fig. 2.18).

The CD-ROM has a diameter of 12 cm (4.72 inches). The reading device in the player (a laser) shines light through the coating and does not physically touch the surface of the disk as it spins. Dust and minor scratches are said not to affect the performance of the disk. It is a CLV device which does lead to a greater storage capacity than a CAV

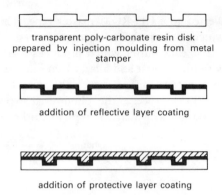

transparent poly-carbonate resin disk prepared by injection moulding from metal stamper

addition of reflective layer coating

addition of protective layer coating

Figure 2.18   CD-ROM final disk treatment (courtesy Sony Corporation).

arrangement but access times are relatively slow. Currently the CD-ROM can store some 550 megabytes of data. Access time is 1–2 seconds and the transfer rate is 1.41 Mbits per second.

It is forecast that prices of CD-ROM players will soon drop from the thousands of dollars now quoted to hundreds of dollars per drive. The cost of mastering is also several thousands of dollars per disk but this, too, is likely to fall as the number of available applications increases. Individual copies can be made for a few dollars each. It is forecast by at least one manufacturer that it will be possible in the near future to store data, images and sound on a single CD-ROM. The term CD-I has been adopted for this device.

2.3.3 Digital optical disks

Video disks and compact disks were originally developed for the entertainment industry and have only subsequently been used for the storage of digital data. A third category of optical disks comprises types of equipment which have been developed especially for use as mass-storage devices for computers.

Digital optical disks fall largely into three categories:

(a) Optical Read Only Memories (OROM),
(b) Write-Once Optical Disks (WOOD),
(c) erasable (re-writable) disks.

Digital optical disk drives are available from a range of suppliers and are already being used for a number of applications. The costs of these drives make them fairly expensive for use with microcomputers, although prices are falling.

Optical read-only memories (OROM): The CD-ROM with its CLV format has a comparatively poor access time and data transfer rate, although it does have the benefit of standard hardware which has been adopted by a number of different manufacturers. The OROM uses the same 13 cm (5.25") size as the floppy disk, together with a CAV approach. This results in a storage capacity of up to 400 Mbytes, and a rotation speed which provides access times in the order of hundreds of milliseconds.

The state of development of OROM disks and drives is behind that of CD-ROMs and it is difficult to see how they could compete with the CD-ROM, in the near term. The entry of one of the big manufacturers of microcomputers into the market, especially IBM, could alter the situation, however.

Write-once optical disks (WOOD): It will clearly be an advantage to be able to write data onto an optical disk as required. A number of manufacturers have produced such disks, but up to the present time, they have tended to be used in larger computer systems. A variety of sizes is available. A significant development is that the 13 cm (5.25") size is being used for write-once disks, as well as for OROMs, and it is likely that OROM and WOOD disks will be usable on the same drive. It is important with write-once optical disks to be able to read data immediately after they are written. The term DRAW (Direct Read After Write) is used to describe disks which have this capability.

2.3.4 Potential uses of optical disks

The potential uses of the optical disk are numerous, for it offers some significant advances in the method of storage and retrieval of information on microcomputers. Important factors are:

(a) the ability to mass-produce some forms of optical disks;
(b) the significant increase in online storage capacities over magnetic disks;
(c) inexpensive equipment;
(d) the medium is protected against wear.
(e) storage of text, video and sound on the same disk.

Admittedly, the shelf life of the disk is not yet proven, but the coming availability of writable disks will enable data to be transferred to new disks should shelflife be a problem.

The optical disk could have a profound impact on the information dissemination process, by allowing a wide range of optical publications to be produced. Already a number of bibliograpical databases are available on optical disk and a small number of optical products containing primary publications are appearing. They are discussed in more detail in Chapter 4.

The optical disk has the potential to replace microfiche in many applications and as a mass storage device for office management systems. A number of document storage and retrieval systems exist which use an optical disk for mass storage but they are still mainly above the microcomputer price range. It will not be long, however, before WOOD and erasable disks are sufficiently inexpensive to justify their use with computers at the low end of the market.

2.4 OTHER PERIPHERAL DEVICES

Just as the MPU can send data to, and receive data from, memory devices such as a magnetic disk, it can similarly communicate with external devices or peripherals such as printers, visual display terminals etc. We usually communicate with the microcomputer using a keyboard, which is rather like that of an electric typewriter, and a visual display terminal, which displays data entered at the keyboard and data retrieved from the microcomputer (see Fig. 2.19). A printed copy of data can be obtained from a printer attached to the microcomputer. A variety of different machines is available and they are discussed in Chapter 9.

Keyboards are usually detached from the microcomputer for ease of use and are able to input a wide range of characters. Visual displays vary in the quality of the image they display. Some will display only characters and not drawings (graphics). Some are no more than glorified television sets. For constant use, a commercially produced unit with good resolution, brightness control, and a large character-set with extra keys on the keyboard to carry out specific functions is recommended. Sometimes the keyboard and display are an integral part of the microcomputer. Other microcomputers are in a separate box and provide the user with a choice of displays (see also Chapter 9). Flat screen displays have become available and are used mainly with portable microcomputers.

The ability to support a graphical display is becoming more important in microcomputers. Machines such as the Apple Macintosh provide easy to use operating systems through the use of graphical displays. Colour graphics is also becoming more available and a range of colour printers is now on offer. Sound and video input/output are available on some machines.

Microcomputers communicate with other devices by means of *interfaces*. The outward signs of these are sockets in the back of the machine. Behind the sockets are some integrated circuits designed to allow the micro-computer to communicate with the outside world in a standard way. *Serial interfaces* are most common; they transmit bits one after another, i.e. serially. A common standard serial interface is the RS232C which takes a 24-pin plug and is commonly used to connect many peripherals including printers and *modems* (which are used to connect to other computers; see below). There are other interfaces to handle video and audio input/output.

Parallel interfaces are also available; they transmit a number of bits simultaneously. They are used, for instance, to connect to printers which

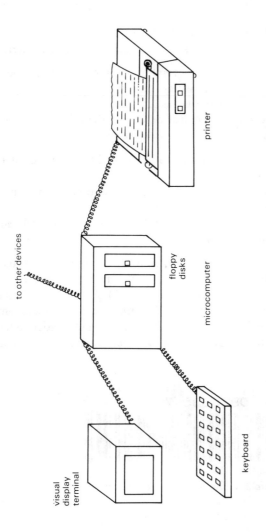

Figure 2.19 Peripherals attached to a microcomputer.

also have a parallel interface; the Centronics parallel is a common example.

To summarize: a typical microcomputer used for serious business purposes will comprise:

(a) a 16-bit MPU with at least 256 Kbytes RAM;
(b) at least two disk drives (two floppies or one floppy and one Winchester);
(c) quality visual display unit and keyboard;
(d) interface ports for connection of other devices, e.g. a printer.

A well-designed machine may have several MPUs for different purposes, for example to manage the visual display terminal, direct memory access. Fig. 2.19 shows an outline of the necessary hardware.

Besides the standard equipment just described there is a range of other peripherals. Examples or other *input equipment* are:

(a) bar-code and optical character readers (for direct reading of text or numbers without using a keyboard);
(b) light pens (often used for selecting one option from a menu of possibilities shown on a screen);
(c) the 'mouse' (a device for controlling the cursor and entering instructions without using the keyboard).

Bar-code readers are frequently used to simplify the issuing and discharge of books in a library. Each book is given a unique number which is coded in vertical bars and placed in the book (see Fig. 2.20). A wand, which can read the number by passing it across the bars, is connected to the microcomputer via one of the interfaces (see Fig. 2.21). Optical character readers operate in a similar way except that they read the numbers themselves, rather than bar-code labels.

Figure 2.20 An example of a bar code label.

Examples of other *output equipment* include:

(a) graphic display terminals (for displaying diagrams and charts) with high resolution;
(b) graph plotters (for printing diagrams and charts);
(c) speech generators.

There are quite a number of other input and output devices for microcomputers, but they are not central to the theme of this book.

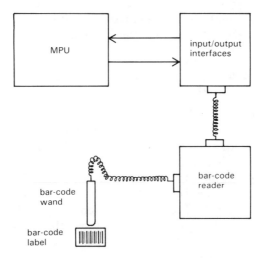

Figure 2.21   Connection of a bar code reader to a microcomputer.

Microcomputers are being used in a wide range of applications such as the control of robots, measurement and control of temperatures, control of metal-working machines etc. All these operations require input and output of data to, and from, the various devices connected to the microcomputer. A fuller description of available hardware is given in Chapter 9.

2.5   TELECOMMUNICATIONS AND NETWORKS

It is possible to connect two microcomputers together using their interfaces. Correctly wired, and with the appropriate programs, data can be transferred from one machine to the other (see Fig. 2.22). This is, in fact, a perfectly feasible way of transferring data to a new machine when the floppy disks are incompatible. Often, no equipment, other than the machines, plugs and wire, is required.

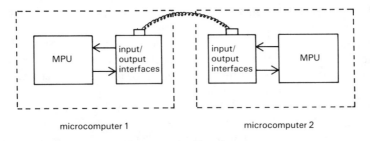

Figure 2.22   Hardware connections of two microcomputers through their interface ports.

To communicate with another computer at a distance will depend on the available line and the *communication protocol*. The types of line will include:

(a) ordinary telephone lines;
(b) private data lines;
(c) public data networks.

Whichever method is used will depend on where the other computer is, what lines that computer is connected to, the transmission speed required (bits per second) and the error rates that can be tolerated. If it is required to connect to a large computer within an organization it is likely that local data lines can be set up. A modem (modulator–demodulator) or a *line-driver* may be necessary to ensure the data can be sent in both directions and correctly interpreted at both ends. The communication protocol used by the large computer will have to be investigated since this is the way that the machine wishes to transmit its data. It is possible that a program will need to be written for the microcomputer in order to comply with the larger computer's protocol. Of course such a program may already exist but it may only be possible to communicate in very simple and unsophisticated ways. At the extreme, it may not even be possible to use a particular microcomputer as a normal simple terminal, without writing some software.

Communication with computers outside the organization usually involves the use of some form of public network, although private lines can be obtained even for long distances. There are two forms of data transmission:

(a) *asynchronous* transmission (in which the transmitting and receiving devices are not in step);
(b) *synchronous* transmission (in which the transmitting and receiving devices are in step).

Asynchronous transmission is a simple low-cost method of transmitting data. It is the most frequently used method of communicating with computers over public networks. The microcomputer's interface is connected to a modem which is connected to the line, often via a normal telephone handset. A device called an *acoustic coupler* can be used in place of a modem. Its advantage is that it does not require any physical connection to the telephone, since communication is through the handset. The likelihood of data transmission errors is greater, however, and it is not recommended for constant use. The equipment for asynchronous transmission is shown in Fig. 2.23. The microcomputer requires a software package which provides the necessary routines for the transmission and reception of data. The use of microcomputers for information retrieval from distant computers is covered in Section 4.3.

The protocol or method of data transmission will be dependent on the modem used. This device converts the data from the microcomputer into a form suitable for transmission to another device (e.g. a host computer). Factors to be considered in selecting a suitable modem include:

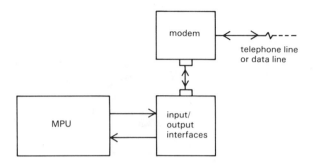

Figure 2.23   Data transmission via a modem and telephone or data lines.

(a) the mode of transmission (synchronous or asynchronous);
(b) the speed of transmission and reception (bits per second);
(c) whether a 'smart' modem is necessary which may have its own microprocessor and ROM containing audodial, autoanswer, telephone number storage and in-built telecommunications software;
(d) whether both full duplex (transmission simultaneously in both directions), or half duplex (transmission in one direction at a time) are needed, or both;
(e) whether the modem is, or can be, part of the microcomputer or needs to be a separate physical device.

Synchronous transmission is a more efficient technique than asynchronous but requires more sophisticated timing equipment to ensure that the transmitting and receiving devices are kept in step. It is normally used with higher transmission speeds and frequently when a whole screen of data is transmitted from the large computer to the terminal.

Transmission of data over long distances can be expensive if normal long-distance telephone lines are used; the use is no different to using the telephone for normal speech. To make data transmission more cost-effective, many countries have introduced public data transmission services. Many of them use a technique called *packet-switching* in which data are sent from transmitter to receiver in small bundles or packets. It is not necessary to set up a fixed line between the two communicating parties and many callers can share the high-capacity networks. In many respects packet-switching is analogous to the motorway or freeway networks in which packets are like trucks sharing a busy route but ultimately going to different destinations. Connection to a network can be by a telephone call to a local *node* (entry point of the network) or it is possible to have a direct line to the node (see Fig. 2.24). The cost of using these networks is often based on the duration of the connection and on the volume of data transmitted but they offer a cheaper and more reliable service than the telephone. For a detailed technical survey of microcomputer telecommunications, the reader is

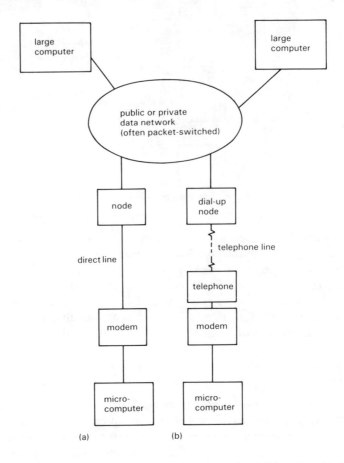

Figure 2.24 Connection of a microcomputer to a network. (a) Direct line; (b) dial-up.

referred to works by Derfler [4] and Shapiro [5]. Schwaderer [6] covers communication techniques for the IBM PC.

Multi-user microcomputers allow a number of operators to share the machine and the complexity of the operations which can be carried out will depend on the size of the machine (RAM, disks etc.) on the power of the MPU and on the operating system (see Chapter 3). Terminals can be at some distance from the processor, thus forming a crude sort of network.

At a more sophisticated level, microcomputer *networks* are available and they are the least expensive sector of the LAN (Local Area Networks) market. A LAN is a communications network which normally operates in a restricted area and provides data transmission speeds often in excess of a million bits per second (see Section 5.11). A variety of equipment can be attached to these networks, such as microcomputers, central disk stores and printing facilities. There are different network configurations; the main ones being star, ring and bus configurations. They are described in detail by

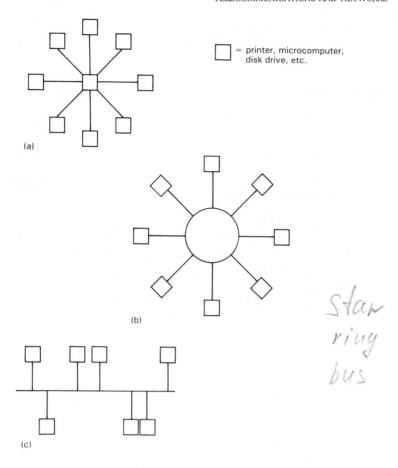

= printer, microcomputer, disk drive, etc.

(a)

(b)

(c)

star
ring
bus

Figure 2.25   Local area network topologies.
(a) Star network; (b) ring network; (c) bus network.

Gee [7] and are shown in Fig. 2.25.

A local area network is really a means of bringing together micro-computers and peripheral devices to create a more powerful computer system than the sum of the individual, unconnected machines. One printer, for example, can serve a number of users. A data base held on one machine can be accessible to another. The growth in the use of microcomputer LANs has been somewhat slow but the entry of IBM into the market could provide some stimulus. System builders will need to be aware of the main reasons for joining microcomputers together and a LAN may not be the right answer in many cases. It may be more cost effective to duplicate equipment, rather than sharing, for example, printers. Duplication of data bases may also be easier. Simple communication, such as just described, or the use of a larger minicomputer may be more effective answers. However, the speed of transmission between machines in a LAN is high and for applications which demand this high volume, a LAN may be the answer.

REFERENCES

1. Osborne, A. and Kane, G. *16-bit Microprocessor Handbook*, Osborne/McGraw-Hill, 1981.
2. Osborne, A. and Kane, G. *Osborne 4-and 8-bit Microprocessor Handbook*, Osborne/McGraw-Hill, 1981.
3. Hendley, T. *Video Discs, Compact Disks and Digital Optical Disks.* Cimtech publications, No. 23, 1985.
4. Derfler, F.J. *Microcomputer Data Communication Systems*, Prentice-Hall, 1982.
5. Shapiro, N.L. *The Small Computer Connection: Telecommunications for the Home and Office*, Micro Lamb/McGraw-Hill, 1983.
6. Schwaderer, W.D. *Digital Communications Programming for the IBM PC*. Wiley IBM PC Series, 1984.
7. Gee, K.C. *Local Area Networks*, NCC Publications, 1982.

3
Software concepts

Programs are the lifeblood of a microcomputer and, fortunately, there is a growing range of software available: the chances are that something can be found to solve a particular problem. Many microcomputer users will therefore never write a single program instruction. Had the programs of interest to them not been available, they would never have bought a microcomputer.

Programs written to satisfy a particular need are called *applications programs*. They are discussed in detail in Chapters 4, 5 and 6. This chapter deals with software other than applications programs and gives a brief glimpse at record and file structures.

There is a range of software essential to the correct functioning of applications and to their development. It includes:

(a) operating systems (which manage the running of the machine);
(b) programming languages (for writing particular applications);
(c) systems software (a range of programs such as editors, to make life easier for the programmer and user);
(d) data base management systems for handling files of data (they are described in Chapter 4).

All these tools are themselves programs and hence have to be written in either an assembly language or a high-level language.

3.1 OPERATING SYSTEMS

An operating system usually comprises a suite of programs that manages the operation of the microcomputer. The facilities offered by individual operating systems vary greatly. Some systems for large computers have had millions of dollars invested in them. Microcomputer operating systems are much more modest but no less important to the running of the machine.

They will, for instance, play a big part in determining whether a certain application will run on a particular machine.

The elements of an operating system are normally held on disk and are loaded into RAM when required, although on some machines the system is permanently stored in ROM. The basic elements of an operating system include:

(a) supervision of, and support for, applications programs;
(b) device handlers — to allow the programmer easy access to the computer's sub-components (e.g. disks);
(c) a file handler — to simplify the handling of files of data (e.g. to support different file organizations, the cataloguing of files, file protection and backup systems);
(d) a command interpreter — to accept and implement user commands (e.g. password management and other commands given by the user).

Simple microcomputer operating systems allow only one program to be run at a time. More sophisticated systems allow more than one program to be run concurrently (sometimes called *multitasking*) and more than one user to operate the computer at one time. The management of the programs for a number of users can be likened to the work of an air traffic controller at an airport who has to share the resources of the airport between the aircraft which are competing for runway, terminal etc. Each program and user makes use of the resources of the computer (disks, interface ports etc.) and each program in the machine will occupy part of the RAM or ROM memory. At a greater level of sophistication, the operating system will be able to swap programs in and out of memory (to disk) in mid-operation in order to let them share the resources of the machine. Each program being run wants to feed its own instructions into the MPU to get them processed. The priorities for deciding which program to process at a particular time will need to be managed. Multiuser and multitasking operating systems should allow the user to decide these priorities. There will be conflicting demands: two programs may want to use the disks simultaneously, for instance, and the order of priority will need to be decided by the operating system. An outline of the storage of programs and data in such a system is shown in Fig. 3.1. The allocation of the memory to a particular program will be under the control of the operating system.

Virtual memory systems are beginning to be seen with microcomputers. With such an arrangement, the amount of memory that a programmer can use is not limited by the physical size of the central memory. Rather, the program and its data areas are divided up into *pages* (a fixed amount of memory). Those pages of a program which are currently needed are stored in the physical memory available to the program. If another page is needed, it is brought in from disk and an unwanted page is put onto disk.

Some microcomputer systems can only be used by one user at a time and will not simultaneously run more than one program. Multitasking machines

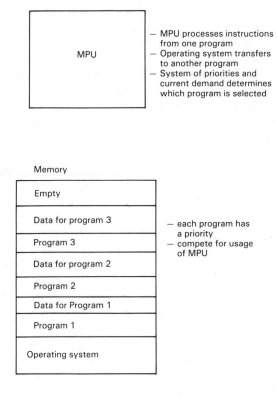

Figure 3.1 Operating system running several programs concurrently.

are likely to be more powerful, and more expensive, and will probably be 16- or 32-bit MPUs to take advantage of the extra power and larger amounts of memory which can be addressed.

An operating system for a machine with disks will include a series of routines to handle the disk files. These are sometimes known as a *DOS* or Disk Operating System, although the term can refer to the whole operating system. Data or programs are stored on files, each of which is given a name. A DOS will provide tools for looking after these disk files, e.g. copying, renaming, cataloguing, storing them on disk and looking after their allocation to free space on the disk. A DOS will release free space after a file is deleted and make it available to another file when needed. The operating system will also make available a number of methods of organizing, and obtaining access to, the data files stored on disk. Various methods of file organization are available, and they are discussed later in this chapter.

An essential feature provided with an operating system is a general *file editor*. Some provide it through a BASIC interpreter (see Section 3.2) but the most useful is a general-purpose program that will simplify the task of input, editing and deletion of programs and data. Editors are mainly used for programming, in particular for the construction of the files containing the program statements. They are not recommended for the input of large amounts of data to files; for this a purpose-built input module is usually available with each application program. Editors broadly fall into two categories, *line* and *screen*, the latter being easier to use because a whole section of the text can be viewed on the screen and the cursor can be used to make the required changes. Line editors show data a line at a time but are preferred by some programmers because they have been available on large computers for many years.

Seemingly as with many of the early developments in microcomputers, the outstanding operating system for 8-bit machines, *CP/M*, was developed in the proverbial garage. CP/M stands for Control Program Monitor but it is most often referred to by its shortened name. Originally developed for the 8080 chip, its use became almost obligatory on machines using the Intel 8080/8085 and Zilog Z-80 MPUs. Its rapid spread was helped by the ease with which it could be adapted to individual manufacturer's machines. Other operating systems, such as those for the Apple II or the PET, were not available for other machines as CP/M was. It thus became the *de facto* standard and its supremacy was enhanced when the stream of applications software began to hit the market. All this applies, of course, to 8-bit machines; with 16-bit MPUs, the situation is much more open as other competitors have entered the market. Hogan [1] describes CP/M in detail.

CP/M is an operating system, then, for single user, single program 8-bit machines. The occupation of 64 K address space is shown in Fig. 3.2. This is sometimes called a *memory map*. The various components which are

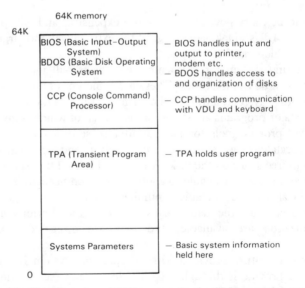

Figure 3.2   The occupation of 64 K memory by the CP/M operating system.

stored in RAM take up about 8 K thus leaving around 56 K for the application program which occupies the transient program area (TPA). Version 3 of the basic system is called CP/M Plus but there are a number of different versions for different purposes and machines. MP/M is one multiuser version of CP/M and CP-Net is another which allows a number of CP/M machines to access central files on disk attached to an MP/M machine. Concurrent CP/M allows a single user to run several tasks simultaneously and gives each task a separate 'window', i.e. its own area of the screen.

CP/M is also available for 16-bit machines with CP/M-86 for the Intel 8086/88 MPU and CP/M-68K for the Motorola MC68000. MP/M-86 is a multiuser version of CP/M for Intel MPUs. However, Microsoft MS-DOS and the IBM version, PC-DOS, are presently the dominant forces in the 16-bit Intel microprocessor market. The adoption of the Microsoft product for the IBM-PC has contributed greatly to this position. The large number of IBM-PCs manufactured and the vast array of available software encouraged other manufacturers to produce IBM-compatible machines, which also operate under MS-DOS.

The availability of more powerful microprocessors has stimulated the development of multi-user, multi-tasking operating systems. Versions of the *Unix* operating system, first developed for minicomputers, are available, e.g. for the MC68000. Microsoft also offers Xenix, a version of Unix, and there are other operating systems which are similar to Unix. Among other systems also worthy of note are Theos (originally Oasis for 8-bit machines) and the USCD P-System, the latter being a Pascal-based system (Pascal is a programming language). It operates by creating a 'virtual machine' inside the real machine. All machines running USCD P-System look the same — they all run P-code (a sort of standard machine code), and all programs, when compiled, become P-code which is then interpreted into the actual machine code. The Pick operating system, with its in-built data base management features, is also available for microcomputers. It is used for library systems for both microcomputers and minicomputers.

A notable development in operating systems was the introduction of graphic display techniques to simplify microcomputer use. The graphical arrangement of information on the screen, together with the use of the mouse to help control operations, has enabled large numbers of unskilled microcomputer users quickly to learn to use microcomputers. The Apple Macintosh operating system is probably currently the most widely used system employing such techniques.

Larger memories and more powerful processors contributed significantly to the development of graphical display techniques for operating systems. Microsoft also has a software package called 'Windows', which is a graphical extension to the MS-DOS operating system. A graphical approach is also evident in the GEM (Graphics Environment Manager) system from Digital Research.

The decision on which operating system to use will be dependent on what the user requires to do. Most machines will be supplied with at least one operating system. This is likely to be the best one to use as more software packages are likely to have been written for the most widely available operating system. It is the ability to run the application program that is probably the most important factor in deciding which operating system to use. However, for program development, one operating system may provide features, for example multiuser operation or the availability of a particular programming language, which make it worthwhile to abandon the normal one. In this area, it will very much depend on how much microcomputer expertise the user has, or is able to get access to.

3.2 COMPILERS, INTERPRETERS AND PROGRAMMING LANGUAGES

It was shown in Chapter 2 how a microcomputer was dependent on computer programs or software to make it work. A small program was written in an assembly language and an assembler was used to translate the program into machine code so that the program could be run. Assembly languages are important for some applications but their use should, in general, be restricted to those special applications when another language would not be satisfactory. Assembly language programs:

(a) normally occupy less memory space than an equivalent program written in another language;
(b) can be executed faster because they are likely to contain fewer instructions to do the same job;
(c) can do some jobs that high-level languages cannot.

However, for most applications one of the high-level languages will be sufficient. It is also possible to use more than one language for a single application; those parts requiring an assembly language can be written in one and the rest can be written in a more convenient high-level language.

One reason for using a high-level language is ease of use. The four line assembly language program to add together two numbers (see Section 2.1.4) could be reduced to one simple instruction such as:

TEMP = 25 + 35

In addition it will be possible to carry out complicated data manipulation operations with single instructions. For example, groups of similar pieces of data can all be processed at the same time by arranging them into lists or 'arrays' (each item being pigeon-holed). There is a range of many different program instructions in a particular language and their power can be augmented by using a data base management system (see Chapter 4). Some languages have specialist applications, e.g. for mathematicians or for processing strings of text, the latter being useful for information retrieval applications.

Compilers: once a computer program is written, the steps to be taken to execute it are:

(a) compilation (translation of the statements of the program into machine instructions);
(b) linking (bringing together all the necessary parts of the final program);
(c) loading (loading the final program into memory ready to run);
(d) execution (running the program).

The operating of a compiler is shown in Fig. 3.3. The compiler sits in memory and operates as a program. The program to be compiled, which is often known as the *source program*, is treated as data by the compiler. The program statements are checked for syntax and logical errors and then, if no

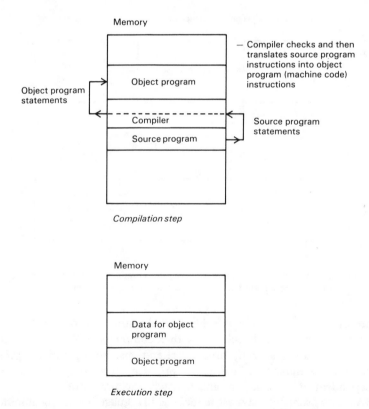

Figure 3.3 Use of memory for compilation and execution of a program.

errors are apparent, each statement is translated into the equivalent machine code instructions. A complete source program may be written in more than one language and each part will need to be compiled separately. In addition, a number of 'subroutines' may be called in by various parts of the program (these are specific pieces of program designed to perform difficult or repetitive tasks). The linking stage brings all these individual parts together into a single *object program* which is loaded into RAM ready to be executed.

Interpreters: these are an alternative method of executing a source program. A good analogy is the difference between the two methods by which humans are helped to communicate in international organizations when they cannot speak each other's language (see Fig. 3.4). Compilation uses a similar process to the translation of a document, which is then read by the other party. Interpreters work in the same way as a simultaneous interpreter in a meeting, translating 'on-the-fly'. Similarly, the source program is loaded into memory and the individual source statements are translated into machine code as they are needed (see Fig. 3.5). The interpreter is kept in memory during the operation of the program.

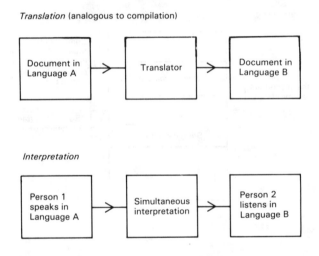

Figure 3.4   Similarity of computer program compilation and interpretation to document translation and interpretation of speech.

Interpreters can be very useful for initial testing of programs because they are quicker and more flexible to use than compilers. Some interpreters have a built-in editor to simplify program alterations. For operational programs, a compiler is important in order to produce object programs that will be independent of the compiler and that will execute more quickly.

BASIC is probably the most highly used language for microcomputers. It is usually available as an interpreter but compilers are also obtainable. It is

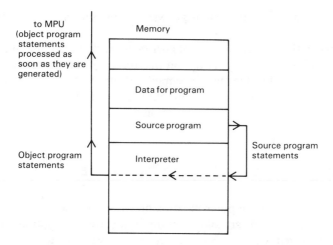

Figure 3.5 Execution of a program using an interpreter.

simple to learn and use and is a general-purpose language with some commands to manipulate strings of characters. Most, if not all, machines have a version of BASIC available but there are a number of different dialects and only minimal standardization, which is important if programs are to be taken from one machine to another (*portability*). BASIC has been criticized for being unsuitable for professional programmers, and rather more suited to use in educational establishments, but it has been successfully applied in many areas, including librarianship. The power of the language varies considerably between the various versions. Another popular language is *Pascal*. It may well be a useful language for library and information retrieval applications because it too has facilities to handle strings of data.

Neither BASIC nor Pascal are favourite languages for mini- and larger computer applications. One that is widely used, at least in the commercial and business world, is COBOL which is short for 'Commercial and Business Oriented Language'. There are versions available for micro-computers. PL/1, a language developed by IBM to satisfy a wide range of data processing needs, is also available for microcomputers. There are other languages available, all of which have some advantages. They include Forth, Lisp (a list processing language) and Fortran (a language used by scientists but also used for other purposes), in addition to others.

A language which is growing in popularity in microcomputers is C. It was originally written for the PDP-11 minicomputer and operated under the Unix operating system. One advantage of C is that it is not tied to a particular brand of hardware and it is very easy to write programs in C which will run on a number of machines. A number of information retrieval systems for microcomputers have been written using C. It has been described as a fairly low-level language but this can provide some of the advantages of an assembly language whilst still offering some powerful programming features.

It is likely that some of the languages in widespread use on larger machines will gain in popularity on microcomputers as the machines become more powerful, the languages more readily available and users more sophisticated. There are also programming languages built into some data base management systems and they are discussed in Chapter 4.

3.3 THE ORGANIZATION OF DATA

Data stored in a microcomputer must be organized in a way that optimizes the performance of hardware and software for a particular application. How data are organized will, of course, depend on what is to be done: an information retrieval system may, for instance, need to locate individual items of data in seconds. In this case the data will have to be organized to make this possible.

Data must be physically stored on a device. Magnetic disks are the usual bulk storage devices used, magnetic tapes being less useful because of the time required to locate data. How data are placed on a device is known as the *physical organization* and this will be limited by the physical layout of the device itself. On a disk, data will have to be stored in the sectors and tracks which have been laid out to hold them. The use of cylinders of data to improve retrieval speed (see Fig. 2.14), and the grouping of records into blocks to save space are two of a number of physical data organization techniques [2]. Fortunately, many of the problems associated with physical organization of data are handled by operating systems.

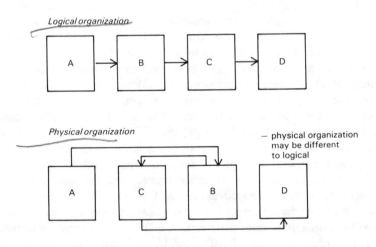

Figure 3.6 Logical and physical organization of data on a disk.

Programmers are usually more concerned with *logical organization:* Fig. 3.6 illustrates the difference between the two forms. A file of data will usually need to be logically organized so that each item has its correct place. From a programming point of view, item B may be logically next to item A. Physically, they may be separated but connected together by links or *pointers* so that the logical arrangement can be presented when required. This arrangement of data would avoid having to sort all the items into the correct order every time new ones were added. The new data could for instance, be put at the end and the pointers rearranged.

Data base management systems can be used to provide complicated logical arrangements of data and they are discussed in Chapter 4.

As might be expected, there are a number of conflicting terms to describe data storage concepts. Terms such as 'record', 'field', 'data element', 'key', 'item' and many others have been used in a variety of contexts. Within that of data base management systems, the terminology is better controlled, but use of it requires a good understanding of a complicated subject.

In the library and information service fields, a number of computer systems have been developed which are commonly called *information retrieval systems*. They tend to employ a relatively simple arrangement of the data to be retrieved, together with some sophisticated indexes to provide fast access to the data. Data for a particular item can be grouped together into a *record*. A common example is to build records to describe a set of documents. This set is called a data base. Each record contains a number of *data elements* (author, title etc.). A place reserved for a data element is sometimes referred to as a *field*. There may be one or more occurrences of each data element (e.g. a document may have two or more authors) and each may be put in a separate field (see Fig. 3.7). The indexes which are built to provide fast access are sometimes referred to as *inverted indexes* or *inverted lists*. The organization of data in information retrieval systems is dealt with in more depth in Chapter 4.

Various computer programs will need to access the data elements within a record and it is necessary to structure the data in a helpful and unambiguous way. The computer thus needs to keep track of where each data element is within the record and how long it is. It is simpler to do this if each record has the same length (*fixed-length records*) and if each

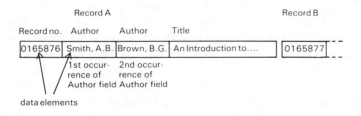

Figure 3.7 Arrangement of data elements into fields within a record.

Record number	Author	Title
0567457	Jones, H.V.	An Introduction to Computers
⊢7 char.⊣	⊢ 16 char. ⊣	⊢ 40 char. ⊣

Figure 3.8   Arrangement of data in fixed-length fields.

occurrence of a data element in different records has the same length (*fixed-length fields*). An example is shown in Fig. 3.8.

Some data elements in a bibliographic data base do have a fixed length, e.g. the date a record was created, but most do not. Placing variable length data elements into fixed-length fields will mean wasting space if the field size is made larger than the longest occurrence of each data element. Otherwise some occurrences will not fit into the space provided and space is still wasted for very short occurrences.

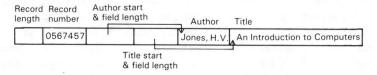

Figure 3.9   Arrangement of data in variable length fields
(note record number is in a fixed-length field).

Records containing variable-length fields will of necessity vary in length. An example is shown in Fig. 3.9. One widely used record structure employs a directory to the record with an entry for each occurrence of a data element. The entry contains details of the type of element, its position in the record and its length. Each record is divided into a number of sections. When the record is created, its length is placed at the beginning of the record and this can be followed by a section containing fixed-length data elements, if required, in order to simplify access to them. A directory is constructed to point to each variable-length data element and then, finally, the variable-length data elements themselves appear. The example shown in Fig. 3.9 is only one of many possible arrangements. The standard one used for distribution of bibliographic data bases has a similar structure to that just described.

The flexibility of variable-length records is bought at a price. A data base of fixed-length records is easier to update since a new record can exactly take the place of an old one, although if new records need to be added at a particular place in the sequence, space will need to be made available. Techniques that allow sophisticated logical and physical arrangements may be needed for updating a file of variable length records or the file may need to be copied, at the same time creating the necessary space. This problem is considered later in the chapter.

The examples shown in Figs. 3.8 and 3.9 are extremely simple data structures. The record structure can become more complicated if some data elements occur more than once. A bibliographic record for a document containing two authors is an example. Single complex fields can also cause problems when processing the data and, in order to avoid ambiguity when processing such a field, it can be split up into sub-fields. In the MARC machine-readable cataloguing system, for example, a personal author's name is recorded (in simplified form) in a single field as follows:

```
100              $aSmith $hWilliam
 |                 |       |
tag              sub-field codes
```

The $a sub-field code marks the surname and $h the first name. The number 100 signifies that the data element is a personal author and is called a *tag*.

A set of records stored on a magnetic disk will normally have a prescribed order. Often this is by the *key field* which is usually part of a record that identifies it uniquely. A record number is a commonly used key field. Using the mechanism of the disk and the disk operating system, an individual record can be retrieved from the disk. The place where the record is stored on the disk is calculated from the key field. Hence although the records may be stored in sequential order, they are accessible, and can be retrieved, individually. A technique called the Index Sequential Access Method (ISAM) was devised which provides a programmer with the ability to build a sequential file on disk but which can be easily updated. The individual records are put together on disk tracks and each cylinder contains an index to all the records stored in the cylinder. If a particular cylinder becomes full, there are one or more tracks or cylinders that have been set aside for overflow records (see Fig. 3.10). Thus new records can be added in their correct place without having to rearrange the whole file. The logical arrangement is maintained although records may not be physically next to each other. In practice, for a large file, a hierarchical system of indexes may be necessary. There might be a *track index* for the records on each track, a *cylinder index* for the records on each cylinder and a *master index* on top (see Fig. 3.11). The ISAM technique provides reasonably fast access to individual records at the same time as keeping the records in sequence, which will be important for processing records in batches, e.g. for printing lists.

In Fig. 3.11, if it is required to locate record number 15, the program would search for the nearest number lower than 15 in the master index. This index would show the location (address) on the disk of the relevant cylinder index. A search would then be made of the cylinder index to find the entry with the nearest lower number, in this case 14. This entry would lead to the point on the disk which contained records starting with 14, in this case 14 to 16. A sequential search of the remaining records would soon locate record number 15. In practice, the number of records would be much larger than is shown in the example.

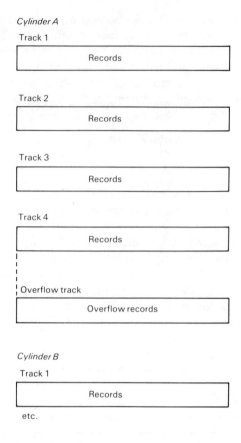

Figure 3.10 Arrangement of data records with tracks to accommodate overflow records.

If it is not important to process records sequentially, they can be organized *randomly* on the disk. The space on the disk is split up into a number of cells (say 1 to *n*). The key field is subjected to a formula that translates it into a cell number. The idea is to invent a formula that translates each key field into a unique cell number so that every record can have its own place on the disk. In practice, there is often a large number of empty cells or, if space is at a premium, it is necessary to have overflow areas when several records generate the same cell number. The process is normally known as *hashing* and the devising of suitable formulae has been the subject of much research.

A simple example of a hashing algorithm is given in Fig. 3.12. It is required to store customer records on disk and use the customer surname to obtain access to a particular record. The hashing algorithm uses the numerical equivalent of the first two letters of the surname. The range of possible combinations is 256 × 256 (each ASCII character occupies 8 bits, giving a range of numbers between 0 and 255). Hence SMITH would

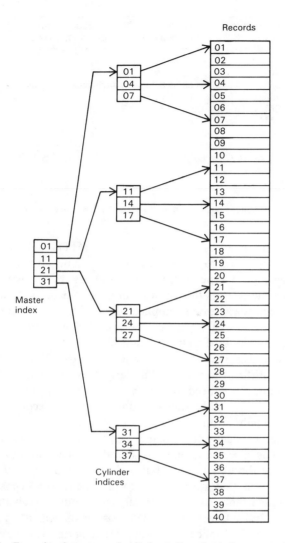

Figure 3.11 Example of master and cylinder indices for index sequential organization.

generate the ASCII code: 83 × 77 (the numbers equivalent to SM).

It is important to know the approximate number of records in the file as the amount of space which should be allocated in an ideal situation would be exactly the amount required to store those records. Assuming there are about 250 records in the example in Fig. 3.12, and multiplying together the two characters from the surname, dividing by 250, then taking the remainder plus one as the location for the record, would produce numbers ranging from 1 to 250. This is equal to the number of records and ideally the arrangement would ensure that each record generated a unique hashing code so that it had its own location.

Record for	Characters for hash	Numerical equivalent	Position on disk (hash code)	Overflow position
Able, J	AB	65 × 66	41	
Brown, T	BR	66 × 82	163	251
Brown, W	BR	66 × 82	251	
Jones, L	JO	74 × 79	97	
Smith, T	SM	83 × 77	142	252
Smith, W	SM	83 × 77	252	
Wills, A	WI	87 × 73	102	

Example: (ABLE, J) AB = 65 × 66   (overflow starts at location 251)
65 × 66/250 = 17 rem. 40
hash code = 40+1 = 41

Figure 3.12 Example of disk file with access by hash coding technique.

There are two occurrences each of the names SMITH and BROWN. An overflow record will need to be created for the second occurrence of each name and its position will be stored next to the first record with the same name. The overflow records themselves will be stored in locations 251 and 252. It can be seen that a more complicated algorithm which included the customer's initial would have reduced the need for overflow records.

The hashing technique, if well designed, provides fast access to data, as normally only one disk read is necessary to locate the data. However, the technique can be difficult to manage with large files which are also growing in size. In addition, if files need to be arranged in different orders, they will need to be sorted. This will be time-consuming, as each record will have to be located individually at different places on the disk.

There are other arrangements of data which provide advantages in certain circumstances. The representation of data on disks is a complicated subject and the foregoing discussion gives but a flavour of the various available techniques. The tools that are provided to programmers to construct data structures are much more advanced on larger computers than they are on microcomputers. Indeed, with some data base management systems (see Chapter 4), extremely complicated logical structures can be devised without worrying about the physical arrangements which are taken care of by the data base software. Often, these logical structures (hierarchies of data etc.) are physically stored by *chaining* records together. A chain is formed by placing the position or *address* of the next or previous record, or both, in the record itself. A record can be part of a number of chains and the process of adding or deleting records can become quite complex.

There is a wide range of books on this topic but for the reader who wants to pursue this subject, those by James Martin are particularly recommended.

REFERENCES

1. Hogan, T. *Osborne CP/M User Guide*, Osborne/McGraw-Hill, 1982.
2. Hanson, O. *Essentials of Computer Data Files*, Pitman, 1985.

4

Systems for information retrieval and data management

This chapter deals with systems for information retrieval on micro-computers. In addition, the features of data base management systems and the use of microcomputers as intelligent terminals for accessing remote data bases are described. Chapter 5 deals mainly with systems for library housekeeping but the line between the two areas is difficult to draw and hence some overlap is inevitable.

4.1   INFORMATION RETRIEVAL SYSTEMS

4.1.1   *Essentials of information retrieval systems*

Online computer-based information retrieval systems were developed in the 1960s, notably by Lockheed Dialog and by Systems Development Corporation (SDC). They were introduced in order to provide fast access to bibliographic records and, at the same time, to improve on the performance of manual search tools such as printed indexes. Bibliographic data bases are, in such systems, stored on disk and searches are made at a terminal connected directly to the computer (see Fig. 4.8 for an outline of the equipment), and answers can be displayed directly on the terminal.

Today, it is possible to connect a computer terminal to a wide range of online computer-stored data around the world. These host computers can store many data bases and have enormous power which is used to service simultaneously many hundreds of users. A few search terms entered at a keyboard can quickly retrieve details of documents or data to satisfy a request.

Information retrieval systems are also available for microcomputers. Their mode of operation is basically similar to those designed for larger computers but they are limited in certain ways in terms of what they can provide. Indeed, some of the systems are scaled-down versions of operational systems for larger machines; for example, BRS, a major online vendor in the USA, sells versions of its retrieval software for mini- and microcomputers. As retrieval systems have become more widespread, they have been used for an ever increasing range of data. In addition to bibliographic records they are used for such applications as real estate sales research projects, online 'yellow pages' etc.

The optimum organization of a data base for retrieval will depend on the particular needs. Of importance will be:

(a) the structural characteristics of the data and their use;
(b) the overall size of the data base;
(c) the speed of retrieval required;
(d) the speed of updating required.

In a classical information retrieval system, data tend to be arranged in a single record as shown in Fig. 3.7. A number of *inverted indexes* which can be likened to those in the back of a book, provide the fast retrieval speeds required. A bibliographic data base can become quite large as documents are often entered into it with only a vague idea of whether they are going to be relevant. A fast retrieval is usually of more importance than a fast updating speed. A *controlled vocabulary* of indexing terms can be used to improve retrieval efficiency (see below) in some circumstances.

Although the online data base vendors, such as Dialog, provide a fast response to queries, updating the data bases themselves is not usually such a time-critical process. Normally a typical data base is updated at weekly or even longer intervals, although there are exceptions. Often, once a record is established, it is not changed or deleted until it is removed with a number of others.

At the other extreme to the large online systems is the single-user microcomputer information retrieval system, the use pattern of which may not have the same constraints. It may, for instance, be possible to make do with a slower retrieval speed in exchange for faster updating. The design of the retrieval system will be very dependent on this decision. However, if a software package is chosen which provides certain features such as fast retrieval speed, it may not be possible to change the system significantly if priorities change. If flexibility is required, it may be better to go for a general-purpose data base management system (see section 4.2) which may offer inferior retrieval functions but more flexible data management features.

Inverted lists or *indexes*: the creation of inverted lists is one mechanism for increasing retrieval speed. Search terms are taken out of each record, or perhaps assigned from a controlled vocabulary, and are entered into lists which are ordered in some way to allow fast matching of a search request against the entries in the lists. There might be different lists for the various types of data, author, title words, terms from a controlled vocabulary etc. or they may all be grouped together. The entries in the inverted lists are often linked to their respective records in the main file through a postings file which stores the record numbers corresponding to the entries in the inverted lists. Fig. 4.1 shows the creation of inverted list entries for three records from a sample bibliographic data base. The files might be arranged and searched as in Fig. 4.2.

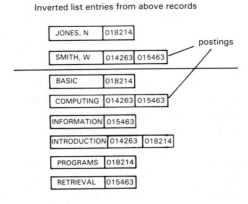

Records in main file (file will contain many more)

| 014263 | SMITH, W | AN INTRODUCTION TO COMPUTING | PRIME PUBL., 1983 |

| 015463 | SMITH, W | INFORMATION RETRIEVAL AND COMPUTING | JAMES, 1982 |

| 018214 | JONES, N | AN INTRODUCTION TO BASIC PROGRAMS | PRIME PUBL., 1984 |

Inverted list entries from above records

| JONES, N | 018214 |

postings

| SMITH, W | 014263 | 015463 |

| BASIC | 018214 |

| COMPUTING | 014263 | 015463 |

| INFORMATION | 015463 |

| INTRODUCTION | 014263 | 018214 |

| PROGRAMS | 018214 |

| RETRIEVAL | 015463 |

Figure 4.1 Inverted list entries generated from records in main file (entries for publisher, record number and date not created).

With this arrangement, searching is usually a two-stage process, the first being to search the inverted lists and the postings file to find the number of records that satisfy the search request. The original records which are retrieved by the search are displayed at a second step and their locations are obtained from the postings file.

The difficulty in updating the data base can be seen from Fig. 4.2. When a record is added or deleted, not only is the main file one of variable-length records but also the entries in the inverted lists and in the postings file have to be altered. The size of these indexes can grow rapidly, especially for bibliographic records, and even more rapidly if an abstract describing the content of a document is also searchable by the inverted list technique.

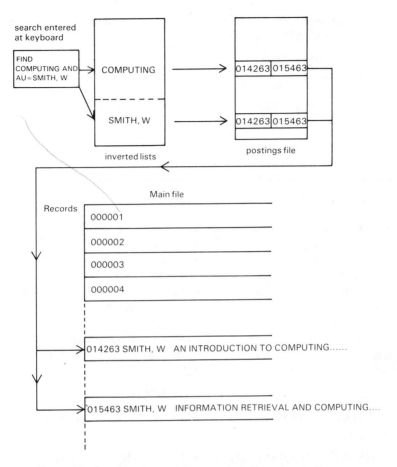

Figure 4.2 Searching inverted lists, postings file and main file.

String searching: the reduction to a minimum of the number of types of data elements which are inverted for searching will reduce the size of the lists and ease the maintenance problem. On some systems, it will still be possible to search on these data elements using a technique known as string searching. The records in the main file are scanned sequentially from the beginning of the file until a match is found. Needless to say, this technique is relatively slow but can be valuable if retrieval speed is not critical. At the extreme, inverted indexes can be dispensed with altogether which, especially with large files, would remove much of the updating headache. Of course, the main file must be updated but the whole process then becomes more manageable. It is likely, as well, that updating of records will be an important factor in in-house systems.

Search strategies: once a data base and its inverted indexes have been set up, a search can be carried out using one or more search terms. In the

Inverted indexes

records shown in Fig. 4.1 a search for all documents containing the word COMPUTING might be as follows:

FIND COMPUTING   (entered at the keyboard)

The answer from the computer would be:

SET 1 : 2 hits   (Fig. 4.1 shows there are two records containing the word COMPUTING)

The search is given a set number so that if the search results need to be displayed or the search refined it can be referred to directly. Hence to display records for set 1:

SHOW S = 1;F = ALL

would be entered. It is sometimes possible to show all or part of the retrieved records. In this case F = ALL means show full records and S = 1 is the set number. The above commands are those adopted for the European Common Command Language (CCL) but they are only a convention and there is a variety of different commands in use. The variety can be quite confusing and its elimination was the main aim behind the development of the CCL.

A more detailed search could be carried out by combining two or more terms using *Boolean logic*, in this case the word COMPUTING and an author W. SMITH (see also Fig. 4.2):

FIND COMPUTING AND AU = SMITH, W

This would retrieve records containing BOTH these terms. The following example:

FIND INTRODUCTION AND (BASIC OR COMPUTING)

would retrieve records containing the word INTRODUCTION together with either the word BASIC or the word COMPUTING.

It is also possible to search for part of a search term. Thus the truncated term COMPUT$, with the dollar sign being the *truncation symbol*, would retrieve records containing words such as COMPUTER, COMPUTING etc. The same symbol can also be put in the middle or to the left of the term in some systems. Records containing a particular term can be eliminated using NOT logic.

All the above searches can be carried out without accessing the main file. Only when the retrieved records are to be seen is it necessary to enter the main file. Other search techniques are possible, such as the string searching mentioned above, and some of them require the main file to be accessed. String searching allows the searcher to specify the relative positions of search terms or that terms should only be searched in a particular type of data element. This can also be done in the inverted data structure if the relevant data are carried in an inverted list or attached to it. Of course, a more complex inverted data structure will add to the maintenance problem, but will speed up searching when more sophisticated search techniques, such as word adjacency, are used.

Controlled vocabularies, thesauri and indexing: the examples of searches just described show the application of what is sometimes called 'free-text' searching. Words or groups of words freely thought up to describe a sought-after subject are matched by the computer against the data in each record. This type of subject search may be sufficient for some questions but not for others. For instance, in a data base of real estate, it may not be possible to retrieve details of all houses which are, say, 'detached' using the data describing the houses if that word is omitted from some of the records. In addition, records describing 'semi-detached' houses may also be retrieved if the retrieval system treats a hyphen as a space. In a similar way, some types of search query, such as those for the subject of a document, are often difficult to match exactly with records for relevant documents; hence the aids to retrieval such as the truncation device described above.

Even with these devices, the retrieval efficiency may not be sufficient. The *recall* (the percentage of relevant records in the collection that are retrieved) and the *precision* (the percentage of retrieved records that are relevant) may not be large enough. Both these measures can be improved in some circumstances by employing a controlled vocabulary. In the real-estate example, a list of 'types of house' would include the words DETACHED and SEMIDETACHED (with no space or hyphen) etc., one of which would be assigned to each house record when it was entered. Thesauri have been produced for a wide range of subject fields.

Controlled vocabularies for subject indexing can become quite extensive for large document collections and techniques are used to ensure that searcher and indexer (the person assigning the terms) use the correct terms. At its simplest the vocabulary can be a simple list of preferred terms, but structural aids, such as showing the relationships between broader, narrower and related terms, can be used. Some vocabularies are based on classifications using a code or notation to describe each subject.

If desired, the controlled terms can be entered into the inverted lists instead of the free-text terms. This may cut down the number of terms in the lists and simplify maintenance. There are disadvantages, however. The vocabulary itself must be maintained and terms assigned to each record. It is also preferable, although not essential, that the retrieval system maintain the vocabulary. If it does not, it can be maintained manually outside the system but this usually means extra work.

A controlled vocabulary can be applied at search time instead of when a record is created. In this case it can be used to help generate the search terms. Most retrieval systems will allow the inverted lists, and, if available, the controlled vocabulary to be displayed online. This can be used both for indexing and searching. There has been considerable debate on whether to use free-text searching or a controlled vocabulary. For further insight into this complex subject, the reader is referred to works by Foskett [1] and by Lancaster and Foyen [2]. If it can be afforded, having both free-text and controlled vocabularies may be useful as they can come into their own in different circumstances. For small collections of records, as may be the case with many microcomputer systems, the user may be able to make do with something quite simple. The final decision will need to be taken on the basis of perceived costs and benefits.

4.1.2 Information retrieval systems for microcomputers

There is a range of available information retrieval systems for micro-computers on the market with a variety of prices. A list of available software is given in Appendix 1. Some of the systems will naturally provide more features than others but it is important to analyse carefully the particular needs and choose the software appropriate for the job. Software features can be divided into those which are necessary, desirable and unnecessary.

Any retrieval system will provide three essential ingredients:

(a) data base creation and management (input of new records, amend-ments and deletions);
(b) search commands, normally in online mode with fast response time (usually a few seconds) and Boolean logic;
(c) display of search results.

Data base creation: one of the first tasks will be to decide on the data elements for the data base and their characteristics. This demands careful consideration because the data base structure may be difficult to change after it has been set up and records have been entered into it.

Most software will have a module to set up the skeleton of the data base. An example of building a data base using the University of London FIRS retrieval system is shown in Appendix 3. Software may also provide a format checker to check such fields as date and record number. The package will have a limit to the size of fields and records and to the total number of records in a data base.

Before input of data, the indexing system will need to be set up. If free-text indexing is used, a decision will need to be taken on which data elements are to be made searchable (see Appendix 3) and how. Elements such as the title of a document will probably require each word to be individually searchable. Authors' names will also be searchable individually but the forenames and surnames will need to be kept together. Some data elements will be searched as a single element (e.g. record number).

The use of a controlled vocabulary will present another level of difficulty as the indexing mechanism will need to be set up. The example in Appendix 3 does not support a computer-stored controlled vocabulary but a manually maintained one could be used in conjunction with it.

Input of data into a record may be onto a preformatted screen, perhaps with reverse video (black on white) characters for the field names and with space next to each field name for the data. More likely, especially if variable-length fields are used, the fields will be presented on the screen one at a time. The first data element is sometimes a record number which is presented by the program. It may be necessary to have a second record number under user control. If a computer-stored controlled vocabulary is used, the assigned terms might be checked automatically and new or mistyped terms would be flagged (marked).

In order to amend a record it is often located using the input/maintenance module by its computer-assigned number and in this case the number must be known. It may be possible to retrieve the record using the retrieval module and then go straight into update mode. Such a feature might be useful if it were convenient to use the retrieval and updating modules together. This approach might also be useful for the deletion of data; for instance, it might be desirable to delete a set of records that satisfy a certain criterion, e.g. older than a certain date. They could be retrieved by the retrieval module and then deleted in one step.

Creation of inverted indexes: when a new record is added to the data base or an existing record amended, the inverted indexes will need to be updated. Some systems may require the whole of the inverted index to be recreated after every change to the master records, but they should be avoided, if possible, as it can be a time-consuming process for large data bases.

Searching and retrieval: following a search it will usually be possible, as a second step, to display results on the screen or to print the records on a printer attached to a microcomputer. Some microcomputers will, if required, print the content of the screen as the data appear. Some systems print or display the entire record only but it might be useful to have a range of user-definable sub-sets of the data base to be extracted and used for other purposes. It may be required to create a report from the results and this could be done using a word processor. The machine-readable records retrieved from the search could be submitted directly to the word processor and edited.

Production of printed catalogues and indexes: production of printed catalogues and indexes may be important, particularly in a library with a larger number of users than (say) a single-user microcomputer could cope with in online mode. It may also be necessary to have access to the data base in different places and the production of multiple copies of catalogues and indexes is one answer to this problem. If multiple terminal online access is required a multiple user system is needed. There are several answers to this hardware problem, one if which is to use a minicomputer!

If printing is required, the software should be examined to see how this can be done. Some systems will allow several different printing formats and sequences. It may be necessary to consider alphabetical filing rules, for example to interfile names such as those beginning with Mc and Mac.

Other features of the software which should be taken into consideration include:

(a) system reminders to create backup copies of data bases (tidy house-keeping procedures are essential to maintaining the integrity of the data base);

(b) access security (different passwords for various categories of user);

(c) user-friendly search facilities (for users unfamiliar with the retrieval system);

(d) software capable of supporting simultaneous use by a number of users;

(e) permanent storage of search strategies;

(f) system recovery procedures to minimize data loss.

Section 4.3 deals with the 'downloading' of machine-readable data from online data base vendors into a microcomputer. Software is available to carry this out but, once the data are in the microcomputer, a retrieval system should be able to take a batch of records directly without the need to re-input it manually. Such a transfer would normally require a format change program to make the records compatible with the local system.

Some information retrieval systems for microcomputers have been derived from mainframe systems developed by online database vendors, others from minicomputer systems for in-house library and information service operation; still others have been devised as original microcomputer systems, and there are undoubtedly other categories. It would be wise when considering selection to examine the history of the development of each system and its current range of applications. If it is expected that the system will have to cope with the range of library housekeeping applications as well (see Chapter 5), some compromises may have to be accepted. As already noted, another approach may be to adopt a data base management system which will probably provide maximum flexibility but will usually require greater knowledge of software. These systems will be discussed in Section 4.2. The use of optical disks in conjunction with microcomputer information retrieval systems will grow in importance and should be taken into account when deciding on a system. Optical disk developments will be considered next.

4.1.3 Information retrieval with optical disks

A growing number of bibliographic data bases are becoming available on CD-ROM and some software producers have been quick to adapt their information retrieval systems to allow searching of these data bases to take

74

place using a microcomputer. It would have seemed amazing just a few years ago to be able to search a data base of hundreds of thousands of records using a microcomputer costing only a few thousand dollars. Bibliographic data bases provided on CD-ROM normally contain both the basic records and the inverted indexes. With a capacity approaching 600 Megabytes, it is easy to see how these huge data bases can be accommodated.

The CD-ROM player can be attached to an existing microcomputer, providing the correct interface is available. Searching is almost identical in most cases to searching a smaller data base stored on magnetic disk on the microcomputer, or similar to an online search of a data base stored on a large host information retrieval service. With such large data bases stored on a microcomputer with CD-ROM, the response time can be slow but the CD-ROM version has other advantages over both the searching of data bases on remote hosts and the use of printed sources. The advantages over online access to remotely stored databases include:

(a) predictable costs compared with paying online connect time charges;
(b) no pressure to search in as short a time as possible;
(c) increasing the number of searches reduces the cost per search;
(d) inexperienced users of online services are more likely to use them;

and over printed publications include:

(a) CD-ROM takes up much less space;
(b) is faster to use;
(c) provides similar sophisticated access paths to those obtained presently with online searching using remote hosts;
(d) multiple copies can be distributed to users at a particular location as they are not expensive to make.

One of the dilemmas faced by the bibliographic data base producers is the possible loss of revenue from other forms of publication of the data base. Widespread distribution of the CD-ROM could reduce the use of online host services, although even this is not clear, as the frequency of updating of a CD-ROM service is not likely to be provided as often as an online host. A further complicating factor is that the CD-ROM could be used to transfer machine-readable records to a local retrieval system on a much larger computer. Thus a user could capture a whole data base for a possibly low price. On the other hand, another type of user might want only to search the CD-ROM file on a single user microcomputer. In this case it would be difficult to justify charging a price much in excess of the cost of the current subscription to a printed index, or what the user currently spends on online charges.

This range of possibilities will demand sophisticated pricing mechanisms and control of the use of records distributed on CD-ROMs. With frequent updating of disks, out of date disks could easily pass into the hands of unauthorized users.

75

Some as yet unknown factors covering the use of CD-ROMs include:

(a) shelf life (10 years minimum is predicted but no CD-ROM has been in existence for that time;

(b) CD-ROMs are only just in production and, although benefiting from volume production of audio compact disks, production prices of the drives have yet to stabilize.

Nevertheless, a growing number of large electronics companies are now producing CD-ROM players. The challenge is to the information community to generate the information products to profit from the evident advantages of the CD-ROM. Indeed, some novel products have already reached the market, such as the CD-ROM version of the Grolier Academic American Encyclopedia.

The optical disk is likely to have an enormous (some say revolutionary) impact on the information dissemination process. The combination of the storage of text, sound and images will provide opportunities for a new approach to information dissemination. The technology is new but already the elements are in place to enable a wide range of CD-ROM products to be marketed, e.g.:

(a) serials,
(b) directories,
(c) encyclopaedias,
(d) reference works,
(e) operations manuals,
(f) student 'texts',
(g) parts lists,
(h) service manuals, etc.

It is the authors' view that, provided manufacturers can produce the CD-ROM at the right price, CD-ROM players will become widely available. The hardware is standardized, file definition standards are being completed, and hence the possibility of using the same CD-ROMs on a variety of hardware is a real one.

The retrieval of information from videodisks using microcomputers is also possible, as described in Chapter 2. Data in machine-readable form can be stored on a videodisk and retrieved in a similar way to that of a CD-ROM. Moving or still images and sound can also form part of the retrieval process. Two early examples of the use of videodisk images, in conjunction with microcomputers and online data bases, are the Pergamon Video-Patsearch and BRS Colleague systems. In the latter, data can be stored in a number of places, including the BRS host computer, a microcomputer with the BRS microcomputer retrieval software and a video disk player containing extracts from a number of medical texts, including diagrams. The Patsearch system was somewhat similar, allowing the retrieval of patent records from the patent data base stored on the Infoline computer, with parts of the original patent being stored on video disk. A major problem with video disks is the cost of production and a number of products have failed in the market place because of this factor alone. It is very likely that the introduction of the CD-ROM, which will also offer text, images and sound on the same disk, will enable a much less costly product to be manufactured. Despite the cost of production, video disks have been successful in interactive training situations and in stores at points of sale.

4.2 DATA BASE MANAGEMENT SYSTEMS

4.2.1 Data base management system features

Data Base Management Systems (DBMSs) do just what the name suggests: manage a computer-stored data base or collection of data. DBMSs were originally developed for large computers to assist with the development, implementation and maintenance of related computer systems.

At first, computer systems were designed around particular applications or departments in organizations. Separate systems were developed for, say, the personnel and payroll departments. It was realized that the data were duplicated in a number of systems, e.g. details of employees' names and addresses. When someone left a company or was promoted, several files had to be altered. In addition, changes in company policy could mean a larger number of changes to all these various independent systems. More seriously, the fact that programs reflected the existing organization made it more difficult to change management structures.

File management systems were introduced to give programmers a consistent set of routines for managing files of computer-stored records. They did not, however, solve many of the fundamental problems of the management of data for the organization. Data base management systems were evolved to provide the sort of assistance required by programmers to enable them to provide more efficient computer systems.

DBMSs for large computers are usually expensive: several tens of thousands of dollars is not an unusual price to pay. The fact that they work indicates the sort of savings and benefits they can bring.

To illustrate the basic principle of how a DBMS centralizes the data for an organization and provides a subset of the data to a relevant department, take as an example the technical service operation of a library. Such a service will be responsible for ordering, receiving, cataloguing, classifying books. Other library departments will require information on different aspects, for example, the book circulation department will need data on users' names and addresses and which books are on loan to whom. A traditional approach to the automation of the various departmental systems might be as shown in

Fig. 4.3. The section responsible for ordering books has a file of books on order and received and a file of suppliers. The cataloguing section maintains a file or catalogue of books in the library. The book circulation department has a file of books for the purpose of controlling circulation, a file of loans and a file of library users.

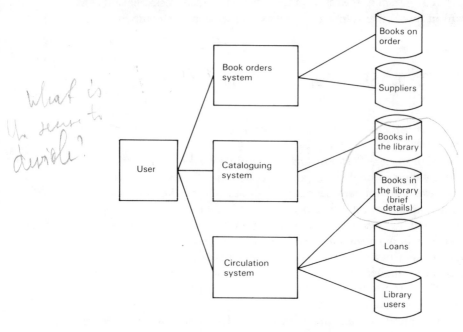

Figure 4.3 A library automation system with separate files for different departmental systems (simplified).

The DBMS approach might look like that shown in Fig. 4.4. All data are centralized into a data base and the various departments in the library enter data and retrieve them according to their interests. The programmer developing a particular application can specify the data needed just for that application. If the design of the whole data base is sensitive to all the library's needs, it can lead to a high level of independence between applications, i.e. changes in one having little or no effect on another. In addition, departments can have access to all the data in the library of interest to them, even that from other departments. Duplication of data is reduced and the result can be a more effective organization for less effort. Just as important, both management and the library user may want an overall picture and can more easily obtain it. For instance, a user interested in a particular book may be happy to wait, if it can be easily determined that it is on order. If the book files are integrated from the user's point of view, this information can be found out with a single online query to the data base. The user can then follow the status of the book as it progresses

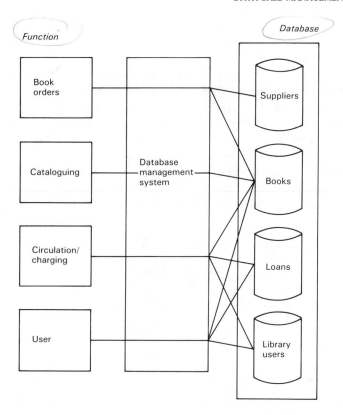

Figure 4.4   The data base approach to a library automation system (simplified).

through the system, i.e. received but not in process, being catalogued, available, on loan etc. A DBMS will comprise a number of modules to operate on the central data base:

(a) a Data Definition Language (DDL), a mechanism for organizing and structuring the data base and defining the data elements;
(b) a Data Manipulation Language (DML), used by programmers to manipulate data, often used in conjunction with a high-level language such as Cobol;
(c) a query language, for users of the data base who need answers to *ad hoc* questions — it should be easy to use and supply answers rapidly;
(d) a report writer, for producing printed, customized reports;
(e) a data input sub-system;
(f) a communications sub-system to support a number of online users.

Of course data base management systems will vary in what they offer but, for large computers, there are generally accepted features which must be available. The term 'database' (without a space) is often used for a collection of data managed by a DBMS.

4.2.2 DBMS data structures

Data base management systems can be characterized by the way they hold or structure their data. Information retrieval systems, such as those described in Section 4.1, generally have a simple structure in the master record where there is often no relationship between data elements other than that they are side-by-side in the record. It can be very like the sort of data structures found in *relational* data bases in which data are arranged in simple tables called relations. The other main category of DBMS uses complex data structures in which elements of data are organized *hierarchically* (one-to-many) or in *networks* (many-to-many).

Book relation *(table)* entities

Order no.	Author	Title	Supplier no.	Date
01625	Brown, T	Computer Systems	124	831211
01626	Able, M	Introduction to PL/1	024	831212
01627	Smith, W	Basic for students	124	831213
01628	Nichols, M	Introduction to Pascal	025	831213
01629	Black, T	Logo for children	024	831214

Supplier relation *(table)* entities

Supplier no.	Supplier name	Address
024	Mount & Son	26 South Street, Anytown
025	Jones and Co.	P.O. Box 1., Westchester
124	Surton Books	246 Time Street, Dounton-on-Sea

Figure 4.5 Books on order and supplier relations in a relational data base.

Relational data base management systems (RDBMS) operate on data tables or relations, an example of which is shown in Fig. 4.5. A relation can be regarded as a matrix, with a number of rows and columns, a row corresponding to a single record in an information retrieval data base (see Fig. 4.1) and a column to all instances of a particular data element. A relational data base can comprise a number of these tables and the RDBMS is able to manipulate them to produce the desired results. Fig. 4.5 shows a simple data base for ordering books which contains a BOOK relation and a SUPPLIER relation. The two relations can be manipulated to produce, for instance, a list of books on order to each of the suppliers. This is shown in Fig. 4.6. The arrangement of data in the two relations avoids the duplication of data. Supplier details are stored once only in a separate relation rather than with each book on order. Thus, if a supplier's address changed, it would only be necessary to change the appropriate entry in the supplier relation. Again, if orders to a particular supplier were changed to another, only the relevant supplier numbers in the BOOK relation would need to be changed. These changes could be made by using the data manipulation tools supplied with the DBMS.

Jones and Co.
Nichols, M   Introduction to Pascal   831213

Mount & Son
Able, M   Introduction to PL/1   831212
Black, T   Logo for children   831214

Surton Books
Brown, T   Computer Systems   831211
Smith, W   Basic for students   831213

Figure 4.6   Production of a report of books on order organized alphabetically by supplier from the relations in Fig. 4.5.

This is only a very simple example of the operation of a relational data base management system. In practice it is necessary to have expertise in this area to take full advantage of them. However, some RDBMSs for microcomputers are fairly easy to use (see below). The analysis of each application requires the construction of relations which are *normalized*. There are different levels of *normal form* of a relation, most of which aim to simplify the relation by, for instance, eliminating repeated data elements and complex links between the key-field and others.

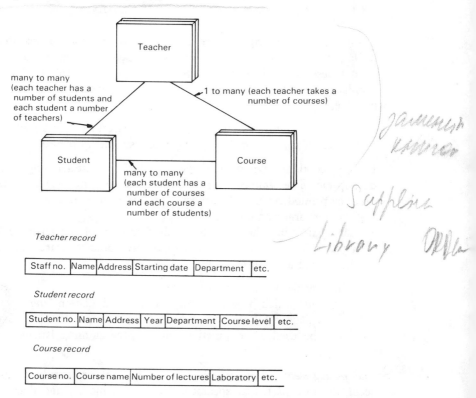

Figure 4.7   Schema for a network data base management system for a teacher-student course data base.

Network and hierarchical data base management systems allow data to be stored in ways which exactly reflect their structures and links. Rather than eliminating the complex links, as relational systems do, the exact desired structures can be supported by hierarchical and network structures. Theoretically, it can be shown that a hierarchy with one-to-many links is a trivial example of a network structure with many-to-many links. These DBMSs allow links to be created and destroyed subject to an overall data base organizational plan called a *schema*. In the example shown in Fig. 4.7, if a teacher takes over an existing course from another, the links between teachers and courses can be broken and re-formed as required. Systems provide rapid access to, and maintenance of, a data base. It is vital, however, to design the data base correctly, as it can be difficult to change the schema significantly if it is not satisfactory once the data base is in operation and of some size. Contrast this with the relational approach in which links are usually implied by common data in different relations (see supplier number in Fig. 4.5).

4.2.3 Data base management systems for microcomputers

DBMSs for microcomputers are, in general, much more modest than those for larger computers and a good deal less expensive. Some of them, in fact, do not deserve the label in the strict sense of the definition. This lack of sophistication can be a positive advantage in some circumstances, however, because:

(a) many applications on microcomputers are themselves fairly modest;
(b) lack of sophistication can also mean simplicity of use.

In practice there is a wide range of DBMSs masquerading under that description. The simplest will do little more than manage a single file to produce printed reports. The most complicated has most of the features of systems for large computers.

Bearing in mind the warning about definition of the term DBMS and taking a wide and pragmatic view of the available software, the packages can be looked at in three groups:

(a) file management systems;
(b) systems which provide a simple data manipulation language;
(c) fully-fledged DBMSs which have a data manipulation language which can be used in conjunction with a programming language such as Cobol.

File management systems provide the ability to create records in a file, according to a particular specification, to add, modify and delete records and sort them into specific orders before printing them in a variety of formats. The procedures to carry out these operations are usually simple to learn.

An information retrieval system, such as described in Section 4.1, will have a file management system built into it. Bibliographic retrieval systems often hold data for a document in a single record and, generally speaking, the data base approach involving, for example, the manipulation of relations as shown in Figs. 4.5 and 4.6 is not a common feature.

There are a number of simple data base management systems which are rather more powerful than file management systems. Some are classed as relational and the authors of some of this last group would claim that the very simplicity lies in the use of relations but that the approach allows the construction of as complicated a data base as the network approach. dBase III is a popular example of the relational approach and, in addition to its data management features, it has a retrieval language which can employ inverted indexes for fast retrieval.

The facilities to be considered when choosing a data base management system in this simple category include:

(a) data element definition: the types of element which can be defined, e.g. alphanumeric, numeric, monetary amount;
(b) record characteristics: maximum field length, number of fields, fixed or variable-length fields/records, maximum record length and records per file;
(c) file handling: multiple file/relation support and manipulation, acceptance of external data base and production of sub-files to take to other systems, ease of redefinition of data base;
(d) searching capabilities: availability of a query language to allow online searching of the data base and its ease of use, including Boolean logic, truncation, support for inverted indexes, range searching, e.g. greater than, less than;
(e) data manipulation language: necessity to use this language in order to make the system work, simplicity of use, power of the language and its function, e.g. is it used for producing reports or is there a separate report generator available?;
(f) integrity and security of data: backup facilities, restart from error condition with minimum loss of data base, if system is multi-user, procedures to ensure same elements of data are not operated on simultaneously;
(g) reports: creation of customized reports, sorting of output on any field, degree of expertise required;
(h) ease of use: easy-to-understand documentation.

Microcomputer DBMSs are becoming more sophisticated with the growing number of 16-bit and 32-bit machines which provide ever greater memory and processing power. When even larger machines become commonplace at microcomputer prices the whole range of existing mainframe software will be exposed to a much larger market. DBMSs for microcomputers are described in detail, with worked examples, by Kruglinski [3, 4].

4.3 MICROCOMPUTER-ASSISTED INFORMATION RETRIEVAL AND DATA COMMUNICATION

4.3.1 The online search process

The process of online searching of remote data bases, in most cases, involves a dialogue between a searcher and a host computer. A computer terminal, operated by the searcher, is connected to the host computer by means of a telecommunication link. An outline of the equipment is shown in Fig. 4.8. The link between terminal and host is often via a packet-switched network (see Chapter 2).

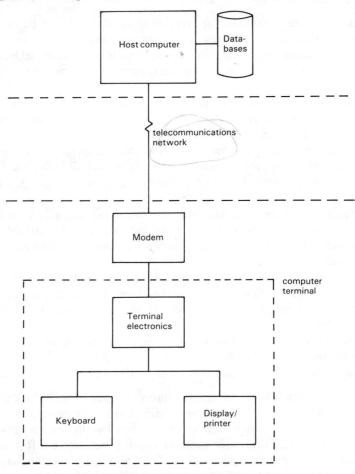

Figure 4.8 Equipment for accessing a remote host computer.

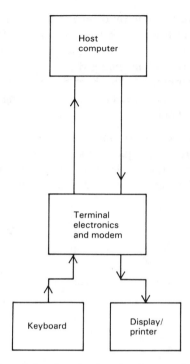

Figure 4.9   Flow of data from keyboard to host and from host to display.

The flow of data is, in one direction, from keyboard to host (requests) and, in the other direction, from host to visual display screen (information), as shown in Fig. 4.9. In this dialogue, the host computer imposes constraints on what the searcher can do and when. For instance, commands must usually be constructed in exactly the required format (see Section 4.1 for examples of the search process) and often it is necessary to wait for a reply from the host before entering the next command, even though the content of that command may not be dependent on the answer to the previous one.

4.3.2   Microcomputer assistance

Inserting a microcomputer between the terminal and the searcher's modem provides computing power to interfere with the streams of data going to and from the host computer (see Fig. 4.10). The microcomputer can be made to manipulate the data which flow in either direction to the benefit of, and under the control of, the searcher. In addition, it can reroute data to and from different devices in the microcomputer, such as magnetic disks, again under the control of the searcher. Recently interest has been shown in the subject of *downloading* or capturing data from a host computer in machine readable form. This can be done by diverting the stream of incoming data onto a storage device such as a disk (see Fig. 4.11). The transmission of data from the microcomputer to another machine is sometimes referred to as *uploading*. If the storage of incoming data and the transmission of data already in the microcomputer to the host can be done conveniently and rapidly, it can provide some advantages over searching techniques with a normal terminal. These include:

(a) simplified procedures for logging-on to the host computer;
(b) 'store and forward' techniques for search data;
(c) storage of search results for later use (in several ways);
(d) automatic transfer and reception of data (unattended);

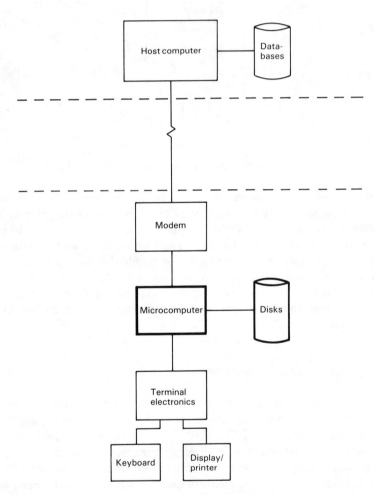

Figure 4.10 Equipment for accessing a remote host computer with microcomputer assistance.

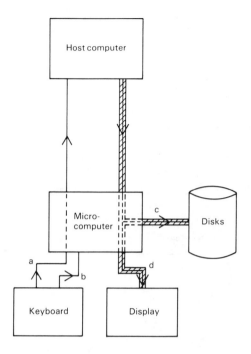

Figure 4.11 Flow of data during downloading operation. (a) Searcher gives instructions to host computer to start to download; (b) gives instructions to microcomputer to collect and store data; (c) downloaded data going onto disk; (d) simultaneous display of downloaded data on screen.

(e) aids to searching such as the provision of advice on using the host computer systems, translation of commands from one host language to another, help to inexperienced users and enhancement of the search strategy.

Perhaps the simplest, and most obvious, use of the microcomputer is for storing data locally in the microcomputer before going online to the host computer and then forwarding the data, as and when required, directly from microcomputer to host computer using simple procedures.

Logging-on through a public data network can be a time-consuming and frustrating task, particularly at busy periods. By permanently storing the network and host user-identifiers and passwords in the microcomputer they can be used to make logging-on a very straightforward process, normally reducing it to a very small number of key-strokes on the keyboard. In addition, auto-dialling can be carried out. 'Smart' modems are available which can store frequently used telephone numbers and even the communications software (see Chapter 2).

The same principle of storing data in the microcomputer before connection to the host can also be applied to search strategies and other

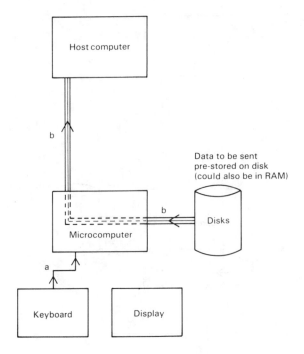

Figure 4.12 Forwarding of pre-stored data from microcomputer to host computer. (a) Searcher gives instruction to microcomputer to send data; (b) microcomputer collects data from disk (if necessary) and sends to host.

commands which are to be sent to the host and which can be worked out in advance (see Fig. 4.12). The advantages of being able to carry out the forwarding of prestored data to the host are evident on analysing the charging policies of many host data base providers. The practice of levying a relatively high charge for online *connect-time* (the time the user is connected to the host), irrespective of whether any searching is actually being done, penalizes the person with poor keyboard skills. Even a proficient typist cannot match the 30 or 120 characters per second that are the usual transmission speeds of the line and at which prestored data can be transmitted. Proceeding at a higher speed, the search can be carried out more quickly, thus saving connect-time or giving extra time for more interactive search operations to be carried out.

A further degree of sophistication is the ability to store data in the microcomputer which are being entered at the keyboard actually during an online session. It then becomes an easy matter to instruct the microcomputer to re-send the data if, say, the message was not correctly received by the host. Similarly, the sending of data can be delayed until a whole line is ready to go, and thus the correction of typing errors by simple backspacing (locally) will again aid input. It must be emphasized, of course, that the microcomputer is usually programmed so as not to interfere with the use of the equipment as a normal terminal.

Downloading: the collection of data from a host computer and its storage in machine-readable form is known as downloading. In order to carry this out effectively, the microcomputer stores the stream of data coming from the host computer (most likely on a disk file), as well as directing it to the visual display screen. Some advantages of downloading are:

(a) Data can usually be stored at the speed they are received and thus the speed of the search is not limited by the speed of the printer; the results can be printed at leisure once the search is finished.
(b) The search results can be edited, possibly to eliminate unwanted references, to make multiple copies, or perhaps to make a more impressive-looking report (a word processor can be used for this).
(c) The search results can be transferred into a local information system, either on the same microcomputer or on some other local computer (see bulk transmission below). Normally a reformatting program that translates the format of the downloaded data into the format of the retrieval system will be needed.
(d) Search results can be transferred from one data base on the host to another, or from one host to another, e.g. a search for chemical compounds in a sub-structure search system which can then be input to (say) a *Chemical Abstracts* bibliographic search.
(e) Retrieved data could be communicated to another computer at another location (a form of electronic mail).

Unattended transmission and reception: it is possible to arrange for data to be transmitted to a host computer at a prearranged time and/or have the microcomputer available to receive data at any time. With this ability advantage can be taken of less expensive, off-peak, telecommunication rates or host charges or to improve the efficiency of the search operation itself. For instance, the M-300 OCLC microcomputer terminal is used to access the OCLC data base, transmit records into the terminal, edit them locally and then re-transmit them back to the OCLC host.

The OCLC data base comprises 10 million plus records in MARC format and is used as a source of catalogue copy for thousands of libraries in the USA and Europe. Searches for catalogue records can be batched together and uploaded when convenient. The records found can then be downloaded when the search is complete without operator intervention, edited in the microcomputer and, if required, uploaded back into the OCLC computer. The whole process saves operator time and takes pressure off the central computer as response time for a particular terminal (microcomputer) is no longer as critical as it was with the previous completely online operation.

A growing number of online retrieval services are providing data manipulation programs for local microcomputers to process downloaded data. McGraw-Hill, through the Data Resources Inc. (DRI) service, provides downloadable economic, financial and business data which can be manipulated on a microcomputer using a spreadsheet program. Such programs are described in Chapter 6. The much talked about problems of permission to use machine-readable records obtained from downloading are at least being tackled, if not yet fully solved.

The microcomputer can be used to provide a number of search aids to the online data base user. Some of them are available on the host computers themselves, but if they are available locally, can be more convenient to use. Other help features are not available on some or all of the hosts and there are a number of them which are clearly designed to be placed in a local microcomputer.

Help data: essential information on command languages, frequently used data bases and other useful facts can be stored in the microcomputer. Once stored, they can be quickly called-up on the screen during a search. An example might be if, having logged-on to a host computer, the searcher needed to know the format of an infrequently used command. Reference to printed manuals would waste time.

Command language translation: some online information services use the same command language (see Section 4.1) and the Commission of the European Communities has sponsored the development of the Common Command Language (CCL). Despite this, there is a plethora of different command languages which present difficulties to the online searcher. In principle it is possible to translate the commands from one service to those of another. In practice not all the commands are likely to match but, nevertheless, software exists which will allow a searcher to use a single language with a number of different hosts when using a microcomputer. For each command entered in one language, the microcomputer can be programmed to analyse and translate it into that of the host to which a connection has been made. Thus:

SS INFORMATION (W) RETRIEVAL (Dialog)

can be translated to:

INFORMATION ADJ RETRIEVAL (BRS/Datastar)

or:

F INFORMATION RETRIEVAL (CCL)

Some systems use a guided approach to development of the query through the use of menus with search terms being entered one at a time. Only when the search is ready for transmission is it translated into the language of the chosen data base and host, which may be selected by the system, rather than the user. Differences in data bases, retrieval systems and data base management system design, together with varying ideas on the setting up of the same or similar data bases on different systems, put a large number of problems in the way of the microcomputer systems designer in this area, but some software has been successful, albeit with some limitations.

Help for inexperienced users: a further level of assistance after command language translation is the provision of searching facilities for a user who is unfamiliar with information retrieval systems. Such a system would:

(a) elicit the question from the user;
(b) decide which data base(s) to search;
(c) decide which host computer to search;
(d) formulate and carry out the search automatically;
(e) display the results to the user.

In practice, this is difficult to carry out for a wide range of different data bases and hosts. The problem of a large number of possible hosts is more acute in Europe than in the United States where there is wide coverage on a limited number of services.

Search enhancement: at its simplest the microcomputer can scan the words or indexing terms which are present in a list of retrieved references and present them to the searcher with the most frequent words appearing first. Those that are relevant and not already in the search can be added to it by the searcher. This feature is the basis of the ZOOM command in the ESA-IRS retrieval service.

Expert systems: In recent years, the study of so-called expert systems has become fashionable. Such systems are designed to solve practicable but complex problems, which normally require an expert to interpret and solve. This is done using a computer model of expert human reasoning with the intention of arriving at the same conclusions that a human expert would reach if faced with the same problem. To date, the success of expert systems has been greatest in fields such as medical diagnosis and treatment, and geological exploration.

Existing expert systems do not completely replace the human in decision making although they do well in some simple applications. Instead, they can be regarded as aids to problem solving and advisory systems that augment the knowledge and expertise of the user.

If the knowledge of the search intermediary could be stored in the microcomputer, it would be possible for an unskilled user to carry out a complex search without the aid of an intermediary. Some of the available search assistance software products are beginning to move in this direction, particularly the database-specific ones. For instance it is difficult or impossible to search an author's name in a particular data base unless a knowledge of the format of that item of data is available to the searcher. Williams [5] claims to have devised a model which describes all the situations which arise when a user searches a data base and has produced a framework in which the decisions a searcher should take can be completely defined. He further claims that it is a systematic interpretation of iterative searching techniques and hopes that it will form a framework for a totally automated search system. The potential for using expert systems for information retrieval is discussed in more detail by Armstrong [6], and by Vickery [7].

Bulk transmission of data: The amount of data usually transferred to the host computer during an online search is relatively small. The microcomputer is capable of transferring much larger amounts of data and this facility can be used as a general-purpose file transfer procedure such as for:

(a) the transmission of inter-library loan requests,
(b) general message transfer or electronic mail.

Electronic mail systems are discussed in Chapter 6.

4.3.3 Software packages for assisting information retrieval

Packages for microcomputers exist at various levels of sophistication, the IBM-PC being clearly the machine for which the most packages are available. There is a group which allows a microcomputer to operate as a computer terminal. It may be just as a single asynchronous terminal, which is sufficient for obtaining access to online hosts. Other packages and/or hardware circuits boards are available to emulate terminals that are used with specific larger computers.

A second group of software products has been designed for general purpose communications and these packages have not, in the main, been programmed with the information retrieval process in mind. For example, some of them can only transmit a whole file of data and not a line at a time, the latter being a useful feature for transmitting search data to an online host. Communications software packages for IBM and compatible microcomputers are covered by Saffady [8] with a US slant whilst Manning [9] compares some of the attributes of the packages in detail when used for online searching.

Some packages require the use of a particular type of modem and care should be taken in selecting both modem and software that they will operate together in a particular local situation. Problems may be experienced, for instance, when some communications software packages, written in one country, are transferred to another.

A third set of packages comprises those especially written to assist the information retrieval process. They may be general purpose in nature, i.e. designed to access all host services, or they may be specifically orientated towards a restricted number of hosts and/or databases. Generally speaking the more features offered, the less generally applicable they are [10, 11].

Some packages are aimed at the experienced searcher and others at the inexperienced user. A list of software packages is given in Appendix 1.

4.3.4 Training in the use of online information retrieval systems

It was explained above how the relatively large connect-time charge can make searching expensive for the inexperienced searcher. Some hosts offer reduced price training files and a few of them are free of charge. Nevertheless, much of a training programme can take place on a microcomputer and a number of systems are available. They are particularly useful for the hands-on training of students. The use of a microcomputer retrieval software package as described in Section 4.1 will demonstrate many of the concepts of online searching and there are several inexpensive systems available. The program for searching the ERIC data base devised by the ERIC Clearinghouse on Information Resources is an example. A subset of the ERIC data base can be obtained on floppy disk, together with retrieval software.

Another interesting approach is to lead a student through a number of worked examples for some of the major host services and data bases. Software has been produced to guide a student through a search of the major hosts (see, for instance, Large and Armstrong [12]). One method is to store examples of searches in the microcomputer, with which a student then interacts. The system acts as a crude form of computer-assisted learning device. Video disks have also been introduced into online training when connected to a microcomputer (Smith [13]).

4.4 CONCLUSIONS

The use of the microcomputer for assisting online searching is probably one of the most successful applications of microcomputers to date, especially with the very apparent gains over the alternative. A wide choice of information retrieval systems and data base management systems is also available. Users have not been slow to report their experiences in the literature and prospective microcomputer users should have little difficulty finding software to manage data bases and retrieve information. Integration of systems along the lines of DRI and BRS will also simplify searching and provide more powerful systems that can better answer users' needs than those currently available. Eventually, data base management systems will be the basis of the more advanced and flexible retrieval systems, giving the data management and retrieval functions required for flexible, integrated library and information retrieval systems. It is also likely that optical disks will eventually have a large impact on the information dissemination process in general.

REFERENCES

1. Foskett, A.C., *The Subject Approach to Information*, 4th ed. Bingley, 1982.
2. Lancaster, F.W. and Fayen, E.G., *Information Retrieval Online*, Melville, 1973.
3. Kruglinski, D., *Data Base Management Systems: A Guide to Microcomputer Software*, Osborne/McGraw-Hill, 1983.
4. Kruglinski, D., *Data Base Management Systems — MS-DOS: Evaluating MS-DOS Database Software*, Osborne/McGraw Hill, 1985.
5. Williams, P.W., A model for an expert system for automated information retrieval, 8th International Online Information Meeting, London, December 1984, Learned Information (Europe) Ltd. pp. 139-149.
6. Armstrong, C.J., Command Languages and the intelligence factor. 8th International Online Meeting, London, 1984, pp. 161-169.
7. Vickery, A., An intelligent interface for online interaction, *Journal of Information Science* **9**, 7-18, 1984.
8. Saffady, W., Communications software packages for the IBM personal computer and compatibles. *Library Technology Reports*, July-August 1985, Volume 21, No. 4.
9. Manning, M., Evaluation of communications software for microcomputers, Information Online 86, First Australian Online Information Conference and Exhibition, 20-22 January 1986, pp. 302-326.
10. Petrie, J.H., The use of microcomputers as friendly assistants for online searching. VALA Third National Conference on Library Automation, Melbourne, November 1985. Vol. 2, pp. 45–66.
11. Spigal, F., Gateway software: A path to the end-user market? *Information Today* vi no. 2, 1985, pp. 6–7.
12. Large, J.A. and Armstrong, C.J., The microcomputer as a training aid for online searching, *Online Review*, 7 (1), 1983, pp. 51–59.
13. Smith, N.R. and Roach, D.K., An interactive videodisc training programme for online information retrieval. 8th International Online Information Meeting, London, December 1984, pp. 493-501.

5

Applications in library and information services

In this and the next chapter, we will examine the ways in which the microcomputer can contribute to the remaining library tasks. For the sake of convenience, these have been divided into discrete topics, but there will be cases where these can be linked for greater efficiency. Indeed, it is a feature of recent library software that such integration is incorporated from the start. A number of packages (discussed below) have been developed as a series of modules, each of which can be bought separately, but which together form a complete integrated library system, providing as a minimum acquisitions, cataloguing and online catalogue, but often adding serials control and some other applications. The library can therefore implement applications as and when required (or as the budget determines), knowing that the software will work with previously established files.

The main objective is to indicate to the librarian the factors which must be considered when investigating automation of one or more of these routines, and to examine how some of the available software deals with this work.

The software available for these applications ranges from general programs for finance and statistics to packages designed for particular library routines: a list of library-specific software is given in Appendix 1.

5.1 SERIALS CONTROL

Serial control *in toto* consists of a number of elements which are more or less closely related. These are:

(a) title;
(b) frequency;
(c) receipt of issues;

    (d) circulation lists;
    (e) holdings and disposal policies;
    (f) locations;
    (g) binding policies and binding records;
    (h) subscription rates and renewal dates;
    (i) supplier;
    (j) former titles.

While not all of these may be in operation (a library might not circulate journals, for example), it is desirable that they be treated as parts of a single serials record, since this will provide a 'one-stop' file containing all the relevant data, and will produce a file with a number of functions. A file like this can be implemented on a DBMS package, a word processor or a dedicated serials management program.

Using a DBMS program, a record will contain the number of fields (lines) necessary to hold the information. Since the software can search each field or a combination of fields, details of outstanding subscriptions, holdings etc. can be found easily, while the report generator can be used to select and print only the fields relevant to a catalogue of holdings, a circulation list or a subscription list. Many other arrangements are, of course, possible — a list of all the journals from a particular supplier, for example, although when using DBMS software, it will be necessary to ensure that a large enough record can be accommodated.

Word processing software will permit a similar structure (indeed, it is free of any constraints on field length and maximum record size), but it will not allow the same flexibility in searching or variety of output, and the data would have to be sorted before it was keyboarded in (though libraries will already have a sorted list). If arranged by title, for example, overdue subscriptions could only be found by scanning the entire file and it will be less easy (though not impossible with a small file) to produce an edited version (of holdings only, say), since any details not relevant to the edited version would first have to be deleted from each record. For these reasons, if word processing software is used, it may be more useful to maintain two files, one of subscription details and one of holdings, even though this means that two files have to be updated with new titles etc. Since this is likely to occur relatively infrequently, it is the sort of 'trade-off' which can usefully be made.

If it is not possible or desirable (for whatever reason) to adopt this single record approach, suitable individual areas for use with either DBMS or word processing software are as follows.

Circulation lists: if journals are circulated to staff on receipt, DBMS software will maintain a file of records containing all the relevant names and 'addresses'. On receipt, keying-in the journal title gives the opportunity to print the record as a label: it can, of course, contain some suitable text such as 'Please pass this journal to the next person on the list'. Stationery is available to allow printing onto adhesive labels for even greater convenience, and the record could contain the date of receipt in order to check the speed of circulation. Such a file would also be machine-searchable to provide lists of the journals which each member of staff receives.

Subscription records: although details of subscriptions could in fact be kept on the spreadsheet programs discussed in Chapter 6, it would be a rather cumbersome method and impossible for large files. It will be better to use DBMS software, particularly if there are a large number of subscriptions, since this offers online searching plus the ability to re-sort the entire file and so to produce output arranged by title, renewal date and price. No predetermined arrangement is necessary for data entry, and overdue subscriptions can be found as easily as listing all titles or finding one supplier. Since most DBMS include mathematical operations, total values can be calculated automatically. Regular searches will indicate subscriptions due in any month or week, as well as those not renewed. If links to word processing software are available, automatic 'chasers' can be sent.

Holdings lists/catalogues: again, both DBMS or word processing software can be used for this application; the former would, as always, offer online searching as well. The aim will be to produce, at appropriate intervals, a catalogue of periodicals, indicating the parts held and the locations where relevant.

Amendments to both are straightforward, and the entire catalogue can be printed rapidly following any amendments. Using a word processor requires that the data be sorted alphabetically first, though libraries will no doubt have such an alphabetical list to hand. With DBMS software, entries can be in random order, with the file being sorted before printing. For the same reason, additions are less difficult to make on DBMS software: to add an entry to a word processor-based list means opening a space in the text at the correct point (which can, in fact, be done with one or two keystrokes).

Which software is used will depend on whether other arrangements of the file will be needed: if they are, a DBMS will be more useful. For example, an alternative listing could be by location, showing serials held in branch libraries.

As has already been suggested, all this information can be held in a single record. Both types of software can be used, but for records with this much detail, any part of which can serve as a sort feature, DBMS software will be preferable. The alternative is to use a dedicated serials control package, a number of which are available (see Appendix 1).

Checkmate is produced by the Capital Systems Group and runs on CP/M systems with a minimum of 64 K RAM and 8″ or Winchester disks. Up to 2000 records can be held on floppy disks and up to 6000 on Winchesters. The user defines the intervals at which each journal is expected and the system then automatically scans the file and prints claim forms for missing parts. In addition, Checkmate prints circulation labels, provides accounts, and can produce alphabetical and subject lists from Boolean searches. In the USA it costs $2500.

Baggarley and McKinney [1] have reported a system using an Apple II for up to 160 journal titles. It can also trace missing issues and subscription details and produces circulation slips. A reported price is $1000, and the authors have claimed an increase in productivity of some 300%.

A complete hardware/software package is available for Blackwell's well-known Pearl subscriptions and serials control system [2]. For an all-in price, Pearl includes a DEC-compatible microcomputer and the software, and this has now been upgraded so that it also contains the Amber package for book acquisitions. This means, therefore, that Pearl is now an integrated package capable of handling all a library's acquisitions (monographs, serials and audiovisual material). A version for the IBM PC is under development at the time of writing.

For serials control, Pearl will handle a maximum of 1000 subscriptions (which do not have to be placed with Blackwell), and it maintains all the relevant information, including receipt of issues, claims and circulation lists. Facilities are also available to control binding operations, and this includes a method of updating the information about holdings when a bound volume is added to stock.

Orders for new journal titles can be transmitted electronically to Blackwell, and the necessary data for such orders can be derived from Blackwell's own serials database, thus reducing the re-keying of data. For libraries which do not use Blackwell as a supplier of serials, orders and claims have to be dispatched to the supplier in hard copy. Pearl also provides facilities for the loan of journals, including reservations and overdue notices.

Swets and Zeitlinger have developed SAILS (Swets Automated Independent Library System), an integrated system which contains a serials control module providing all the standard features required. In this case, microcomputers can be used as front ends in a local area network based around a minicomputer or mainframe environment. In this configuration, it can support over 200 terminals, and a microcomputer-based version is also under development.

Logical Choice have added a serials control module to their Bookshelf series of programs. This too provides all the features required for serials handling, and includes provision for multiple copies of titles with shelf location, binding and photocopy requirements, as well as ISSN and CODEN.

The Serials Management Services of the Dawson Group now offer their Serials Management System PC-SMS running on an IBM PC or compatible equipment. As with Pearl, there is an option to provide telecommunications with Dawson's serials database, in order to derive records for ordering and holdings files, and this facility can, in fact, be used to access other databases through the PSS network. PC-SMS provides a number of facilities for serials control, not the least being a comprehensive set of report options which the library can adapt to local requirements (although the standard reports are, it is claimed, normally adequate for most applications). These reports can include analyses of circulation lists by borrower or department, lists of subscriptions due to expire and details of titles by relevant funding code or section. At the time of writing, PC-SMS is one of the few systems for which an inexpensive demonstration disk is available, the full cost of which is refunded in the event of the library purchasing the complete system.

A system new to the United Kingdom is Faxon's MicroLinx Check-in program for the IBM XT and AT range. This is unusual in providing bar code reading facilities for checking in serials issues, where these have a bar code printed on the cover. Passing the reader over the code calls up the relevant check-in record, thus eliminating one element of keyboarding. Faxon have also announced their investigation of the use of CD-ROM players for serials control. The Library of Congress MARC-S serials file is available on CD-ROM, and Faxon software can link this file with its MicroLinx check-in package, thus permitting the rapid transfer of serials records from the MARC files to the library's own files. All that has to be added to the transferred record are details of library-specific information such as holdings.

An equally significant development is the provision by a bibliographic utility of serials handling software, utilizing its own online database. OCLC'S Serials Control System (SC350) runs on an IBM PC or OCLC's own M300 Workstation (an adapted IBM PC) and can be used in a stand-alone mode or with a telecommunications link to the OCLC serials records. Up to 20 000 serials records can be handled, with all the required facilities. Users can transfer records from OCLC's online union catalogue or from an existing serials control system, or can create them locally where records do not otherwise exist. Records can be suitably edited, no matter what their origin, in order to create a local serials control file, and there are a variety of report features available [3].

It can be seen, we suggest, that serials control packages for micro-computers have developed significantly in the recent past. Serials control has been something of a neglected application: it lacks the glamour and 'visibility' of an online public access catalogue, and still requires some time and effort to create the necessary files. It may be, however, that as library and information workers develop their awareness and experience of microcomputers for their work, they will eventually turn to serials handling as an application.

Of the integrated packages referred to above, one other currently provides a serials control module. Pyramid's Computer Aided Library Management (CALM) requires the librarian to specify items as 'serials', whereupon records can be constructed to indicate the start date for a title and to record the receipt of issues. Two running 'totals' are then maintained, of the number of issues received and of the shelf holdings at any time [4].

5.2 CIRCULATION CONTROL

For this, one of the most popular microcomputer applications, there are a number of programs available, including some for specific areas within circulation control. The basic requirements of an issue system are: to record books which are on loan and to whom, to find and 'trap' books requested, and to indicate overdue books. An additional facility will be to provide regular statistics. The ability to print or display messages appropriate to the operation is also necessary: these will indicate errors, overdue or reserved items, and so on.

Most microcomputer packages for circulation control use bar-code readers as the simplest and most effective way of matching reader and book [5]. Alternatives such as keying-in names and book titles at each transaction, or even readers' numbers and book numbers, would be too time-consuming in all but the smallest library, and too prone to operator error. It may, however, be possible to use DBMS software in a small library (see below).

The system hardly differs from existing bar-code readers operating on minicomputers and mainframes: the 'pen' is passed over the labels on the reader's card and on the book, thus recording a loan. Requested books are sought by number and are 'flagged' so that, on return, a message is displayed. Overdue items are sought by the date due and notices can be printed automatically. To aid the standard operations such as flagging reserved books, some systems provide 'command' bar-code labels which tell the system to carry out a preset operation on the number which follows (for example, 'the next number to be entered is that of a book which has to be reserved'). Fig. 5.1 shows a bar-code reader with light pen attached.

For microcomputer systems, the bar-codes can now be generated by an ordinary dot matrix printer, rather than the very expensive printers previously necessary, and Fig. 5.2 shows some bar-codes produced in this way.

There are two basic approaches to a microcomputer-based issue system. the simplest method is to record a book number and a reader number at the time of the loan. The complete loans file will then contain only a record of books on loan and who has them. Manual lists (accessions registers etc.) will be needed to translate these numbers when necessary.

The alternative is to store details of the library's entire holdings (in abbreviated form), and then to record loans against these book records. In this case, translation of author and short title is carried out by the microcomputer.

The former is easier to set up, but the time involved in translation for overdue and reservation notices will have to be balanced against the initial savings. The second approach will be more expensive, since greater storage capacity is needed. Time will be saved in the preparation of notices, but it

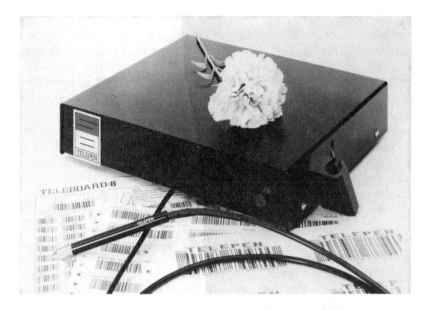

Figure 5.1   A bar code reader (courtesy of SB Electronic Systems).

Figure 5.2   Examples of bar codes (courtesy of SB Electronic Systems).

will take longer to set up the system. Generally speaking, the second approach will be more suitable for the library with a large number of transactions, while the first will be feasible in the smaller library. A decision on which to adopt will have to be based on a careful analysis of the circulation system and is indicative of the fact that microcomputer-based systems require just as much in the way of systems analysis as do larger projects.

There are a number of points to bear in mind, other than the obvious one of whether the package has the capacity of handle all the library's loan records. One is relatively minor and concerns the number of messages which can be displayed. Suggested as vital are: 'book overdue' (perhaps with the amount of any fine) and 'book reserved'. This last will require a list of readers who have requested the book and this may have to be maintained manually.

Other useful messages will indicate that a reader has too many books out, membership has expired, a reader has overdue items (not necessarily the ones currently being returned) or that the book is required for, say, the reserve collection. A system will also have to cope with different loan facilities for different categories of user, and different loan periods for various types of material. As suggested above, it will be important to consider how reader and book numbers will be translated into names and titles, as it will be most unsatisfactory simply to send out a notice to the effect that 'book number 123456 is now available'.

If access to a minicomputer or mainframe is possible, a microcomputer system can be used as a terminal, with loan records being uploaded daily or weekly. This will increase the power of the issue system, though some online access to records will still be required. An alternative to this arrangement is to use the microcomputer as a backup system when the computer that normally handles loans is down.

Mid-Cornwall College of Further Education is using two programs in what the librarian describes as a 'symbiotic system' to provide both a computerized catalogue and an automated issue system. G&G Software's College Library Accessions System Software maintains loan records of 2250 borrowers and 20 000 books on a North Star Horizon with 20 Mb hard disk [6]. However, the system will cope with up to 10 000 borrowers and 60 000 items. A complete package costs approximately £5000, while the software alone costs £750.

This system does not use a bar-code reader: instead, the operator keys in numbers for book and borrowers, and so an accessions register and a register of readers are maintained to translate numbers. Automatic printing of overdue notices is provided and this can be on adhesive labels which can then be fixed to postcards. The system will also provide a list of all books or groups of books on loan, and a similar list of borrowers with details of the books they have borrowed.

The same program is in use at Harper Adams Agricultural College in

Shropshire [7]. In this instance, the option to use bar codes and a light pen has been taken up and the total system uses a five-terminal multi-user system, some of the terminals being used with the online catalogue (see Section 5.4.2 below). This was accompanied by a programme of retrospective conversion, and the librarian has reported a 46% increase in loans following implementation [8].

Wood [9] has described the use of the Information System Design's Circulation Control System at Stockport College of Technology. In this application, an Epson HX-20 portable micro is used as a barcode data capture unit and is linked to an ACT Apricot xi with, typically, a 10 Mb hard disk on which all data files are stored. As an indication of the capabilities of such microcomputer-based circulation control systems, we can note that it will allow up to eight categories of borrower and of book, each of which has its own lending period. Standard notices for overdue and recall can be produced, and the system will also produce statistics on stock use, so that the librarian can, for example, determine which are the least borrowed items. The Circulation Control System can have up to 10 000 borrowers and 260 000 books on file.

Bookshelf includes a module for circulation control in its suite of programs. It is integrated with the online catalogue, so that loans are recorded against the catalogue entry. Thus, consulting the catalogue will indicate whether or not the book is on loan. There is also automatic display for each borrower of that borrower's entitlement, any reserved items and any fines due.

One aspect of circulation control which often causes problems is the short loan or reserve collection of books which are in great demand for a limited period (e.g. for tutorials) and which are therefore removed from the open shelves and loaned for limited periods — sometimes by the hour. When the demand finishes, they are returned to their normal status.

These books are, therefore, a shifting population, often subject to very stringent control. If loan periods are not standardized, staff will have to know what periods apply to which books, how long the books have to be kept on reserve, and so on. It is also useful to know who has recommended these books, since a common enquiry is for 'Dr X's recommended book(s)', when the reader does not know the author or title. For the same reasons, it is helpful to record the course or subject for which the books are used. The University of Oklahoma has reported an in-house program which offers seven access points to the reserve collection [10]. Among other features, library staff can quickly check on titles due for removal, a not insignificant point when it is realized that books can number hundreds, and storage space is probably limited.

Paisley College of Technology library has used dBase II to solve some of the problems associated with its reserve collection. The system stores titles and authors and has improved the maintenance of the collection. The library has plans to extend the system to provide statistics on the number of times a book is in the collection and on the number of loans per book [11].

It is theoretically possible to use DBMS software for an issue system based on book and reader's numbers which are translated as required. A record would contain reader and book number, return date and a field to take messages such as 'reserved'; the reader number and book number would have to be keyed in at each transaction. Searches could be made for each element, so tracing overdue items and reserved books would be speeded up, but production of notices would not be noticeably improved unless there was a link with word processing software to produce the letter.

Normally, circulation control will require a dedicated system, since transactions can be made at any time — and there is always the risk with a non-dedicated system that the computer is tied up (in a lengthy sort, for example) just when it is needed.

A feasible alternative for libraries with a low daily issue would be to batch the transaction records and key them in at the end of the day. This will free the system for other uses during the day, but it does require some (temporary) means of recording loans and the duplication of work may reduce savings in other areas.

5.3 ACQUISITIONS

An acquisitions file is intended to indicate the status of each title on order, together with information on its ordering (supplier, date etc.), for whom it was ordered, and the heading or budget to which the cost is to be debited. It will also indicate overdue titles, with any reasons for the delay, and it will answer enquiries from readers about the progress of books they have ordered.

Acquisitions is often an automated routine because it is not unusual to find the same information being repeated at various stages during the ordering process. The same details of author(s), title, publisher etc. can appear on record cards, official order forms, lists of overdue titles etc., which is why many libraries use multipart order slips for each title, slips being filed where appropriate. The microcomputer simply extends this principle and offers many more access points to the file.

Because word processing software does not offer online searching for, say, overdue titles, it is not generally suitable for acquisitions, though it does offer a simple way to produce copies of printed orders, complete with headings and additional text. In addition, the entire file can be printed out to serve as a reference list. If the file is very large, it may be possible to divide it in some useful way, e.g. by departments.

DBMS software provides much greater flexibility for acquisitions files, not least because lists of overdue titles can be produced simply by searching for a suitable date. To produce a similar list with word processing software means scanning the whole file (unless it is arranged by date), which would make it suitable for relatively small files only. Since DBMS programs normally include mathematical operations, the value of individual orders, the total cost of multiple copies etc. can all be calculated automatically. This is a facility less common in word processing software.

The file could, if storage space is adequate, act as a progress record *after* receipt of the book, but *before* it found its way on to the shelves. This will mean including in the record structure a field or fields to contain information such as 'date received', 'cataloguing', 'classification', 'binding' etc. Once the book was placed on the shelves, the record could be deleted or transferred to an accessions or archive file, in which case it could be used, in a shortened form, to produce a list of recent additions to the library.

It is suggested that this type of linked application is a very valuable one which is easy to implement on a microcomputer. In the case of acquisitions, provided the record is constructed to contain all the fields which will be needed, a single basic record could go through a series of amendments as the book is ordered, received, catalogued, classified etc., finally to produce the catalogue cards and the accessions list entry (see Section 5.4).

This, in fact, is the basic principle behind much of the integrated software now available. Logical Choice's Bookshelf, for example, contains an acquisitions module which accepts details of each title ordered. The individual records can be displayed in response to catalogue enquiries (see Section 5.4.2 below) to show titles on order, but serves primarily as an order record containing all the relevant information. Claims for outstanding items can be created, and the system will cope with full or part supply of titles on an order. The module will also handle donations and exchange items, and when a title is received, there is an automatic procedure to provide accession numbers, labels and bar codes. From the records of titles received, it is possible to create accessions lists of recent additions.

A much more straightforward program which simply creates an order is Orderit from Right On Programs. All that is required is to type in details of author, title, publisher, data and price in response to screen prompts. An order can then be printed and sent to the supplier. Records are deleted on receipt of the book, and the updated file can be reprinted. This level of automation could be achieved using DBMS software, though this would probably be more expensive (Orderit costs $40), but the program has the advantage of being simple to use and does not require a record format to be devised first.

In all the systems described so far, the actual order to the chosen supplier has to be generated in hard copy and then posted. A system which approaches total automation of the acquisitions file is the microcomputer version of Blackwell's well-known Bookline system. This is now available on a DEC Professional 350 with 5 Mb hard disk and all the software for approximately £13 900 (if the Perline system is also included (see Section 5.1), the total cost is £16 900).

Bookline will handle up to 1000 book orders, and 'candidate' titles can be derived from printed sources or directly from machine-readable records such as Blackwell's own Bookfile of 850 000 items. Orders, in turn, can be transmitted to Blackwell, and the progress of orders can be checked in the Order File there — although Blackwell stress that users are not compelled to place orders with them, since orders can be printed for posting to any supplier. The system includes facilities for claiming overdues and maintaining accounts.

A variation on a complete acquisitions file is Accessions Plus from Right On Programs. This simple program asks for author, title and subject of new books and then prints an accessions list arranged by any of these elements as required. It can also be used to prepare reading lists and bibliographies.

5.4   CATALOGUING AND CATALOGUE CARD PRODUCTION

It is necessary to make a distinction between an automated, online catalogue held on a microcomputer, and the use of the microcomputer to print catalogue entries for a traditional catalogue (cards, sheaf or book). A number of programs are now available for the former application, and this should be seen as a logical development, particularly if circulation control and acquisitions are already automated. However, it is possible to implement systems to produce catalogue cards only: such programs tend to be less expensive, though in many ways this method of working does not make full use of the microcomputer's abilities and power.

It should also be said that the intellectual effort of the cataloguer is still required: while some programs will supply punctuation, formatting etc., decisions on choice of headings, form of names etc. will still have to be made by the (human) operator, based on a knowledge of the relevant cataloguing code and library practice.

5.4.1   Catalogue card production

Word processing software can be used to produce entries for a card or sheaf catalogue, and even a small book catalogue. However, since the production of additional entries with author(s), titles, series and classification numbers as 'headings' means editing each entry so as to bring the required part to the heading position, it will be more effective to use the software to print a number of copies of the unit entry and then to add the headings with an ordinary typewriter. This at least saves the effort of typing a number of cards which are identical apart from the heading.

Automatic production of all catalogue entries is easier with DBMS software, provided that adequate report generator facilities are included with the program. A format for a unit entry will be required which will contain all the elements demanded by local practice. Once the unit entry has been created, the report generator will bring the contents of each heading field to the heading position (which will usually be the top left-hand corner). This method has the advantage of being fully automatic: once the report generator formats have been set up, they can be run in turn to produce all the required entries. However, there are drawbacks to this approach.

A number of such report generator formats will have to be created – in fact, one for each potential heading – and the operator will have to 'call up' each format in turn, which means that the system cannot simply be started up and then left to run to the end. It also means that copies of the entries will be produced regardless of whether a field contains data and therefore whether an additional card is needed. For a work of single authorship and no series statement, this could result in six entries being printed when only three (author, title and classified) are needed. Of course, the alternative of simply printing enough copies of the unit entry could be equally wasteful, since here too it will be necessary to print, say, six copies and then discard any unused cards. This is a situation in which the librarian will have to balance the time saved against the cost of stationery to determine the best approach with DBMS software.

There are two ways to resolve this problem. One is to examine each entry to determine how many copies are needed and then to print only that number. Needless to say, this will be very time-consuming, and may negate any savings in time. Alternatively, it may be possible to adapt the program in such a way that it ignores any records that do not have data in the relevant field. This is a relatively simple piece of programming and it will be worthwhile consulting the software supplier about having it done.

Use of the microcomputer in this way, and particularly with DBMS software, raises the possibility of the return of the book catalogue, at least for small collections. Rather than produce a number of catalogue cards — some of which may be wasted and all of which will have to be filed — it may be feasible to hold the catalogue entries on disk (though without public access) and to add new entries as books are catalogued. At suitable intervals, the entire amended file can be sorted by all the relevant fields in turn (additional authors, series etc.) and the various sequences thus created merged to print the book catalogue. If merging is not possible with the DBMS (which may be the case with less expensive or less powerful programs), a sort/merge program can be used, or the various sequences could be printed separately, though this is a less satisfactory solution. While most libraries will wish to separate the classified sequence, it will be desirable to have only one place in which to search for other elements in an entry. Given that the total size of the catalogue is suitable for this approach, it is possible to offer more access points than might otherwise be possible with a manual system, though it will be necessary to establish precisely which entry points will be useful.

The commercial software now available for catalogue card production operates on these same general principles, although some also offer a degree of 'automated cataloguing' by appropriate formatting to a cataloguing code or by inserting the necessary punctuation.

The Capital Systems Group Card software, for example, prompts the user for data elements and then arranges the elements correctly according to either AACR2 or the earlier Anglo-American Cataloguing Rules. The required punctuation is added automatically and the system will produce the correct number of cards with headings, i.e. it ignores blank fields for which no additional entry is needed. The layout of the cards produced with this software is such that the classification number (which the software refers to as a call number) stands on its own to the upper left of the card, and this will probably be acceptable in most cases (see Fig. 5.3). Similarly, Right On's Catalogit asks for the relevant card details and then prints author and title cards, plus up to four subject cards. Again, the subject cards are for a dictionary catalogue, but they could be used for additional authors, series etc.

Two variations on the theme of catalogue card production are AV Catalog Writer and Avcat, which, as their names suggest, are intended for audio-visual media. The former prints a book catalogue, while the latter produces catalogue cards.

As we suggested above, the production of catalogue cards does not represent the best possible use of the microcomputer's power, since it treats the system essentially as a sophisticated printing device. This approach is understandable, since it is relatively easy to implement, is quickly understood by library staff, and the costs of software tend to be low. However, the current trend is towards full-scale use of the microcomputer to create an online catalogue for public use.

5.4.2   Online catalogues

Online catalogues of holdings are the logical extension of automating catalogue card production, since such automation requires that a catalogue entry be set up in the first place. An online catalogue will store this entry, but requires no further entries to be made, since the software will search for all elements (or most of the elements) within the 'unit entry'. Of course, it also eliminates the need to file catalogue cards — a major source of error in most libraries!

An online catalogue will, in larger libraries at least, require a number of terminals if lengthy queues are to be avoided; ideally, these will be part of a multi-user system or network. The software will have to be very 'user-friendly', with clear, simple instructions and, as far as possible, user

```
R
973.08        Aldrich, Gene
Aldr              America's treasured documents,
c1                1776-1976
c2            Oklahoma City, Okla.:  Metro
              Press, 1975
                60p.


                1. U.S.-History-Addresses
              and essays. 2. U.S.-Government
              publications.  I. Title.
```

```
                America's treasured documents,
R                 1776-1976
973.08        Aldrich, Gene
Aldr              America's treasured documents,
c1                1776-1976
c2            Oklahoma City, Okla.:  Metro
              Press, 1975
                60p.


                1. U.S.-History-Addresses
              and essays. 2. U.S.-Government
              publications.  I. Title.
```

```
                U.S.-HISTORY-ADDRESSES AND
R                 ESSAYS.
973.08        Aldrich, Gene
Aldr              America's treasured documents,
c1                1776-1976
c2            Oklahoma City, Okla.:  Metro
              Press, 1975
                60p.


              1, U.S.-History-Addresses
              and essays. 2. U.S.-Government
              publications.  I. Title.
```

Figure 5.3   Catalogue cards produced with commercial software (courtesy of EDUCOMP).

responses should be with single keystrokes. Systems are now available which utilize touch sensitive screens, thus eliminating even the need to press keys. Users simply touch the relevant part of the screen display to invoke an operation such as searching for an author or title keyword, or to browse through a set of entries. Software used for either system will have to offer fast access times for standard enquiries by author or subject, although slower response times may be acceptable for more complex searches. Security will be important, since it will not be desirable to have library users amending or deleting catalogue entries! In this context, it will be useful if passwords etc. can be changed to minimize the danger of someone learning the password.

It is unlikely that a monograph catalogue could be stored on floppy disks, unless the collection is very small: a 1 Mb disk will hold less than 4000 250-character records, because space is needed not only for the entries themselves, but also for any indexes required by the system (see Section 4.1.1). Space requirements are often misjudged: it is normally necessary to reckon on at least a 1 : 1 relationship between the file of records and the indexes. That is, the storage space required by indexes will be at least as much as that needed for the records alone: in most cases, it will be considerably more, and a safer estimate would derive from a 2 : 1 or 2.5 : 1 ratio.

An example of an online catalogue is Computer Cat from Colorado Computer Systems. This runs on an Apple II Plus, with between 5 Mb and 10 Mb hard disk storage (for 8000–54 000 titles), although floppy disks are used to create entries which are then transferred in batch mode to the hard disk. Standard online search enquiries can be for author, title or subject, but records can be retrieved and printed by searches on any field or combination of fields.

Records can be a maximum of 238 characters, but field lengths appear to be fixed at what many libraries will consider to be inadequate amounts: 29 characters are available for author (and only one author field is provided), and 30 characters for the title. Copyright, i.e. date of publication, receives 14 characters, 9 of which are taken up by the word 'copyright'! However, claimed response time for an online enquiry is less than 3 seconds.

A similar system is marketed in the UK by G&G Software and is in use at Mid-Cornwall College of Further Education. The Catalogue and Retrieval System is an online catalogue in which entries consist of author(s), title, classification number, ISBN, accession number and a short publisher statement. Primary and instant access to records is by accession number, but the program creates indexes to all other elements in an entry (except publisher), and these can also be used for searching.

The program can be used in conjunction with the same company's circulation control software (see Section 5.2), in which case a search for a book will also reveal whether or not it is on loan. Used by itself, it allows entry and deletion of records, searching and printing. It will be noted that, apart from a classification number (Dewey Decimal), no subject entries are possible, so the program provides an element of subject indexing by creating indexes to all keywords in the title: these can then be used for searching. It does not seem to be possible to combine search terms other than title keywords (e.g. an author and a subject), but it should be remembered that Boolean searches are not a feature of a monograph catalogue, as distinct from a data base.

The program can accommodate 60 000 books and 110 characters are available for author(s), title and publisher. The suppliers claim that tests show this to be sufficient for 98% of all entries, the remainder requiring a certain amount of abbreviation.

This same package is in use at Harper Adams Agricultural College, where it is used with five public access terminals, in conjunction with the integrated circulation control module. Some problems have been encountered here with the limit on characters available for author, titles and publisher: the literature of agriculture has many corporate authors, and it has been necessary to abbreviate some entries[12].

Figure 5.4 shows screens from the CARS system at Harper Adams College, including searches for author and for title word.

Boolean searches are possible with the Catalogue and Enquiry Module of Logical Choice's Bookshelf software. This can be integrated with the companion module for circulation control, so that the full catalogue record or selected fields can be retrieved during circulation control desk enquiries. The full catalogue record is not limited in size, nor are any of the fields, so cataloguing can be as full or as short as required by the library. Boolean operators can operate on any field in the record, and right hand truncation is also feasible. Bookshelf also offers a feature which is novel (at the time of writing): the library can define which fields it wishes to use for searching and which are therefore indexed by the system. A default list of fields operates if the library does not take up this option, but this default list contains those fields which one would normally expect to be able to search in an online enquiry, i.e. author, title, keywords and classification number, together with a number of other fields. Figure 5.5 shows the screen output for Bookshelf's catalogue maintenance program.

An additional facility is the ability to specify various combinations of searchable fields for different media. This would allow the library, for example, to indicate that the collation field for maps was to be indexed (and therefore searchable), but not the collation field for books. Searches on Bookshelf are remembered by the system, so that sets created earlier in the search session can be used in new search strategies: there is even the facility to store and recall searches from earlier sessions, if this is required.

Search results are 'browsable' on screen, using either a standard format or one defined by the user. This would allow the user to stipulate which fields he wished to see displayed, and facilitates browsing, where the full record could be confusing.

Bookshelf also contains an output facility to print catalogue cards or to direct the catalogue output onto magnetic tape [13].

Like Bookshelf, Ocelot has an online catalogue module which interfaces to a companion circulation control system, using bar codes. The Catalogue Module establishes an online catalogue which can be searched by author, subject or title. It also offers a facility to generate 'see' and 'see also' references for subjects and names in bibliographic records. Preferred terms and cross-references can be displayed online, while 'see also' references are automatically checked to ensure that they do, in fact, exist. If, in the course of an online search, no records are found for an enquiry, any 'see'

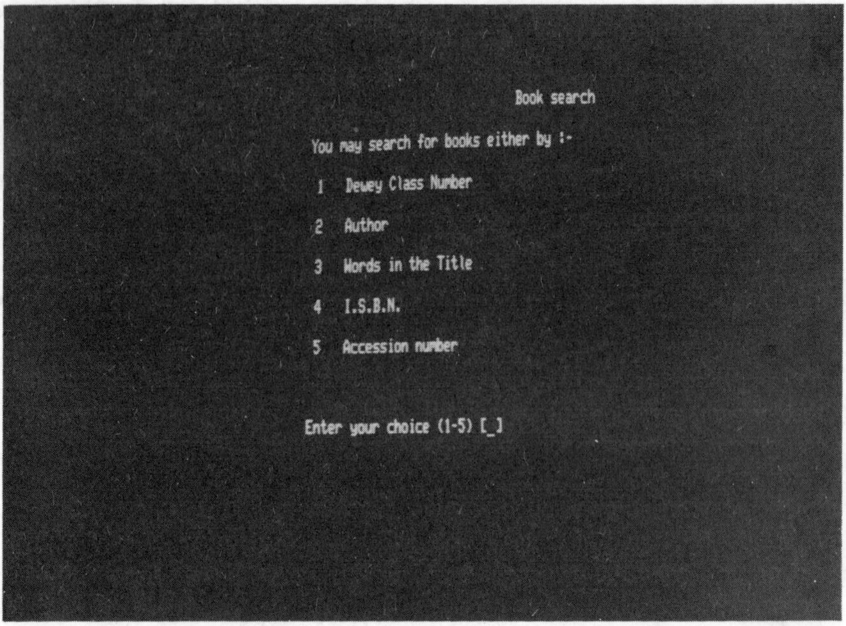

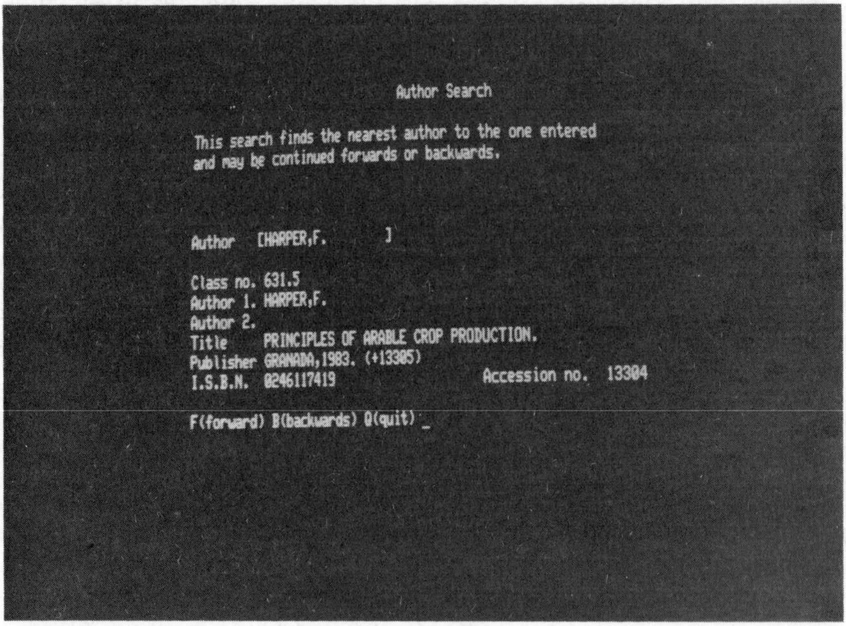

Figure 5.4   Screen displays from Catalogue and Retrieval System (Courtesy of the Librarian, Harper Adams Agricultural College).

CATALOGUING AND CARD PRODUCTION

```
                    Search for words in the title

     After entering a word the system will search for that word and display
     the nearest. You may then either accept that word or move backwards
     or forwards until an acceptable word is found. On entering a second
     word the search will be restricted to books containing both words.
     To finish entering words just press the return key. The book details
     will then be displayed.

     Word to find [EARTHWORM      ] EARTHWORM        Occurs  1  Matches  1

     Found  1



     Class no. 636.087
     Author 1. NIAE
     Author 2. FOOTE,N.
     Title     EARTHWORM CULTURE FOR FEED PRODUCTION & ANIMAL WASTE CONVERSION.
     Publisher NIAE,1982.  [PAMPHLET]
     I.S.B.N.                        Accession no.  17100


     F(forward) B(backwards) Q(quit) _
```

references are searched automatically, thus eliminating the need for the user
to re-enter alternatives for the search. Similarly, 'see also' references can be
used for a search without re-entering them: they are simply selected from
the display provided. From the catalogue entry, it is possible to ascertain
the loan status of a title, so the user can not only verify that a title is in
stock, but also whether it is, in fact in the library at the time of the search.

Ocelot also provides a MARC interface, which can be used to trap MARC
records and incorporate them into the online catalogue. MARC-compatible
records can be produced using the data entry facility: a simplified MARC
tag system is used.

An alternative and, it might be said, a more 'traditional' approach to an
online catalogue is provided by Eurotec's LIBRARIAN software. This also
contains an element of tailoring of the catalogue record to the requirements
of the individual library. LIBRARIAN comes in two forms, one suitable for
monograph records and the other for journal indexes, providing, as it does,
for an abstract. The online catalogue can be configured to a library's needs,
by specifying which information is to be stored online, and which fields are
to be used for searching. LIBRARIAN also provides an alternative method
of searching, in that authors and/or titles can be represented by codes
derived from the first four letters of the author's surname and the first four
letters of the title. Provided that the appropriate detail has been included in
the record, searches can also be based on type of publication.

Subject searching with LIBRARIAN is based on classification number,
though numbers can be combined with author and title codes, if required.

```
Bookshelf                                                        05 MAR 86
                           CATALOGUE MAINTENANCE

1) Standard No. A21_____      2) GMD T      3) Class WA 108____

4) Title  1 Lecture notes on epidemiology and community medicine_____
          2 _____

5) Init.  6) Surname
   1      RDT  Farmer_____
   2       DL  Miller_____

7) Edition 2nd ed. _____        8) Editor _____

9) Place              10) Publisher                          11) Year
   Oxford_____   Blackwell_____   1983

12) Accession      Location    Status  Due date        No. of
    1 C13572....   JR:SL.....   A       ........        copies
    2 C13649....   JR:SL.....   A       ........        7
    3 C13650....   JR:SL.....   A       ........

Please enter a standard number (an ISBN or other, if prefixed by a letter)


Bookshelf                                                        05 MAR 86
                        CATALOGUE MAINTENANCE (cont'd)

13) Collation _____      14) ISSN _____    Entry date 28 AUG 84

15) Series title _____
16) Series no.   _____

17) Notes  1 _____
           2 _____

18) Keywords                             19) Subjects
    1 Community medicine_____          1 _____
    2 Epidemiology_____          2 _____
    3 _____           3 _____

20) Recommenders        21) Reservers                       22) Groups
    1 ...................    1 ...................               1 ____
    2 ...................    2 ...................               2 ____

23) Source _____   24) Price _____

Enter any free text relating to the physical description
                              . . . . . .
```

Figure 5.5   Screen displays from Bookshelf Catalogue Maintenance Module (Courtesy of
Logical Choice Ltd).

As catalogue entries are added, the program builds up its own classification
schedule. The terms indexed can be consulted online, thus providing the
user with the equivalent of the classified index to a card catalogue.
Classification numbers obtained in this way can then be used for online
searching of the main catalogue sequence.

One of the first users of LIBRARIAN was the Library of the University
of Buckingham, where some 60 000 entries have been created in the
classified index [14].

A further integrated package which includes online catalogue access is
Micro Library, from SPS Software Services. Micro Library has four core
modules which include cataloguing, together with additional modules for
circulation control, acquisitions, serials control and a MARC interface. Data
for any record in Micro Library are stored once only: these data can then be
accessed by relevant modules as required. There are pre-determined lengths

to fields, though fields can carry any name the library wishes, and it is possible to add unlimited free text, using a facility called AIM. This allows certain fields in a record to be indexed and used for searching with very powerful features: three characters are sufficient for retrieval, and left- and right-hand truncation can be included [15].

A move towards even greater sophistication of online catalogue software is demonstrated by the ADLIB-2 system, which is supplied in versions for microcomputers and minicomputers using the UNIX operating system. ADLIB-2 includes the necessary features for an online catalogue, plus free text searching on any significant word in the record. The system also maintains a thesaurus (which can be in-house or a standard thesaurus) which is used during searches to select the relevant terms. ADLIB-2 is also an integrated set of packages, since it provides acquisitions, serials control and circulation control, in addition to the online catalogue function.

Apart from specific cataloguing software, it is possible to use information retrieval for online catalogues and catalogue card production. All of these programs offer searching facilities of greater or lesser complexity and will accommodate a record of the likely size of a catalogue entry. A number of libraries in both the UK and North America have adopted this software for their catalogue, with successful results. It is, for example, being used at the Turing Institute in Glasgow for a combined catalogue and database of holdings. The Institute Library has a relatively small book stock, but subscribes to a number of journals and reports in the area of artificial intelligence. Reports and journals are indexed analytically, and so the database contains entries for all journal articles, conference proceedings and reports. The database is searched using BRS/Search software from terminals located in the library and throughout the Institute and offers searching on author, title keywords, journal title and abstract terms. An example of the output is provided in Figure 5.6.

There are many similar programs available, often offering very sophisticated facilities for information storage and retrieval: not surprisingly, such programs tend to be more expensive, though prices are comparable to some of the software discussed above. Four packages are derived from minicomputer or mainframe software, and their ancestry shows in their power. The four programs are BRS/Search (discussed above), Micro-CAIRS, Micro-STATUS and ASSASSIN PC. These programs provide for maximum records of considerable size, certainly more than would normally be needed in a monograph catalogue. Micro-CAIRS, for example, will accept records up to 16 000 characters in length and with a maximum of 80 fields per record. Possibly its most powerful feature is the ability to create a thesaurus as an aid to searching the database. This thesaurus provides all the usual facilities of broader, narrower and related terms and it can be 'browsed' by the searcher, in order to select search terms [16].

Smaller packages (i.e. with more limited record maxima, etc.) are also

accession 000001475 location Journals

Title
Detection and three-dimensional localization by stereoscopic visual sensor and its application to a robot for picking asparagus.

Author
BAYLOU, P., EL HADJ AMOR, B., MONSION, M., BOUVET, C. and BOUSSEAU, G.

Notes
In: Pattern Recognition 1984: 17 (4). 377-384.

Abstract

This paper describes a three-dimensional localization process used on an agricultural robot designed to pick white asparagus. The system uses two cameras (CCD and Newvicon). Thanks to diascopic lighting, the images can easily be binarized. The threshold of digitilization is determined automatically by the system. A statistical study of the different shapes of asparagus tips allowed us to determine certain discriminating parameters to detect the tips as they appear on the silhouette of the mound of earth. The localization is done stereometrically with two cameras. As the robot carrying the system moves, the images are altered and decision criteria modified. A study of the images from mobile objects produced by both tube and CCD cameras was carried out. A simulation of this phenomenon has been done to determine the modifications concerning object shapes, thresholding levels and decision parameters as a function of robot speed. Key words are robot stereometry, mobile image acquisition and automatic white asparagus harvesting

TI Library for julie 20 Jun Item 1 of 1

(1)
accession 000001475 location Journals

BAYLOU, P., EL HADJ AMOR, B., MONSION, M., BOUVET, C. and BOUSSEAU, G.

Detection and three-dimensional localization by stereoscopic visual sensor and its application to a robot for picking asparagus.

In: Pattern Recognition 1984: 17 (4). 377-384.

TI Library for julie 20 Jun 1

Figure 5.6 Output from a database using IR software (courtesy of the Turing Institute Library)

available, at a range of prices. Aquila/Eagle, for example, will handle 2000-character records, and offers both fixed length and free text fields. MIRABILIS will cope with records of up to 3750 characters, and also includes truncation of search terms, word adjacency and Boolean searching. Of interest is the fact that an acquisitions module is also available.

A significant development in the way in which this type of program operates is shown by IME's TINman software, which is being used in the Department of Information Science at Strathclyde University in a variety of ways. Although a database management system in essence, TINman structures the database in such a way that it is possible not only to browse through items selected in response to a search, but also to 'navigate' from record to record, extracting related information (the TIN of TINman is thought to stand for The Information Navigator!). The navigation concept allows the searcher to link items in a number of ways, dependent largely on the record and the information it contains. For example, a search could begin with a known author, the results of which would include the subjects of that author's books or articles. A link to the subjects would then reveal other books on the same subject, and from there a further link would provide the authors of those books [17]. There is thus a greater freedom to work through the entire database at more or less specific levels, depending on the search and the interests of the searcher.

However, in many cases these programs may be considered too sophisticated for a standard catalogue, which contains clearly defined elements. This is because the software is intended for more complex applications such as bibliographic data bases in which the entries include keywords, free text abstracts etc. This is not, of course, to be construed as criticism of these programs, but is merely to emphasize the need to use the right software for the particular application. Many of these information retrieval programs contain facilities which are simply not needed in a catalogue of monograph holdings which users will approach by a few, well-defined access points (usually author, title or (simple) subject).

Some reasons can, however, be put forward for using this kind of software. If the particular program is already in use for a data base of some kind, it will be convenient to use it for an online catalogue as well. Staff will be accustomed to its operation and will not have to switch from one program to another to answer enquiries. It may even be considered useful to combine in a single file both the monograph catalogue and any other data base or index which the library maintains (provided storage capacity is sufficient). Users will benefit because there is then a single enquiry point which will indicate everything the library holds that is relevant to the question. It must, of course, be considered whether users will want this kind of response: if all that is required is a standard textbook, it will waste time to provide in addition a selection of articles on the same topic. This could be avoided if the software allows the user to specify the required format (book or article), but this may be considered an unnecessary complexity. However, as suggested above, this approach has proved successful at the Turing Institute.

An important point to consider will be the ease with which users can search *without assistance* — indeed, this is an important feature of any software that is used by the library's public. Ideally, screen prompts should be in a natural language and should be answerable by a single keystroke as often as possible. Prompts should lead the user logically to a display of relevant items, and a 'help' feature will be useful. Users cannot be expected to have read all the documentation. It should not be forgotten that many users will not consult the catalogue frequently and so will not become familiar with the system. The touch sensitive screen mentioned above is one approach to solving the problems of user-friendliness.

All software suppliers claim that their products are user-friendly, but some are more friendly than others. It may be possible to have relevant parts of the software customized by the supplier to make it easier to use, but because of the extra cost (if it can be done at all), the best approach may be to select a catalogue program which has simplicity of operation built in from the start.

This, by and large, is the case with the integrated software discussed above, and it is almost certain that the immediate future will see a major growth in the number of online public access catalogues (OPACs) being created. As was suggested at the beginning of this section, it is a logical development. It provides the library with the opportunity to create a library database (rather than a simple record of monograph holdings), with links to circulation control and other relevant files. OPACs are the subject of much research at present, both in the UK and the USA. Many aspects of their creation and operation were considered at a conference in Bath in 1984 [18] and a follow up in 1986, and the British Library have funded a research programme at Central London Polytechnic aimed at developing an OPAC on a local area network [19]. Initial developments in this area were, effectively, online versions of card catalogues, but as experience grew, so more innovative approaches were introduced which had the objective of more fully utilizing the power of computer-based systems.

Particular attention has been paid to the question of subject access to collections via OPACs. The 'traditional' methods of subject access via classification number and/or subject keywords were often found to be inadequate, once users became familiar with the power and flexibility of computer searching. Suggestions have, therefore, been made to improve subject access by, for example, including keywords from contents pages and chapter headings and even from back-of-book indexes, in a bid to improve subject recall of monographs [20]. Such an arrangement would allow the library to include detailed analytical entries for chapters with little extra effort, and, it is claimed, would greatly improve the user's ability to find material on a subject basis.

This research is not, of course, restricted to microcomputer-based systems, but it is here that we may see major advances, if only because microcomputer-based OPACs are set to become a major growth area.

5.4.3 Retrospective catalogue conversion

Once the librarian has implemented an online catalogue, he is faced with the dilemma of what to do about the existing catalogue records. There are two possible solutions. The first simply closes the existing card catalogue: no further entries are made, and all new stock is recorded in the online catalogue. This leaves users with two places to look, although as the card catalogue gets older, it is likely that less and less use will be made of it, and it will gradually atrophy. The alternative is to convert all existing records to the new online catalogue, either before the new catalogue comes online, or as an ongoing process after implementation. This is, in theory, the better alternative, since it eliminates the problem of two places to search, and gives the opportunity to amend entries if required. It also provides an occasion for stock editing. It is not, however, a task which is undertaken lightly in any but the smallest library. It involves a considerable amount of work, essentially keyboarding all the existing entries, along with error checking, etc. It may not be possible to spare all the time required, with the result that the conversion drags on and on, and may never be finished.

Given, however, that online catalogues could be adopted by more and more libraries in the coming years, it is a problem which will grow. Fortunately, some assistance is provided by microcomputer-based retrospective conversion systems which, though they are not a completely automated answer, do offer considerable assistance.

Retrospective conversion can be accomplished in one of two ways. It is, first, possible to use one of the centralized or shared cataloguing services to obtain records for the library's existing stock which are downloaded to the library's microcomputer, re-formatted as required and merged with the existing online catalogue. This is clearly very fast (assuming that the base records are available from the cataloguing service), and involves the minimum of keyboarding. It does, however, require software to re-format the records.

Two systems available for retrospective conversion which have been described are MITINET/retro and REMARC. Both utilize the MARC database of records, though in slightly different ways. Using MITINET/-retro, a library can avoid a great deal of keyboarding by matching its records against an existing catalogue. This has been the method used by, for example, Wisconsin Libraries in order to allow all the state's libraries to access the state library database and to convert their catalogues to MARC format [21]. When a library finds a record on the MARC file which matches an in-house record, a unique number is written to the in-house record.

MITINET/retro then offers a series of menus from which the operator chooses and enters information relating to the titles to be entered. This information is then recorded on a disk.

Full disks are sent to a bureau service, where they are transferred to hard disk for storage. When the hard disk is full, the records are transferred again to tape and then merged with the state union catalogue.

If a library's record is not available on the union catalogue files, it can be found by the system on a microfiche version of the Library of Congress MARC files. The record from this is then pulled from the database and merged with the union catalogue. Records which are not on either file can be entered from scratch by the library. It is then added to the floppy disk which is sent to the bureau service at intervals.

In the Wisconsin Libraries system, MITINET/retro is running on Apple II microcomputers with the relevant software. It requires, in addition, a customized edition of the LC MARC file on microfiche.

The REMARC system is being used at the University of Edinburgh Library to complete the task of retrospective conversion for its Geac online catalogue. In fact, the task is seen as one of creating a single machine-readable data base from the numerous sections to the university library which is accessible from terminals located throughout the campus. This has meant coping with a wide variety of formats, cataloguing rules and classification schemes. The retrospective conversion project is expected to take at least five to seven years, by which time a fully networked library database will be available from over 700 terminals throughout the university.

The REMARC system for retrospective conversion uses Apple micro-computers and a database consisting of Library of Congress bibliographic records in order to create an online catalogue [22]. At Johns Hopkins University, search requests made up of the Library of Congress number and the first two words of the title are stored on disk on the Apple, together with details of the library's holdings and uniform titles. Full disks are matched with the database by the Carrollton Press, which is in the process of creating the machine readable REMARC files. Searches which are matched on the database are sent back to the library on magnetic tape for uploading onto the library's BLIS-based catalogue. Titles which are not found on the REMARC files, duplicates and any other queries are sent back in the form of printed lists which have to be checked manually. Titles not on the database will have to be keyed in separately, but Johns Hopkins expect that this will not involve more than about 25% of the total holdings.

Finally, we can note that some of the integrated software packages referred to above (Section 5.4.2) have the ability to at least assist the process of retrospective conversion. In this case, all records would have to be entered from the keyboard, but using a 'pro-forma' cataloguing template on screen eases the task of creating the necessary records from a (printed) shelf list or catalogue cards. Algoma University College Library have found that, after an initial training and practice period, records could be entered in this way at a rate of one every three minutes, using the Ocelot cataloguing software mentioned earlier [23]. It is also possible to download suitable records from a commercial online database such as Dialog (subject, of course, to an appropriate agreement), thus easing or eliminating the task of keyboarding all the required entries.

5.5 INDEXING

The primary concern of this section is with the microcomputer as an aid to the subject indexing of documents. We will, however, look first at a related topic, namely the preparation of back-of-book indexes.

5.5.1 Book indexing

In order to automate the production of an index to a book, report or similar document, once a decision has been made about which terms are to be included (usually by marking the terms on a proof copy of the text), all that is needed is the ability to enter each term and page number as it occurs, without having to worry about alphabetical or numerical order. The software should then sort the terms into the correct sequence, simultaneously eliminating duplicate terms and assigning their numbers to a single reference. An additional feature is the ability to include modifiers and/or subdivisions of the main term and to sort these as well. Output should be printed and it must be possible to correct entries from a draft copy of the index.

Capital Systems Group produce a program called Bookdex which meets these requirements, as do Electronic Aids (Tewkesbury) and Farestead Associates (the latter also offer an indexing service using their software). The Electronic Aids software will handle a maximum of 900 terms, plus page numbers, and indexes can be called from disk and merged with other indexes if necessary. Bookdex offers the additional facility to abbreviate for data entry any frequently used terms, which are expanded by the program when the index is printed. A similar program, Newsdex, produces indexes to journals, and newspapers from terms assigned to each article. It is possible to produce a monthly index to daily newspapers, and the indexes can be searched online.

Macrex is a very powerful back-of-book indexing program produced by A.H. and D.M.E. Calvert. It is used in a variety of ways in the Department of Information Science of the University of Strathclyde, and has been used to produce the index to this book.

Using Macrex, terms to be indexed are simply typed in as they occur in the proofs. Once all terms have been entered, the entire index can be sorted alphabetically, during which process duplicate entries are removed and the page numbers assigned to a single reference. The index can then be inspected and edited as necessary, prior to printing. A variety of print formats are possible, and Macrex can incorporate some word processing control characters, so that various enhancements such as double strike printing are possible. Alternatively, the entire index can be reformatted as a word processing file, thus providing the opportunity to incorporate the full range of the word processor's facilities for text output.

```
D
data,
    information, knowledge 2.1
    satellite derived 4.7
data collection, analysis,
  presentation 2.5
data protection 3.18
databanks, databases 4.12
database management systems
  1.10, 1.9
databases 3.8
    databanks 4.12
determinants of use/non-use,
  information 2.9
diffusion, ideas 2.9
disciplinary procedure, staff
  5.7
document delivery, electronic
  3.13
document delivery systems 4.18
downloading 1.13

E
economics, information transfer
  3.9
editing 3.4
education 4.22-25
electronic,
    bulletin boards 3.12
    document delivery 3.13
    information exchange systems
    3.15
    information market place 2.7
    journals 3.12
    publishing 1.11, 3.7
electronic information,
  archiving 3.17
electronic sources 4.1
enumerative classification
  schemes 1.7
equipment, evaluation &
  purchase 1.17
ethics,
    censorship 5.17
    confidentiality 5.17
evaluation 5.13
    information sources 4.1
expertise directories 4.14

F
faceted classification schemes
  1.7
file structures 1.10, 1.12,
  1.14, 1.16, 1.18
```

```
financial control 5.11
formats, cataloguing codes 1.13
freedom of information 2.2
full text retrieval services 3.8

G
general bibliography 4.19-22
goals objectives functions,
  management 5.2
government sources, national &
  international 4.3
grey literature 4.9
grievance procedure, staff 5.7
guides, literature 4.11

H
health care bibliography 4.22-25
historical bibliography 3.18-25
housekeeping systems, automated
  & integrated 1.12
humanities, scholarship 3.10
humanities & social sciences,
  bibliography 4.19-22

I
ideas,
    adoption 2.9
    diffusion 2.9
    innovation 2.9
indexes 4.11
    computer produced 1.17
indexing, special
    classification schemes 1.19-25
indexing theory 1.1
industrial relations 5.8
information,
    analysis synthesis
    repackaging 4.1
    careers 5.8
    control 2.2
    cost price value 2.6
    data, knowledge 2.1
    determinants of use/non-use
    2.9
    networks 4.17
information audit 5.9
information exchange systems,
  electronic 3.15
information explosion 3.6
    libraries 3.12
    research & scholarship 3.16
information flow analysis 5.10
information industry 2.6
information market place,
  electronic 2.7
```

Figure 5.7 An index produced using Macrex Software.

A particularly useful feature of Macrex is the ability to utilize 'macros' during the input stage. Macros can be used to represent terms or strings of letters which occur frequently in the text being indexed. Rather than having to type all of these terms each time they occur, they can be represented by a symbol (chosen by the operator): thereafter, only the symbol need be typed. Macrex automatically converts these macros into the term or string which they represent. For example, the index to this book contains a number of references to the Apple microcomputer which are scattered throughout the text. When constructing the index, the word 'Apple' was represented by a single symbol, which was entered each time the word was encountered in the proofs. Macrex will also cope with various styles of index, so that it is possible to have sub-entries running on or indented. An example of Macrex is shown in Figure 5.7.

Purton [24] has described the use of the microcomputer for book indexing and has some salient points to make about the software. He rightly points out that the typical sorting capabilities of a microcomputer are such that entries in upper case only will be filed before everything else in the

```
Govt Print Off %        Hazardous materials regulations 1982
Grab B. %               Basic television. 4th ed.
Green D. %              Digital electronic technology
Green D.                electronics II - self tester
H.S.E.                  Guidance note GS21
H.S.E.                  Publications catalogue 1983
Hanson J. %             Textbook of economics.
Hartley M.              Microelectronics and microcomputer
Hatch L.                From hydrocarbons to petrochemicals
Hawker P                Amateur radio techniques
Henderson J.            Audiovisual and microcomputer
Heyworth Ff. %          Disussions
Hindmarsh J. %          Electrical machines and their
Holmes T.               The semaphore
Hughes O.               Ship structural design
HMSO %                  SI 1983 no.808
HMSO %                  Health and safety at work (diving
HMSO %                  Dangerous substances in harbour areas
HMSO %                  Dumping at sea act 1974
HMSO %                  Explosives act 1975
HMSO %                  SI 1983 no.1398
HMSO %                  Boiler corrosion and water treatment

Library Ass. %          Libraries in the UK and Republic of
Lister  E.              Electric circuits and machines
Lowe A.                 The law of the sea
Marcham P.              Guide to telecommunications
Mason J. %              BASIC numerical mathematics
Massenburg J.           Handbook on marine hull insurance
Mateosian R. %          Programming the Z8000
Mathias P.              The first industrial nation
Matthewson D.           Revolutionary technology
McQuillin %             Exploring the geology of the shelf
Meek B.                 Guide to good programming practice
Met Office              Handbook of weather messages Vol.1
Met Office              Handbook of weather messages. Part II
Milan M.                Disk drive projects for micros
Milne P.                Underwater acoustic positioning
Mitson R. %             Fisheries sonar
Molle W.                Industrial location and regional
Morton T. %             Motor engineering knowledge for marine
```

Figure 5.8 A sorted index from commercial software: note the effect of full stops and the position of 'McQuillin'.

sequence. Any indexing program will also have to cope with the standard library practice of filing 'Mac' and 'Mc' together and at the beginning of the M sequence. As an example of the difficulties faced when producing lists etc. consider Fig 5.8. This is an 'unretouched' sorted index from Petaid, a DBMS for the Pet. Note the effect of including full stops between initials and how 'Mac' and 'Mc' are separated. The abbreviation 'St.' (for Saint) will cause similar problems.

Such difficulties are not insuperable: it may be possible to amend the sorting routine in the program to take account of such practices, but librarians should be aware that the amendment will be necessary in standard commercial software.

An alternative to book indexing software is to use a DBMS program. This will not be as convenient in that, for each occurrence of a term, it will be necessary to amend the existing 'record' for that term. The user will also have to maintain the page numbers in the correct order under each term. However, if a DBMS is already in use within the library, it would seem sensible to use it in this way, should the need arise. Hines and Winkel [25] have described yet another method, which uses software written by them in conjunction with a word processing program. The latter creates the initial entries, which are then sorted and merged, with duplicate references being removed as the final step. The authors point out that a great deal can be done with just a sort/merge program and a word processor.

5.5.2 Subject indexing

Here we shall consider the use of the microcomputer to create subject indexes of various types. This involves the manipulation of index terms or title words by the program in order to produce all the index entries required for a document. In the case of index terms, these will be assigned by a (human) indexer working from the document and probably a thesaurus or authority file. Programs which produce indexes from title words require only that the title be entered and an indication of how the words are to be manipulated in order to produce the index entries.

There is an important distinction, however, between the automatic manipulation of title words and manipulation of terms assigned by the indexer. A number of writers have pointed out [26] that the former approach of derivative indexing offers an economical way to index documents at the expense of increased effort during the search stage. Derived indexes such as Key Word in Context (KWIC) and Key Word Out of Context (KWOC) all depend on titles being fully representative of content, an often unwarranted assumption, particularly in the fields of the humanities and social sciences. These indexes will also fail to bring together references if the title uses synonyms — and few searchers would consider a KWIC index to have any great aesthetic qualities as a printed index.

They remain, however, a quick and simple way to produce an index, and they are ideally suited to machine manipulation. Almost the only other facility required is a stop list of words not to be used for index arrangements.

Assigned indexing, on the other hand, requires considerable intellectual effort at the entry stage, but offers consequent savings during searching. It is, however, less amenable to automation, precisely because of this level of intellectual effort.

Examples of the two approaches may be found in work carried out at the College of Librarianship, Wales, where staff have developed a Key Word And Context (KWAC) indexing teaching package [27]. This is essentially the same as a KWOC index, although the KWAC system repeats the lead term in the full statement. The package also uses T.C. Craven's NEsted PHrase Indexing System (NEPHIS), and students can compare the effects of the two methods on the index entries they create.

Students enter index terms or phrases coded in accordance with the indexing system they have preselected (KWAC or NEPHIS). The program then manipulates the appropriate coding symbols to produce the index. The KWAC system uses only angular brackets (‹ ›) as symbols: these enclose the word or phrase which is to be taken out of the full context to create the lead term. Various print formats can also be selected for the index so that, for example, the lead term is printed in upper case, with the full title on the next line and in lower case, thus:

‹MICROCOMPUTERS› FOR ‹‹INFORMATION› RETRIEVAL›
produces the following entries:

INFORMATION
— microcomputers for information retrieval
INFORMATION RETRIEVAL
— microcomputers for information retrieval
MICROCOMPUTERS
— microcomputers for information retrieval

NEPHIS was also designed for computer manipulation: terms in the form of noun phrases or single words are 'tagged' with angular brackets ‹ and ›, a question mark? or the @ symbol, and the program responds to these (they are the only four symbols required by NEPHIS) by permuting the phrases in various ways (depending on the symbol) in order to produce the index [28].

The package is essentially for teaching, and so the number of index terms which can be generated is limited (samples of up to 100 are possible in various formats), but the program listing and the program on cassette are available from the College of Librarianship. However, the package does demonstrate the potential of the microcomputer in the production of detailed subject indexes to a variety of document types.

Using a CBM Pet, Craven has explored many aspects of his NEPHIS system, not all of which are relevant here. He has also applied NEPHIS to titles in a bid to produce index entries, i.e. a return to derived indexing. Obviously it works best with what Craven calls 'descriptive titles' [29]: these are automatically coded using the NEPHIS symbols to produce index entries which the program then permutes. However, it is a pragmatic approach to the problem, in that before the entries are permuted, the coding is checked by a human indexer, who can, if necessary, correct any errors. The emphasis is on rapid indexing for the majority of titles, using the speed of the computer: the slower human indexer is required only to amend the few titles that are wrongly coded. This has been taken a step further by using a screen editor on the Pet to 'prevent the human indexer or coder from making syntactic errors in the first place' [30]. The indexer types in each term, together with the NEPHIS symbols, and at each entry of a symbol, the editor checks to ensure that this will not produce unacceptable NEPHIS syntax. False instructions are not acted on, so the operator can see immediately that something is wrong. *Potentially* false instructions are highlighted: if, at a later stage, a symbol is added which matches up and thus produces acceptable syntax, the highlighting is deleted. Simultaneously, the screen displays the entries that will result from the input at each stage, providing total feedback to the operator.

Craven does not give any indication of the size of document collection which might conveniently be indexed using his methods, although he himself has produced an index to a set of 3000 documents, using titles alone.

One of the most successful indexing systems has been PRECIS (PREserved Context Index System), used in the *British National Bibliography*. PRECIS was designed from the start for machine manipulation of terms in a way that maintains the context in which the terms are used, so that the searcher can enter the index by any significant term and can see immediately the precise context(s) in which that term has been used in the collection. Role operators and codes are used as the commands for the manipulation of the index string.

PRECIS is a system requiring a great deal of operator training, but its basic principles have been used by Yerkey to produce PERMDEX, which is a preserved context system for microcomputers. It was developed on a TRS-80 Model III, and a listing can be ordered from Yerkey [31]. PERMDEX has simplified role indicators and more straightforward string manipulation to produce what the author describes as a computer-assisted, but not automatic, indexing system. Terms are first assigned during a preliminary analysis of the document, and the indexer is then prompted by the program for each term, its role and whether or not the term should be a lead term. Unlike PRECIS, the indexer does not have to work out the necessary strings and tags.

From this point, the program creates a string and a shunting routine creates the index entries by passing the terms through the same Lead-Qualifier-Display position that PRECIS uses. The entries are then stored on disk until the printed version is required. PERMDEX does not claim to be as sophisticated as PRECIS, and input can be a slow process (although single key choices are provided). It does, however, aim to produce an index of PRECIS quality within the overall limitations of a microcomputer, for a moderately sized collection and without the need for intensive operator training — though, of course, the indexer must still be prepared to contribute the intellectual effort of assigning index terms.

It is possible to use DBMS software to create a subject index, particularly if reference is simply to a document number, rather than to a complete bibliographic citation. This is not, however, indexing *per se*, since the software will not permute the index terms, but it will allow a precoordinated index of words or phrases to be set up. The collection of documents will have to be analysed not only for terms, but also for the likely number of documents which could have the same term(s) assigned, as this will indicate how large the record structure for a term plus the document numbers will have to be. Record numbers could occupy individual fields (one per number) or numbers could be entered in a series of fields of the maximum permitted length, the numbers being entered in order. This last method will permit more numbers to be entered, but it would be difficult to sort the file by record number, should that ever be required.

An index of this type is possible with Micro-CAIRS, which is a microcomputer version of the well-known CAIRS software for mini-computers. A complete record in a Micro-CAIRS file can contain an abstract and descriptors and an index of descriptors plus document numbers is prepared automatically (Fig. 5.9a). Alternatively, the index can be printed with the full citation as well (Fig. 5.9b).

Batty [32] has made the point that, to date, many microcomputer systems have been used merely as substitutes for manual indexing systems, with the result that the more sophisticated features of indexes, such as cross-references or the development of thesauri for vocabulary control, have been ignored. Batty sees the microcomputer as capable of much more than that, and has described how, using dBase II, he was able to develop, with little effort, a vocabulary and thesaurus of some 200 terms for a very specific subject area. His claim is that up to 2000 terms could be manipulated with little extra effort. Certainly, the point that microcomputers have, until recently, largely been used simply to create electronic versions of existing manual systems is one we have already made. However, it seems likely that library and information workers are becoming more ambitious and are using the automation process as an opportunity critically to examine procedures in order to make the best possible use of the microcomputer's power.

There is great value in a newspaper index, since the materials contained in newspapers are topical and timely, but newspaper indexes pose many problems. Most newspapers are, of course, daily publications, which means that the sheer quantity of material is very high. Each issue may, in addition, contain a great deal of information which has to be preserved and retrieved at a later date.

The library of the University of Maine has begun an index to the weekly *Maine Times*, using the DBMS program dBase II [33]. This is a relatively simple application, in that each record consists of only the subject keywords associated with a report and the citation details. The library has described the command files which it has set up to use dBase II in this way, and has suggested that, simple though the file may be, it serves a very useful purpose in answering enquiries.

On a much larger scale, the *Glasgow Herald* Indexing Project, which is located in the Department of Information Science at Strathclyde University, is currently creating an index to the *Glasgow Herald* for the years 1968 to 1984. In this instance, a number of IBM PCs are being used with software created in-house, and the objective is to produce a printed, multi-volume

	8310912
BONITO	8311978
CARCASES	8311987
CHEESE	8311979
CHEWING GUM	8310911
CHEWING GUM	8310914
CHEWING GUM	8310915
CHEWING GUM	8310916
CHEWING GUM	8310930
CHEWING GUM	8310932
COCONUT	8310884
CONDENSED MILK	8311982
DRESSINGS	8310893
ELECTRICAL STIMULATION	8311968
FATS	8310891
FATS	8310896
FRUCTOSE	8310919
FRUIT PRODUCT	8310941
GLUCOSE	8310917
ICE CREAM	8311986
JUICE	8310938
LACTOSE HYDROLYSIS	8311984
MARGARINE	8310899
MEAT	8311973
MEAT	8311981
MEAT	8311983
MEAT PRODUCT	8311977
OILS	8310889
ONION PRODUCT	8310945
RENDERING	8311967
SAUSAGE	8311980
SAUSAGES	8311964
SAUSAGES	8311972
SHELLFISH	8311971
SHRIMP SUBSTITUTE	8311985
SOYA CONCENTRATE	8310887
STUNNING	8311969
SUGAR	8310907
SUGAR	8310936
SUGARS	8310901
SUGARS	8310933
TABLETTING	8310908
TUNA	8311976

Figure 5.9   (Above) A short printed index from Micro-CAIRS. (Right) A printed index with full record from Micro-CAIRS (courtesy of Food Research Association).

8311982N P
Borden Inc, (Williams A.W.)
Sweetened condensed milk. U.S. PATENT 4:362:756. X.

DRESSINGS 8310893
8310893N P
General Foods Corp, (Wood R.W.)
Stabilised dressings. U.S. PATENT 4:352:832 X.

ELECTRICAL STIMULATION 8311968
8311968N P
VAN ZANDT M.M.
Meat tenderizing, (electrical stimulation using a rectal probe)
U.S.
PATENT 4:358:872 X.

FATS 8310891
8310891N P
International Octrool Maatschappij BV, (Rek J.H.M.)
Mixed plastic fats. U.S. PATENT 4:350:715 X.

FATS 8310896
8310896N P
Unilever NV.
Hard fats. WEST GERMAN PATENT 2:265:747 (De). X.

FRUCTOSE 8310919
8310919N P
DDS-Kroeyer AS
Fructose syrups. WEST GERMAN PATENT 3:145:185 (De). X.

FRUIT PRODUCT 8310941
8310941N P
Rich Products Corp, (Kahn M.L.)
Infusion of fruit. U.S. PATENT 4:350:711. X.

GLUCOSE 8310917
8310917N P
Werner and Pfleiderer
Glucose production. WEST GERMAN PATENT 3:048:802 (De). X.

ICE CREAM 8311986
8311986N P
Lotte KK.
Ice cream, (off-flavours masking by means of cyclodextrins). JAP
ANESE
PATENT 46:348:82 (Ja). X.

JUICE 8310938
8310938N P
Josef Willmes GmbH, (Braun O.)
Fruit juice press. U.S. PATENT 4:350:089 X.

LACTOSE HYDROLYSIS 8311984
8311984N P
Rohm GmbH.
Lactose hydrolysis, (in milk by means of immobilised fungal lact
ase). WEST
GERMAN PATENT 3:112:336 (De). X.

MARGARINE 8310899

index to all the articles in the newspaper (excluding certain items such as the weather reports and sports results) (see Fig. 5.10). Although the eventual end-product will be a printed index, it is possible to search the floppy disks used for data input, and the whole project indicates the potential of microcomputer-based systems for such an application [34].

Sidlaw in North Sea,Mar 28,19e.
ABERDEEN Stevedoring Co. Ltd.:
Labour:
[Supplies to N Sea rigs jeopardised by threatened strike], Jun 14,3e.
ABERDEEN Town Council:
Dispute over Labour advert on Housing Act,Sep 28,3b.
Parks and Recreation Committee:
Aberdeen looks at park site for sports centre,May 30,11e.
ABERDEEN Trust Ltd.:
Aberdeen delayed by merger [with East of Scotland Trust Ltd.],Dec 6 23c.
ABERDEEN Zoo:
Boy [Alexander Laing] bitten as he tried to pat wolf,Jul 12,9f;Potato menu for monkeys [because of dock strike],Aug 5,1d.
ABERDEEN and District Engineering Employers' Association:
[Aberdeen and Fraserburgh engineers strike continues],Jun 16 3g.
ABERDEEN, Marquis of:
Marquis leaves £79,000,Jul 8,3h.
ABERDEEN-ANGUS Cattle Society:
Angus Society's £10,000 profit,Jan 7,5c;Angus society back to Paris after 90 years,Feb 28,14c;[James Biggar to judge show],Apr 18,2h; [Society to send team to Paris Agricultural Exhibition],May 20,2g From bull ring to beef ring,May 25 6g,P;[Visit by American party],Sep 19,17i.
ABERDEENSHIRE County Council:
Alexander Hall to build County offices,Jan 24,14d;Council to

acquire 850 acres in N-E,Jul 22,5e
Litter slogan row,Sep 9,2g.
Planning Committee:
Old [Deeside] line "becoming a midden",Feb 26,2c;New industries attracted to the North-East [of Scotland],Apr 28,8b,F,P;[Cruden Bay to Grangemouth] pipeline go-ahead,Apr 29,14h.
Roads Committee:
Progress on road for Glenfeshie, Nov 25,3c.
ABERLADY Nature Reserve:
Pesticides continue to endanger bird life,Jul 28,10c,P.
ABERLOUR Town Council:
40p rates rise,Sep 9,3d.
ABERLOUR Trust:
Aberlour Trust to expand,Jul 28,7a
ABERNETHY (Perthshire):
Twin towers of antiquity,Oct 28,1e P.
ABORTION:
450 gns paid for abortion, says consultant,Feb 1,16g;Biggest abortion clinic ordered to close, Feb 29,3b;Changes women want in Abortion Act,Feb 29,8e;Scottish abortion rate up,Mar 1,3h; Abortions warning by BMA president [Sir John Peel],Mar 21,2d;Foreign women's abortions [in Britain],Apr 19,11d;Community need,May 6,6a,L; Free advice for women,May 6,7e; Increase in abortions [in Scotland],May 12,22d;Backing for research use of aborted foetuses, May 24,18e;Efforts to curb abortion urged [by Scottish Episcopal Church],May 26,31;Ex-nurse [Christine Grant] fined for

attempted abortion,Jun 21,9g; ,Jul 17,6e,1; ,Jul 22,6g,1; ,Jul 25,8e, 1;Thousand more abortions in Scotland,Jul 27,8g; ,Jul 28,10b,1 ,Aug 2,6a,1;Woman [May Mulholland] jailed for abortion attempt,Aug 2, 7e; ,Aug 7,6d,1; ,Aug 14,6d,1; Abortions add to work of midwives, Aug 21,7h;MP urges nurses to protest on abortion,Nov 11,16e;UK abortion illegal in Germany,Nov 16 11g;Great regional variations in the availability of abortion,Nov 24,12b,P; ,Nov 27,8b,1; ,Nov 28, 10f,1; ,Nov 29,10f,1;Big rises in violence, divorces, and abortions, Nov 30,7d; ,Dec 2,6b,1; ,Dec 2,6b; ,Dec 2,6c,1; ,Dec 11,8g,1;Sir John Peel hits at abortion exploiters, Dec 23,7e; ,Dec 25,6e,1.
ABORTION Act (1967):
Longer waiting lists [in Dundee because of Abortion Act],Jan 13,2e Kirk attack on working of Abortion Act,May 4,2h.
ABRAM, John W.H.:
[Society],Sep 5,10d,1;[Trade Unions],Sep 14,8f,1.
ABRAMS, Creighton:
New US Army Chief of Staff,Jun 21, 11e.
ABRINES, Samuel:
[Trade Unions],Dec 23,6c,1.
ABRONHILL Parish Church:
Committee for the Advancement of Churches in Cumbernauld:
Church opened,Sep 16,7e.

Figure 5.10   Printed output from a newspaper index (courtesy of the Glasgow Herald Index Project, Department of Information Science).

In the last year or so, we have seen the development of a number of packages which go beyond what might be regarded as standard or typical indexing procedures and which offer full text retrieval of documents prepared electronically. In such cases, the emphasis is more on rapid searching of a 'library' of documents which have previously been indexed by the program itself. The index terms can be displayed on screen, if required, but the main intention in creating such an index is simply to allow the program to search rapidly for the required piece of text. Recall, for example, will accept documents which have been prepared using Wordstar or one of a number of word processing packages. The only requirement when using word processors other than Wordstar is that the text files can be made available in ASCII format (see Section 1.7). These text files are accepted by Recall and each word is indexed, using a stop list of common words.

When searching, the user enters the term or terms required and Recall will search the library until it finds all the documents which contain the term or terms. Boolean logic is supported, and Recall can display the term requested in its sentence, paragraph or document context, thus providing some flexibility in presentation of results. In some cases, Recall's limits are those of the hardware: using a hard disk will obviously allow larger files to be established. However, the maximum limits are quite generous: a library can hold up to 1000 documents each of 32 000 paragraphs, and each paragraph can contain up to 256 sentences of 256 words. Maximum length of a word for searching purposes is 12 characters: longer words can be traced using truncation.

Recall, and similar packages such as Concord and ZyIndex [35] can therefore accept a variety of word processed material such as letters, reports, memoranda, etc. and retrieve them on the basis of only a word or two which is known to be associated with them. Thus, vague enquiries for 'the report on micros in libraries' can be answered more easily and, of course, such packages offer what is still a relatively novel facility, namely retrieval of the document and not simply of a bibliographic record. Clearly, it would hardly be feasible to transfer a book collection to run under Recall (even if copyright did not prevent it!), but given that more and more use is being made of word processors to create documents such as reports, their storage and retrieval is greatly improved.

5.6   CURRENT AWARENESS AND SELECTIVE DISSEMINATION OF INFORMATION

Current awareness and selective dissemination of information (SDI) have as their overall aim the provision of information about new library material of potential interest to users: in some cases, neither need be restricted to publications, since they can also advise on new product literature or forthcoming conferences and meetings. The essence of the service, however, is in keeping users up to date: many librarians would only differentiate on the basis that SDI is usually a service to an *individual* user, while current awareness may be aimed at the *general body* of library users. The distinction, however, is not a hard and fast one.

For SDI to be 'selective', it has to be matched against the known subject interests of the individual, i.e. a subject profile, so that the user receives only information that is relevant: a major aim of SDI is to save the user's time.

In order to do so, two files must be maintained on disk. One contains profiles of users' subject interests, while the other holds the bibliographic or non-bibliographic information relevant to the total user population. The profiles are actually individual search strategies which are stored on disk and can therefore be recalled at any time after the record file is updated:

this ability to store regularly used searches is a feature of many DBMS programs. For subject searches it will also be necessary, as is the case with a manual system, to have an authority file or thesaurus of keywords. A uniform set of journal titles may also be useful, as will some form of date indicator (a running number, for example) which can be added to the strategy so that only new records are retrieved each time.

Search strategies can be stored under the user's name, and are easily amended if interests change. An SDI system of this type will normally be linked to the operation of an online index to periodicals received, but if such an index is not maintained, it will be necessary, when scanning journals, to assign keywords to articles which are then matched with user profiles stored on disk. In other words, this method works rather like a circulation list but with subjects instead of journal titles, and it prints a list of those users who are interested in the topics represented by the keywords. The record which is printed as a result of a search must contain space to include the citation as well as the name and address of the user. This would only be a feasible solution with small files, since it will be necessary to search in turn for each keyword.

An online index to periodicals can also be the basis for a current awareness service by producing, for distribution to all the library's users, a list of articles in journals recently received. The list can be created by searching the updated file for the current date: output can be arranged by subject (assuming keywords were assigned) or by journal title (a current contents list). The first approach also requires a thesaurus or authority file of keywords. A current awareness list like this can be distributed as a publication in its own right, particularly if it is a lengthy document, or it could be included in a regular library bulletin.

As we have said, SDI need not be limited to periodical articles. Conferences, product literature and similar 'grey' material can be included, provided that the DBMS software used is flexible enough to include the variety of fields which these kinds of material will require.

SDI, by definition, requires searching facilities, so it is not likely that many word processing programs will be able to operate the service, but current awareness lists could be prepared with this software, when its editing and formatting features will simplify the production of good copy.

Current awareness can also extend to the production of bibliographies, (select) lists of holdings and similar publications. These should be distinguished from the complete library catalogue of holdings, though it may be possible to establish links between the two, particularly if the catalogue is online (see Section 5.4).

Catalogues and lists like this are probably best produced on word processing software, since they tend to be 'one off' productions which will go through various drafting and correction stages. Unless the full catalogue is held on hard disk, it will be difficult to extract via a microcomputer the necessary records for such lists, although it may be possible to use a microcomputer-based acquisitions file such as that described above (Section 5.3) to produce a catalogue of 'recent additions on the subject of. . .'. This will, however, require another field in the acquisitions record, or selection from the file (using DBMS software) could be based on classification numbers, where it is assumed that entries with classification numbers are new titles.

Commercial software such as Accession Plus can produce lists of new titles arranged by author, title or subject, together with brief annotations. Records for this program, however, have to be entered from scratch: it is not possible to use records set up in other files or other programs, such as an acquisitions file.

Even if entries cannot be derived from another, machine-held file, but have to be keyboarded in, DBMS will offer the opportunity to produce several arrangements of the list or the bibliography (author, subject, date), depending on the need for such alternative approaches. If they are not needed, word processing software will be the best way to produce a professional product, with annotations, introduction etc. The bibliography to this book is an example of the possibilities of word processing for this application, since it is stored using a program called Easywriter. In the original version, each entry is annotated: the annotations were removed using the editing facilities to create the bibliography included here. Word processing software is sufficient for this application because there is no requirement to search the bibliography online. Perhaps the ideal solution would be to use DBMS files with integrated word processing software.

The various information retrieval programs offer an alternative method of producing lists, bibliographies etc. They offer at least the same facilities as DBMS in terms of sorting to produce multiple arrangements of records, and many will also accommodate abstracts or annotations, sometimes in variable length fields.

As an example of this approach, the Foreign and Commonwealth Office Library has used Cardbox Plus to create an index to its legal periodicals on an Equinox SX8000 microcomputer [36]. In the Library, legal journals are scanned as they arrive for material of interest to the Office's Legal Advisers and lists of this material are circulated. Using a manual system, it was only possible to produce such lists quarterly, and there was no provision for searching the card file by anything other than standard subject headings.

Using Cardbox Plus, the Library has been able to increase the frequency of the circulated lists to a monthly distribution and to improve the production of the printed lists. These can now be produced directly from the printout, without further rekeying. Equally important is the fact that the file can be searched for any term in any field, with a print-out for the user. The library is in the process of transferring the old card index to the new system in order to provide a more comprehensive online facility together with the current awareness service.

In addition, two programs specifically for bibliography compilation are known. Bibliography Compiler is an inexpensive ($20) cassette-based program for a variety of hardware, while Bibliography Writer is available for the Apple II and TRS-80. These are simple programs requiring records to be keyboarded in: the records are then sorted and printed as required.

5.7   INTER-LIBRARY LOANS

In the last two or three years, a number of programs have been developed to assist with inter-library lending routines [37]. Among the first was Roy Adam's Administration of Interlending by Microcomputer (AIM), developed as a result of a project sponsored by the British Library Lending Division (now the British Library Document Supply Centre). This package evolved from a commercial DBMS, Compsoft's DMS, and runs under MS-DOS or on Commodore equipment. AIM provides a wide variety of facilities for inter-library loans, including request creation and automatic transmission of requests to BLDSC either through Telex or ARTTel. Loan of material to the library's users is recorded, together with return date, and overdue notices can be produced automatically. AIM will also handle loans to other libraries and maintains an archive file of all ILL transactions for management analysis. These analyses can include type of material requested, journal titles by frequency of request, etc.

In a typical application. AIM is thought to be able to cope with approximately 10 000 requests per year[38].

The problems of inter-library lending in a small library which nevertheless had a large borrowing rate were exemplified by the Resource Center of MacNeal Hospital in Illinois. Here, a package called FILLS (Fast Inter-Library Loans and Statistics) was developed primarily to reduce the time staff spent on completing ILL forms [39, 40]. Running on the IBM PC range of microcomputers, FILLS enables the operator to fill in a screen display which is formatted in a way similar to that of the standard American Library Association ILL form. The request can be printed onto an ALA form, with the automatic addition of the borrowing library's name and address. FILLS also maintains records of items on loan to users, together with various reports which show the usage of inter-library lending. Unlike AIM, however, there are no archiving facilities; when loans are satisfied, the data are removed from the disk in order to save space. This would not be a problem if a hard disk was used.

FILLS is an example of a package developed in-house and then used and marketed (it has an installed user base of over 50 libraries), unlike AIM, which is based on a commercial package. Other systems which use commercial software include AFRIKA from Linköping University Library (based on Ericsson's Combi/Step software) and a package developed at the University of North Carolina, which derives from dBase II [41].

As a major bibliographic utility, OCLC is naturally involved in inter-library lending, and has developed its ILL Micro Enhancer as part of its range of programs available for use on IBM PCs and its own M300 Workstation. Using the Micro Enchancer, libraries can locate references on OCLC's database (12 000 000 records plus) together with locations for those titles. The system will automatically approach up to five locations in turn until it receives a positive reply, which is posted in the ordering library's mail box on the system, together with any conditions attaching to the loan. The ILL Micro Enhancer is particularly suited to batch processing of requests and answers to requests, since instructions can be entered in batch mode and are 'distributed' by the OCLC system to the correct mail box files. This is useful if a number of messages all contain the same information regarding conditions of loan, return date etc., and it allows the library to utilize off-peak periods when connection charges are lower, thus freeing the microcomputer for other work at other times.

Another aspect of the new technology which can be of use in inter-library loans is electronic mail. This can be of most value in transmitting requests to other libraries (branch libraries, members of a cooperative group etc.), and it has been reported briefly by librarians in Bedfordshire [42]. The development of the Teletex system in the UK will greatly enhance the possibilities, while BT Gold and similar electronic mail services now coming onstream provide libraries with the opportunity for relatively low cost automation of request transmission, although libraries will still have to maintain their own records of usage, return dates, loans, etc. It will also depend, of course, on many more libraries being able to justify the cost of subscribing to such services! America has The Source and Tymnet, among other networks, and the latter has been used by libraries in Montana for inter-library lending, using standard applications software. There are some drawbacks — the software will not sort, for example — but many of these have been overcome by the use of word processing software first [43].

A more detailed consideration of electronic mail and Teletex will be found in Section 6.3.

5.8 NON-BIBLIOGRAPHIC DATA BASES

Data bases of this type differ considerably in the kind and quantity of information which they contain, although searching requirements are roughly parallel to those of bibliographic data bases.

Non-bibliographic data bases are essentially files of factual information which are provided as part of the library's reference service. They can therefore contain such diverse data as the opening hours of public buildings and offices, the names and telephone numbers of local officials, brief facts about local buildings or personalities associated with the area, and so on, together with references to sources of more information. Within a large library system or a cooperative group, a file could provide details of particular staff subject specialisms or the strengths of subject collections.

In brief, a non-bibliographic data base can contain almost any information that is sought either by library staff or users, and there is a particular value in using such a data base for the kind of information that changes regularly or frequently. As will no doubt be clear by now, storing such data on disk makes amendment very much easier, and this in turn ensures that the information is kept up to date more easily. Nor will it come as any surprise to learn that this type of data base can be maintained on DBMS, word processing or information retrieval software.

However, since an important feature of these data bases is currency, it may well be advisable to provide online access via a terminal at the reference enquiry point, rather than a printout of the file. Information of this kind is normally required instantly: it can, of course, be provided from a printed list as well as from a VDU, but printed versions may be time-consuming to produce and keep up to date, particularly if the information changes frequently.

If the information is of this type, then DBMS or information retrieval software will be more suitable than a word processing program. Amendments can be made easily and the file can be searched for all elements, though in practice some will be needed more than others. As in all applications, a careful study of the information on file and the ways in which it is used will indicate which is the most suitable software.

However, this kind of data will pose some problems for DBMS software, and in particular the less powerful programs. The information is very varied in its structure: a single record could contain, for example, telephone numbers, addresses and free-text explanatory notes, together with references to sources of further information. For easy data entry, therefore, the DBMS software should ideally permit the use of both fixed- and variable-length fields and it should be possible to search both types. Variable-length fields will also be more economical of disk space. It will not be impossible to use DBMS with fixed-length fields, particularly if the maximum field length is high (256 characters per field is not unusual), but it may place some restrictions on how the data are presented.

This will not be a problem with word processing software, but searching for anything other than the element under which the information is filed will be difficult. If such searches are not required, then word processing may be the best way to avoid restrictions on field lengths.

Woodrow has described the use of an Apple II with DB Master and Visdex software for in-house files in a large public library [44]. This work has subsequently become more sophisticated with the introduction of an IBM PC using dBase II to create, store and retrieve information from local and community information files. These files contain basic information relating to the community, including for example details of local dentists, doctors and chemists, the availability of translation facilities, etc. This information is now provided online within the reference library, and it is an easy task to maintain the files and keep them up to date. Woodrow has also developed command files with dBase II which make searching more straightforward for the inexperienced user, and it is worth noting that these files can be provided by Woodrow to any librarian with the appropriate equipment, for the price of a suitable disk. Such examples of cooperation are valuable, since it prevents the now legendary re-invention of the wheel in the area of microcomputer applications in libraries and information services [45].

A similar system has been established in Motherwell District Libraries, in this case using an Apple II and software created for the task by staff of the Scottish Community Education Microelectronic Project [46]. In this instance, the files contained details of local organizations, and the library was almost overwhelmed by the response from the public. Unfortunately, the hardware was only on loan for a trial period, but staff felt that, in the time they were able to provide the service, they demonstrated quite clearly the effectiveness and value of the system, as well as gaining valuable experience in the creation and maintainence of the files. Such an arrangement may be relevant to many libraries otherwise unable to purchase the necessary hardware and software.

In a totally different application, staff of the College of Librarianship, Wales have created a microcomputer-based index to library suppliers' literature, a collection of which is maintained for the use of students. The index, which uses dBase II and a number of command files, allows the student to search by product or supplier (including listing suppliers in any one country). Because dBase II can work with two files simultaneously, the system was able to store supplier information in one file, with product details in a second file. The two files could be linked by a common field containing the product number [47].

Bivins [48] makes the useful observation that non-bibliographic files can be a valuable aid to library staff who are unfamiliar with the total resources of the reference section, perhaps because they work there for short periods or only infrequently (covering for illness, for example). Files like these can then be a first 'port of call' in an enquiry, particularly if they indicate other sources of information.

Non-bibliographic information can also be recorded using the micro-computer to download data from public data bases, where this is permitted. An obvious example is the Prestel system: as noted in Section 6.3, Prestel pages can be downloaded and they could be edited and stored as part of a non-bibliographic data base. Editing will allow the data to be linked with related information from other sources, providing a more comprehensive data base.

Given that the requirements are analysed carefully, microcomputer-based non-bibliographic files can save a great deal of time and effort, at least in the initial stages of an enquiry or when brief, factual information is needed. It may also be worth pointing out that a service of this kind could enhance the library's image as well as the quality of reference service.

5.9 UNION CATALOGUES

A major problem with union catalogues is often the sheer size of the final printed catalogue, and the need to make amendments at more or less

```
                          PERIODICALS
                          -----------
         Title                               Holdings
         -----                               --------


Marine Engineering/Log               5 (1978 - )/ 14 / 16 (1972 - )
                                     18 (1962 - )

Marine Engineers Review              3 (1976 - 1980) / 5 (1971 - ) / 14
                                     16 (1971 - ) imp. / 18 (1971 - )

Marine Geology                       2 (1963 - )

Marine Geotechnology                 3 (1975 - )

Marine Observer                      5 (1970 - )

Marine Policy                        3 (1979 - 1981) / 18

Marine Pollution Bulletin            3 (1979 - )

Marine Product Guide                 5 (1973 - 1975)

In Multihull International from 1975
Marine Propulsion International       5 (1979 - ) / 14 / 16 (1980 - )
                                     18 (1980 - )

Marine Technology                    5 (1964 - 1973) imp. / 3 (1978)
                                     14 / 16 (1964 - ) / 18 (1957 - )

Marine Technology Society Journal    15 (1973 - )
                                     3 (1973 - )

Marine Week                          5 (1974 - 1980) / 14/ 15 (1974 - 1980)
                                     16 (1974 - 1980)/ 18 (1974 - 1979)
Ceased publication
Mariner                              5 (1970 - )
                                     14

Mariners" Mirror                     5 (1968 - )

Mariners" Weather Log                5 (1970 - )

Maritime Defence                     14

Maritime Policy and Management       5 ( 1976 - )/14
                                     15 (1976 - )/16 (1977 - )
Formerly Maritime Studies & Management
Maritime Sediments and Atlantic      2 (1982 - )
Geology
```

regular intervals in order to produce a revised edition.

The contribution of the microcomputer is to ease the production of each new edition. The initial data entry task will still be a major one, as it would be in a manual system. However, the microcomputer can then print the catalogue much faster than any typist and, of course, the need to retype the entire amended list at regular intervals is eliminated. Amendments can be made as they are notified to the central agency responsible for the catalogue or they can be batched immediately prior to the production of the new edition.

Since this is the case, either DBMS or word processing software can be used. The former will not require entries to be sorted prior to input, and it offers online search facilities. A significant problem with a large catalogue — and union catalogues tend to be large, almost by defini- tion — will, however, be the number of (floppy) disks required to hold the complete file: this will make online searching cumbersome (though in fact this may not be needed at all). Moore [49] has described the creation of a

```
CADIG                                                      ELECTRON
DATE  11 APRIL 1983                                        PAGE NO.  144

ELECTRONICS LETTERS
    CL 5YR:  EA 1977- :  LP 1965- :  MI 1965- :  RP 2YR:  UW 1965- :
ELECTRONICS QUARTERLY
    MI 1963- :
    C OF INSTITUTION OF ELECTRICAL ENGINEERS PROC
ELECTRONICS RELIABILITY AND MICROMINIATURISATION
    GT 1962-63:
    C AS MICROELECTRONICS AND RELIABILITY
ELECTRONICS SALES OF PASSIVE COMPONENTS
    UW 1969- :
ELECTRONICS TODAY
    LP 1976- :
ELECTRONICS TODAY INTERNATIONAL
    CL 1978- :  CT CURRENT:  GF 1YR:  LL 3YR:  NW CURRENT:
ELECTRONICS WEEKLY
    CL 1YR:  CT CURRENT:  EE 1YR:  EW CURRENT:  GR 6MTH:  GT 1974- :  IF 1981*,1982- :  LP 6MTH:
    RP 3MTH:  UW 1967- :  WG CURRENT:
ELECTRONICS WORLD
    GT 1959-71:
    C AS POPULAR ELECTRONICS
ELECTROPLATING AND METAL FINISHING
    AN 1947-76:  BC 1975-76:  GT 1970-76:
    INCORPORATES METAL FINISHING JNL
    C AS FINISHING INDUSTRIES
ELECTROTECHNOLOGY
    CT CURRENT:  LP 1970- :  RR 1978- :
ELEGANTISSIMA
    EW CURRENT:
ELEKTOR
    CL 1976*,1977- :  LP 1976- :
ELEKTRICHESTVO
    SEE ELECTRIC TECHNOLOGY U.S.S.R.
ELEKTRIZITATWIRTSCHAFT
    EE 10YR:
ELEKTROKHIMIYA
    SEE SOVIET ELECTROCHEMISTRY
ELEKTRONISCHE RUNDSCHAU
    GT 1955-61:
ELEKTROTECHNISCHE ZEITSCHRIFT
    SEE E T Z
ELEKTROTEHNISKI VESTNIK
    GT 1967- :
ELEMENTARY SCHOOL JNL
    WL 1964- :
ELIN ZEITSCHRIFT
    EA 1974-80*,1981- :
ELIZABETHAN
    NF CURRENT:
EMANCIPATION NATIONALE
    UW 1936-40:
EMBALLAGES
    AN 5YR:
```

Figure 5.11   (Left) Union Catalogue entries using DBMS software. (Above) Union catalogue entries using word processing software (courtesy of CADIG).

large union catalogue with 1200 titles and 8000 locations which is spread over five disks: it uses DB Master on an Apple II. Using DBMS software for a union catalogue also means a large record size may be needed in order to cope with the (potentially) numerous locations: these will certainly have to be coded in some way, although this is common practice with manual systems.

Generally speaking, unless it is useful to print the whole catalogue in more than one arrangement (sorted by location, for example) or it is necessary to offer online access, word processing software will be the most straightforward approach. Although entries will have to be sorted prior to keyboarding, it will not be necessary to devise a record format capable of containing all the potential locations. Coventry and District Information Group (CADIG) has produced a union catalogue of 10 000 entries and 464 pages using the SELECT word processing software on a Sirius 1. It maintains 26 files (one for each letter of the alphabet) on two disks.

Fig. 5.11 shows entries from two union catalogues: 5.11a was produced with a DBMS program, while 5.11b used word processing software.

5.10 USER EDUCATION

It seems natural to employ the microcomputer for user education, since computer-aided learning (CAL) is one of the principal ways in which microcomputers are used in schools and colleges.

The methods used are the relatively well-established ones of CAL. Either a preliminary course of instruction can be reinforced by a microcomputer program which assesses how much the student has learned and retained, or the computer program can give the instruction and then pose relevant questions. For example, details of the content and coverage of journals or the use of reference works can be followed by specific questions relating to those journals or works. Use of the catalogue can be treated in a similar way.

Programs of this type tend to be used by individuals rather than classes and, like most CAL programs, they allow the user to proceed at his or her own speed. They can also be used as a 'refresher course' when appropriate. Since, like all user education, programs must be linked to a specific library context, this is one area in which off-the-shelf software will be of little use, except perhaps for very general introductions. Twelve such introductory programs are available from Right On Programs. These present information on a variety of topics, followed by a number of questions. In some cases, the questions are posed in the form of a game, with 'rewards' for correct answers. The subjects range from the principles of the Dewey Decimal Classification Scheme (using the Sport schedule as an example), through the use of the card catalogue, to programs on how to use a book index and the table of contents. There is even a program on the copyright notice! These appear to be quite simple programs which could be used to advantage in general and introductory user education.

Because of their library-specific orientation, programs will often have to be written in-house (by library staff or computer programming personnel) or commissioned, and the problems of these approaches are discussed in Section 8.2. Their content and overall approach will also be a matter for individual librarians, since this too will be influenced by the user population served. The main point to bear in mind will be to use the established techniques of CAL, and if staff are available who are well versed in those techniques, they should be closely involved in the preparation of the program(s). The programs, like traditional methods of user education, can consist of general introductions to the library (library orientation) as well as more detailed guidance on specific subjects or aspects of the library (information sources in medicine, or the use of the catalogue, for example).

A further use of the microcomputer is suggested by the need for plans of the layout of large libraries, which are displayed at suitable points in order to guide users to the areas they seek. At an American school of information science, a program called Library Tour [50] has been developed which responds to the user's input on possible movements within the library, and indicates which library services or section of stock will be found at the point reached. Movement can be in any one of four directions (North, South, East and West), combined with 'up' or 'down'. Entering the desired direction of movement produces a statement of where this will take the user and what facilities will be found in that area. The statements are relatively simple ('You are standing next to the catalogue: to your right is the reference section') but it is possible to go on a complete tour of the library. The program also knows the location of walls, doors and stairs: if the user attempts an impossible move, the computer responds with a comment such as 'You can't walk through walls, can you?' However, this is only a *tour* of the library: it does not answer specific questions such as 'Where are the books on microprocessors?' A more useful approach will be to provide *directions* to specific areas, perhaps even employing graphics to show the way. It will also be more convenient to locate a number of terminals at suitable points around the library, though each terminal will then either have to contain a version of the program specific to that location, or the instructions will have to be couched in general terms (e.g. 'Physics books are on floor 2' rather than 'For physics, turn right at the enquiry desk').

In a similar way, Wayne State University Library have solved some of the problems associated with their use of several call number schemes which had proved to be confusing to library users. Using an Apple II Plus with an in-house package called Education Library Locator (ELL), the user can now trace the stack number for any call number he derives from the catalogue. In addition, a floor plan can be displayed on which is indicated the exact location of that particular stack [51].

A very different application has been developed at the University of Stirling Library to assist in user education for abstracting and indexing reference works. Using a BBC Micro and Microtext software, the library staff have created a number of modules for use with such works as Biological Abstracts, Chemical Abstracts and Science Citation Index. Microtext can almost be considered an authoring language for such applications, and it has allowed inexperienced library staff to develop these user education aids which are then made accessible to library users [52]. This seems to be a particularly valuable application of the microcomputer, freeing library staff to cope with the more complex enquiries, while allowing users to learn at their own pace. Since such training modules are always 'on call', the user can also take a quick refresher course at any time, should the need arise.

A particularly interesting use of the microcomputer in user education has been reported from the Chicago Public Library [53]. Like many libraries, it sought to provide a quick guide to the most requested subjects and their classification numbers — in this case, for both Dewey Decimal Classification and Library of Congress schemes.

It proved possible to use commercial software in this instance: Data Factory, a DBMS program running on an Apple II, produces a large wall chart showing both the LCC and DC classification numbers together with the relevant subjects. The chart can be arranged by classification number or subject, and where appropriate, one scheme can be left out altogether. The advantages of the system lie in the ease with which new subjects and numbers can be added to produce a revised chart. The librarian (aptly named Dewey!) reports that the wall chart has improved public awareness and use of the libraries, and has saved between one-third and one-half of all the reference enquires received in one of the libraries in the system. Copies of the chart have been used as teaching aids on school visits by the children's librarian.

The application suggests the possibility of producing other notices and guides with a microcomputer. Diagrams illustrating the use of the catalogue, for example, could be printed using word processing software, although these will be more effective if enhanced characters can be produced on the printer: otherwise, the result will probably be too small and insipid to be of any real use. (See Section 6.2.4).

The microcomputer has proved particularly useful in the schools of librarianship, primarily as an inexpensive way of teaching online searching. Previously, the schools had to incur all the expense of actually using the data bases (though a number of these do offer training or educational files at cheaper rates). Now many schools have developed microcomputer-based simulations of the online hosts, complete with a file of references, which students can use to practise search techniques without incurring any charges.

The CALLISTO Project maintains a record of these simulations and other software used in the education of library and information professionals, which is published in hard copy and is available online at Newcastle Polytechnic. In its online form, it can be searched for application, hardware and software [54].

The advantages, other than the savings in costs, are those of all CAL packages: they allow the student to progress at an individual pace and can reinforce what is learned in the classroom. It has also been pointed out [55] that such simulations can be used by infrequent users of the data bases to refresh their knowledge, and the programs could therefore be of value to the practising librarian as well.

Programs like these are not necessarily easy to develop [56], and ideally it should be possible to include some form of student assessment or to monitor the student's progress. In addition, of course, a data base of references must be set up, though it may be possible to download a selection of references from the commercial host for this purpose. This will require the cooperation and consent of the host, but if this can be done at regular intervals it will ensure that an up to date data base is maintained.

At the Department of Information Science of Strathclyde University, developmental work is being carried out on the potential of expert systems for teaching such subjects as cataloguing and classification. One of the major advantages of using expert systems is that they contain a built-in explanation facility, which the student can use to ask why a particular line of questioning is being followed. In addition, expert systems, if properly constructed, can display their 'reasoning' up to a given point, and it is possible to record the progress of a student for later analysis by a member of staff. This can indicate whether a student has missed some important point in the exercise and is thus going in completely the wrong direction. It also allows staff to modify the exercises, if it is discovered that students are absorbing ideas more rapidly than expected — a situation more common than many cynics may think!

Another topic in the professional training of librarians and information scientists, indexing, is the subject of a teaching package developed at the College of Librarianship, Wales. This teaches two indexing techniques (KWAC and NEPHIS) and is considered in more detail in Section 5.5.

5.11 LOCAL AREA NETWORKS

We have already discussed the technology of networks in Section 2.3, and this section will indicate some of the ways in which a local area network (LAN) can contribute to the library service.

A LAN could operate in one of two ways: either the library is a node on a network which runs throughout the parent organization, or the LAN operates within the library itself. In fact, it would be perfectly feasible to have both in operation, since the library network can be linked to the larger network through a gateway. The library-based network will probably only be necessary and economical in larger libraries, particularly those occupying a number of floors in a building or on multiple sites, though a LAN cannot be ruled out entirely for smaller libraries wishing to offer online access to its users.

In the first configuration, the library's database (i.e. its catalogue, indexes and possibly acquisitions or accessions file) will be part of the LAN and will therefore be accessible online from terminals located throughout the organization in offices, workrooms, laboratories and so on. Users at these terminals will be able to consult the catalogue or indexes and can send messages to the library about the books or references they trace in this way. Requests for books can also be transmitted from terminals, while the library can send information to individuals, as part of the SDI service, or to the entire organization (current awareness bulletins, for example).

As suggested above, the library's data base could include the acquisitions file, and users could consult this to see which books are on order and, if required, ask to see these when they are available. Access to the issue system may also be possible, though this will have to be restricted to viewing by an individual of only the books which he or she has on loan.

Obviously, with such open access to files and records, security will be an important feature of any system. It should not be possible for users to alter records (or to delete them!), except perhaps to add their name to an order record. It will, therefore, be desirable to prohibit access to parts of some records or to entire files and to limit operations on records by users: the same problem arose when we discussed online catalogues. For example, users could view the authors and titles of books in the acquisitions file, but would be locked out of the accounting and ordering details of those records.

If the LAN operates within the library, much of the above will still be applicable, except that terminals will be located within the library only. This means, of course, that SDI services will not be possible, although current awareness could still be offered, perhaps in the form of a library bulletin board. Equally, it will be possible to place reservations and requests for information, though this may not be considered necessary, since staff will always be available.

This ability on the part of users to enter requests via terminals does, of course, imply a regular routine on the part of library staff to check for such requests and to act upon them. The library's image will not be enhanced if reservations disappear into an electronic limbo, never to be acted upon! Putting the library online in this way will also require uncomplicated operating instructions. Although this will be largely determined by the particular LAN used, those available tend to be based on the assumption that users are not expert operators, and operation is correspondingly straightforward.

An important consideration will be the maximum number of terminals and peripherals that the network can support. Although this can number in the hundreds, some may be limited to less than 100, and while this will normally be sufficient for a library-based LAN, it may be too small for a very large organization.

If the LAN is to be within the library, the librarian will be able to choose the most suitable for the proposed application(s). However, if the library is to be a node on an organization-wide network, the choice will be out of the librarian's hands, except insofar as he can advise on the library's requirements. This, of course, means active participation from the start in the investigation and implementation of a LAN, so that the library's particular needs can be considered along with those of all the other sections involved.

Collier has studied the possibilities of LANs for library and information services [57] and has concluded that the area likely to benefit most is that of readers' services, since users will have more ready access to records of the library's holdings and can communicate with the library from workroom terminals, etc. There has, however, been little indication to date of library and information services implementing local area networks, particularly in the UK. This is no doubt due primarily to the cost involved, which can be considerable, but some work has been carried out to investigate the potential in a practical way at both Aslib and the Polytechnic of Central London.

At Aslib, the LAN was a small-scale one, employing three workstations on a Zynar network of Apple II microcomputers. The main aim in this project was to assess the value of LANs for information processing and transfer, including sharing information between participants. Thus, the network provided electronic mail facilities, an electronic diary of events and manipulation of online search results (using Wordstar), together with a database management package, Condor. The use of an Apple II microcomputer posed some problems, due largely to its (by now) dated capabilities, but on the whole the project team felt that they had gained valuable experience of the implications of LANs for information work. One of the most significant points to emerge from the project was the need for a network system manager with responsibility for overseeing the system and ensuring uniformity in data preparation and input and regular housekeeping such as archiving of files, back-ups, etc. [58, 59]. This has also been the experience of the Department of Information Science at Strathclyde, where a local area network of IBM PCs has been installed both as an administrational aid and to assist in the teaching of library and information professionals. One member of the staff has responsibility for the overall operation and maintenance of the system, thus ensuring that important tasks such as backing up of centrally held files is carried out on a regular basis.

The Library Services of the Polytechnic of Central London were awarded a BLR&D research grant to investigate a larger-scale application of a LAN

for particular library operations, including cataloguing, information retrieval etc. The first area studied was the provision of an online public
access catalogue (OPAC), since very little work had been carried out on this
in the UK. The network finally established was a PLAN 4000 (also from
Zynar) which had a central hard disk store of 137 Mb. User terminals
consisted of either Apple IIs or IBM PCs and some 15 of these were
eventually installed. The project also increased in size as the capabilities of
the network were explored: the initial 6000 records installed as a 'test bed'
were soon augmented by the entire Polytechnic union catalogue of
approximately 90 000 records, which were transferred using in-house
software which read and re-formatted the records. A database of this size
does much to indicate the potential of a LAN for libraries of some size.

Since one of the main aims of the OPAC was that it could be used easily
by those lacking either training or experience, much emphasis was placed
on the investigation of user reaction and interaction with the system. The
full details of the project are contained in the final report to the British
Library [60], but here we can say that use of the system is aided by
coloured function keys for command such as 'help', 'interrupt' or 'browse
backwards' and considerable attention was given to the method by which
the OPAC carried out searches. The working prototype, incidentally, has
been named Okapi, which is, ostensibly, an acronym for Online Keyword
Access to Public Information, but was also chosen 'because the okapi is a
rare, shy, fast-moving animal with a long gestation period'!

A number of American libraries have installed local area networks of
various types and are providing a range of functions through the network
[61]. Some, for example, are realizing the situation described above, in that
access to the library's files is available from terminals located in offices of
the parent organization, and the files provided include an online catalogue.
Some public libraries are currently limiting their application to a network
which supports circulation control, but others plan to provide a network
which supplies local information to supplement that available from the
centralized service.

One novel application is the provision by an academic library of
microcomputer software. This is stored in a library on hard disk, but can be
called up by library users from microcomputers which are the terminals of
the network.

It is also interesting to note that, of the libraries considered in Levert's
survey, only the special libraries were endeavouring to provide a fully
integrated system containing acquisitions, circulation control, online
catalogue and serials control. No indication of size is given by Levert, but
we can speculate that such integration at this stage was only possible in
these smaller special libraries. It may therefore take larger libraries (public
and university, for example) some time to develop integrated systems on a
local area network, though the work at Central London Polytechnic
suggests that size is not as critical a factor as might be thought.

Figure 5.12 Local area network system (courtesy of Research Machines Ltd).

Figure 5.12 shows a microcomputer system designed *ab initio* for a LAN configuration.

REFERENCES

1. Baggarley, R. and McKinney, J., Microcomputerized periodical management, Proceedings of the 44th ASIS Annual Meeting. Vol. 18, pp. 248–249, 1981.
2. Holmes, P., PERLINE on a microcomputer, *Program*, **19**(1), 64–66, 1985.
3. Serials control from OCLC Europe, *Vine* (60), 40–46, 1985.
4. Dyer, H., CALM: computer aided library management, *Electronic Library*, **3**(4), 242–248, 1985.
5. Evans, P.W. Barcodes, readers and printers for library applications, *Program*, **17**(12), 160–171, 1983.
6. Reed, M., Mid-Cornwall College of Further Education computer program (CLASS), *CoFHE Bulletin*, (36), 5–6, 1983.
7. Taylor, D., An online catalogue and issue system for smaller college libraries, *Library Micromation News*, (5), 14–15, 1984.
8. Taylor, D., Progress with G&G software: an update on Harper Adams Agricultural College library's computerisation programme, *Library Micromation News*, (8), 3–6, 1985.
9. Wood, L.R., A circulation control system on an ACT Apricot, *Vine*, (57), 4–12, 1984.

10. Miller, L. and Choi, K.P., A microcomputer based reserve system for university branch libraries, Proceedings of the 45th ASIS Annual Meeting, Vol. 19, pp.195–196, 1982.
11. Millar, P. and Cochrane, J. Administration of a reserve collection at Paisley College using dBase II, *Program*, **19**(3), 262–270, 1985.
12. Taylor, D., Progress with G&G Software . . . *op.cit.*
13. Bookshelf: an integrated, modular package for the smaller library, *Vine*, (54), 37–38, 1984.
14. Pemberton, J., Cataloguing on a micro with LIBRARIAN, *Library Micromation News*, (3), 7–14, 1984.
15. Pegg, N.; Micro Library: an integrated system for small to medium sized libraries, *Vine*, (59), 26–34, 1985.
16. Cline, G.N. Information retrieval for the 80's: CAIRS and Micro-CAIRS', in, The application of mini- and micro-computers in information, documentation and libraries. Proceedings of the International Conference . . . Tel-Aviv, 1983. Edited by Carl Keren and Linda Perlmutter. North Holland, 57–62, 1983.
17. Noerr, P.L. and Noerr, K.T.B., Browse and navigate: an advance in database access methods, *Information Processing and Management*, **21**(3), 205–213, 1985.
18. Online Public Access to Library Files: the proceedings of a conference held at the University of Bath . . . 1984. Edited by Janet Kinsella, Elsevier International Bulletins, 1985 (ISBN 0–946395–18–7).
19. Mitev, N.N., Venner G.M. and Walker, S., Designing an online public access catalogue. British Library, 1985 (LIR Report 39) (ISBN 0–7123–3058–5).
20. Wormell, I., SAP — a new way to produce subject descriptions of books, *Journal of Information Science*, 3, 39–43, 1981.
21. Bocher, R., MITINET/Retro in Wisconsin libraries, *Information Technology and Libraries*, 3(13), 267–274, 1984.
22. Drake, V. and Smith, M.P., Retrospective conversion with REMARC at Johns Hopkins University, *Information Technology and Libraries*, 3(3), 282–286, 1984.
23. Bazillion, R.J., Microcomputer-based recon with Ocelot: a case study, *Library Software Review*, **4**(3), 125–127, 1985.
24. Purton, A.C., Microcomputers for home indexing: a report and guide, *The Indexer*, **13**(4), 27–37, 1982.
25. Hines, T.C. and Winkel, L. Microcomputer aided production of indexes, *The Indexer*, **11**(4), 198–201, 1979.
26. See, for example, Foskett, A.C., *The Subject Approach to Information*, 4th edn, Bingley, 1982.
27. Armstrong, C.J. and Keen, E.M., *Microcomputer Printed Subject Indexes Teaching Package*, 2 volumes (BLR&D Report nos. 5710, 5711), British Library, 1982.
28. Craven, T.C., Microcomputer simulation of large permuted indexes, (*Proceedings of the 42nd ASIS Annual Meeting*, Vol. 16, pp. 168–173, 1979.
29. Craven, T.C., Automatic NEPHIS coding of descriptive titles for permuted index generation, *Journal of the American Society of Information Science*, (March 1982), 97–101.
30. Craven, T.C., A NEPHIS screen editor as an aid in permuted index generation, *Journal of Information Science*, **5**(5), 187–191, 1983.
31. Yerkey, A.N., A preserved context indexing system for microcomputers: PERMDEX, *Information Processing and Management*, **19**(3), 165–171, 1983.
32. Batty, D., Microcomputers in index language design and development, *Microcomputers for Information Management*, **1**(4), 303–312, 1984.
33. Flaver, E. and Mechen, G., A simple newspaper index using dBase II, *Small Computers in Libraries*, **4**(10), 6–8, 1984.

34. Baird, P., Gibb, F. and McAdams, F., A newspaper's index finger, *Times Higher Education Supplement*, (672), 17, 1985.
35. Portoghese, C. and Schrader, D.B., ZyINDEX: a powerful indexing and searching package, *Electronic Library* 3(1), 30–33, 1985.
36. Callow, M., Producing an index to legal periodicals in the Foreign and Commonwealth Office library using Cardbox, *Program*, 19(3), 251–261, 1985.
37. Ede, S.J. and Wheatley, M.L., The use of microcomputers in interlibrary lending, *Interlending and Document Supply*, 13(3), 63–70, 1985.
38. Gadsden, S.R. and Adams, R.J., The Administration of Interlending by Microcomputer, LIR Report No. 30 (0–7123–3044–5). British Library, 1984.
39. Brooks, J.A., F.I.L.L.S. Fast Interlibrary Loans and Statistics, *Electronic Library*, 3(1), 28–29, 1985.
40. Witters, M., Interlibrary loans with a micro: clean and quick, *Online*, 8(6), 53–61, 1984.
41. Evans, E.A., Microcomputers: an interlibrary loan application, *Special Libraries*, 75(1), 17–27, 1984.
42. Williams, M., Electronic mail, *Educational Computing*, 3(2), 26–27, 1982.
43. Givens, B., Micros and interlibrary loans in Montana, *Access: Microcomputers in Libraries*, 2(3), 5–7, 24, 1982.
44. Woodrow, M. Application of the Apple, *Library Association Record*, 84(1), 21–22, 1982.
45. Woodrow, M., Community information on the IBM PC, *Library Micromation News*, (4), 17, 1984.
46. Bennett, C., A bite off the Apple, *SLA News*, (180), 7–8, 1984.
47. Bordwell, S., dBase II — library use of a microcomputer database management system, *Program*, 18(2), 157–165, 1984.
48. Bivins, K.T., A microcomputer alternative for information handling — REFLES, *Information Processing and Management*, 17(2), 97–101, 1981.
49. Moore, B., Microcomputer data base management for union listing, *Technicalities*, 2(9), 8–9, 1982.
50. Schoenly, S.B., A library tour and orientation program for small microcomputers, *Software Review*, 1(1), 44–57, 1982.
51. Bacsanyi, K., ELL: Education Library Locator, *Education Libraries*, 9(1/2), 25, 29, 1984.
52. Snell, M.J. and Duggua, H., Microtext — electronic blackboard, expert system or teaching package, *Library Micromation News*, (8), 9–10, 1985.
53. Dewey, P.R., Easy to use microcomputer generated 'subject guide' wall chart, *Online*, 7(2), 32–43, 1983.
54. Day, J.M. and Tedd, L.A., Computer software for education and training: developments in UK schools of librarianship and information science, in, 7th International Online Information Meeting, 471–481, 1983.
55. Marx, B., Ghirardi, L. and Wolf-Terroine, M., A computer-aided instruction program for developing use of data bases, in, 6th International Online Information Meeting, 135–142, 1982.
56. Large, J.A. and Armstrong, C.J., The development of a microcomputer emulation for teaching online bibliographic searching, *International Forum on Information and Documentation*, 8(2), 14–17, 1983.
57. Collier, M., Local area networks: the implications for library and information science. LIR Report No. 19 (0–7123–3028–39), British Library, 1984.
58. Copeland, J.M. and Flood, S., Users and local area networks: opportunities for information transfer, *Electronic Library*, 2(4), 273–277, 1984.
59. Copeland, J.M. and Flood, S., Database software for a local area network, *Library Micromation News*, (5), 11–13, 1984.

60. Mitev, N., Venner, G.M. and Walker, S., *op. cit.*
61. Levert, V.M., Applications of local area networks of microcomputers in libraries, *Information Technology and Libraries*, 4(1), 9–18, 1985.

6

Administration of library and information services

Over and above information retrieval and the related routines of a library or information unit, there is an element of work which arises simply from the fact that libraries are, in their own way, small businesses. There are budgets to be prepared and accounts to be kept, statistical information to be collated and presented, correspondence and reports to be prepared, and so on. How much there is will depend largely on the size of the library, but every library will have an element of this kind of work.

Given that software has been developed to handle almost every aspect of business work, from budgetary control to Statutory Sick Pay records, then this is one area in which the library can automate with little or no difficulty: information retrieval may place some strains on software primarily intended for the business world, but the office work will not be significantly different.

In addition, libraries and information units have their own, often unique problems of resource management, which, though it can be as prosaic as shelf guiding and stock taking, it is still a time consuming business. As we shall see below, a number of librarians have developed some innovative and imaginative applications of microcomputers in these areas.

6.1 WORD AND TEXT PROCESSING

For this, the obvious answer is the ubiquitous word processor, versions of which exist for almost every microcomputer. We will only consider here the 'microcomputer-as-word-processor', because this is a combination which generally offers the best of both worlds: we should not, however, forget the existence of dedicated word processors, which will be a better choice if report and correspondence writing are a significant part of the library's housekeeping [1].

The advantages of word processing can be summarized as.

(a) Storage and production of standard documents to which minor changes are made to 'personalize' them.

(b) Storage and production of draft documents which can be quickly and easily amended to produce perfect copy.

(c) Storage and production of lists, catalogues etc. which are amended at intervals, so that up-to-date versions can be produced with the minimum of retyping.

Uses can thus be summarized as any textual information which has to be replicated at regular intervals or in quantity, with or without amendments. As in the early days of computers, there is a tendency towards the 'we can't do it that way, because it wouldn't suit the word processor' syndrome. Forcing text to suit the software should be avoided, since it will almost certainly result in poorer documents, if it will not 'fit' the word processor, then the wrong software has been chosen. There is a wide selection available and it should be examined with a detailed knowledge of the library's requirements.

Most word processing software, almost by definition, offers the same basic set of facilities, while additional features are available on the more expensive programs: prices range from £20 to around £700 for very powerful and complex programs.

Standard features of word processing software are:

(a) *Text formatting*: left and right margins, line spacing, justification (i.e. a straight edge to text at the right-hand side), page size, page numbering, centred text (headings).

(b) *Text editing*: delete single words or blocks of text, transfer lines or blocks of text to another position, append text from disk, insert space for new text, 'global search and replace', (i.e. find all occurrences of a word and replace it with another word), paging backwards and forwards through text, automatic links with succeeding text.

Programs differ in how they carry out some of these operations. Most will allow the operator to specify an overall format of margins, line spacing and so on, and to change these where necessary with instructions 'embedded' in the text. Text can be deleted by positioning the cursor over the text and pressing a delete key, or by defining the text in some way (using brackets at the start and finish, for example) and then pressing the delete key. After a portion has been taken out, remaining text is readjusted.

Inserting new text can be done in two ways. For small amounts of new material, it is possible to open up the text at the appropriate point and then simply type in the new material. Larger amounts of text can be entered at the end of the document and then transferred *en bloc* to the correct position, usually by defining the text, moving the cursor to the desired location and pressing the 'transfer' key. Describing the process almost takes longer than doing it: once a document has been drafted onto the screen, text can be edited in this way with two or three key-strokes only.

Programs may handle text as 'pages' (actually more than an A4 page) or as a continuous document to the maximum allowed, which is usually several tens of thousands of characters. The latter is more flexible, particularly for long documents: any changes, such as insertions or deletions will produce a readjustment of text which will carry through to the end of the text. Programs based on 'pages' may readjust only to the end of the page, and this will throw succeeding text out of alignment. However, the page-based software tends to be more suitable for letters and shorter documents.

All programs will allow the operator to move through the text one line at a time, but it is also useful to be able to move a screen of text at a time with a single key-stroke, in order to 'page' rapidly from one part to the other.

Presentation of the text on the screen is important, because that is normally how initial corrections and checks are made. Some programs simply stop screen printing at the end of a line and start at the next line, with the result that words are broken up. While they will be printed properly, it makes screen viewing unpleasant: it is better to have words that will not fit placed in the next line.

The advanced features of the software are:

(a) *Mathematics*: it may be possible to carry out calculations on figures included in the text. This can range from simple adding of columns to automatic recalculation of all related figures when one is changed (as in a spreadsheet; see below).

(b) *Record merging*: this usually involves calling up a name and address from a file and merging it with a piece of text (often a standard letter). Some programs have the added facility of selecting names from the file on the basis of some relevant criterion. It would then be possible, for example, to send a letter only to the members of one department or section.

(c) *Spelling checks*: a dictionary is included which automatically checks spellings and highlights words not in the dictionary. (Highlighted words may not always be misspelled, since the dictionaries are limited in scope.)

(d) *Background printing*: also known as concurrent printing, this facility allows the operator to work with one piece of text while another document is being printed, thus eliminating the need to wait while each document is printed.

There are one or two other features which should be considered. Most contemporary word processing software provides facilities for enhancing the printed output of documents, provided that the printer is capable of accepting such commands. The range of such options available naturally varies with the program, but it is now usual to find that underlining, super- and sub-scripts, bold, italic, double-size and condensed printing are possible: Fig 6.1 illustrates these possibilities in a short piece of text (admittedly specially created for the occasion!).

The Delphi Technique

Can be used for informed speculation about future developments in any management context, in industry, commerce, socio-economic arenas, etc.

It is not only **speculative**, but also **predictive**: value of predictions will depend on thoroughness of procedures and standing and knowledge of experts involved.

Techniques developed in early 50's '4', but has been criticised as lacking in any sound theoretical basis. Results may not always be successful, but some useful data have been derived.

Advantages of the technique have been stated to be:

1. Systematic
2. Gathers opinions of majority of experts in panel
3. Allows feedback
4. Prevents domination of survey by one or two experts
5. Avoids bandwagon effect and influence of public opinion.
6. Of value in problems which are not amemnable to precise techniques
7. Collects information and data from respondents whose views are irreconcilable or are physically separate
8. Supplements data from traditional sources and past experience.

Delphi technique can be applied in:

1. Technological forecasting
2. determining values and preferences
3. Socio-economic predictions (the value of life)
4. Stimulating decision-making
5. Encouraging development of innovation

Note 4: There has been much refinement of the technique since then.

Figure 6.1 Word processor output with various typefaces.

Programs also vary in how the commands which determine such print features as margins, typeface, line spacing, and so on are incorporated in the document. In some cases, all the necessary commands have to be inserted at the start of the document: any changes which may be wanted in the body of the text have to be inserted at the appropriate points, and then the original values must be re-inserted. In other cases, a set of default options operate for margins, line spacing, and so on, and the operator need only insert commands when these have to be changed. In such cases, it is also common practice to be able to 'switch off' these inserted commands with a single character, whereupon the program reverts to the default options. This is obviously an easier system to operate (provided that the operator remembers to insert the 'switch off' command!), but the reader should note that, in programs imported from North America, the default options may not always be suitable in a UK context. For example, the typical default page size on IBM's Easywriter word processing package is 66 lines, with 55 lines of print per page, to comply with the size of standard

North American paper. This means that, for UK paper of A4 size, the operator must always incorporate commands to change the page size to approximately 70 lines, of which some 60 lines will contain print.

In some cases, commands for these and other operations have to be inserted using a combination of keys (e.g. a control key and one other): this can be cumbersome and can lead to errors. Dedicated word processors usually have single keys for such operations, as do some microcomputers. It may be possible for the operator to define certain keys (which are otherwise little used) for specific functions within the software. These 'macros' can therefore make some operations less error-prone.

As with all software, features over and above the 'standard' ones will have to be selected on the basis of what will be needed or useful in a specific context.

One of the first uses of word processors was to produce standard letters, each with a different name and address, so that each letter looked as though it had been individually typed. However, the uses which are outlined above mean that, within a library, the software can be used to produce catalogues, bibliographies, etc., in fact any document which, with a standard typewriter, would have to be retyped a number of times to produce a perfect version and (perhaps of even greater use) documents which need a considerable amount of retyping at intervals. For example, a polytechnic library has over 1000 video tapes which it lists in a separate index: large numbers of new tapes are added each year and dated ones are removed. By producing the index on a word processor, the library has eliminated the need to retype a lengthy list each time a new edition is required: in fact, it is now possible to produce the index more frequently and thus to ensure that it is more up to date. Similar remarks can be made about union catalogues (see section 5.9).

6.2 ADMINISTRATION, STATISTICS AND FINANCE

All libraries have to operate within a budget (be it large or small) and probably all libraries keep some statistical information on loans, numbers of readers etc. How much effort is put into the recording of this will often depend on the time available, the expertise of the librarian and the amount of information needed. Even if there is a limited amount of such work, it may well be useful to use microcomputer-based techniques to reduce the work involved, and the software may also offer the opportunity to carry out additional operations not otherwise possible.

6.2.1 Administration

Library administration covers a number of topics, ranging from those paralleling the business world, such as personnel records and salaries, to routines more peculiar to the library world. Many libraries may also be involved in maintaining booking records of one type or another: in college libraries these often relate to instructional films hired during term.

Of course, a number of these routines may be handled by other departments within the parent organization — the personnel office or the salaries section, for example — and the library will have no need of payroll software or programs to calculate Statutory Sick Pay, though it will have to maintain records of staff illness, annual leave and so on. There are business programs to cover all of these possibilities, but, because the library may rarely be involved in many of them, we shall concentrate on those routines that are maintained by the library.

A long-term staffing exercise has been carried out on a microcomputer at Texas A&M University. Models of the requirements of the processing section have been used to draw up a 5-year plan for staffing [2]. The microcomputer provides a simulation of the processing department based on a number of factors, such as volume of material received, staffing, amount of OCLC terminal processing etc. Best, worst and most likely cases are entered for these, and it is also possible to put 'what if?' questions to the system, e.g. 'What if productivity were increased by 5%', or 'What if staffing grades change, with consequent changes in the possible levels of processing?' The information provided is used to support the decision-making process: it does not, of itself, provide the answer.

If a library regularly sends out mail on an established list (accessions bulletins, for example), it can be a tedious chore to address large numbers of envelopes. Mailing list software elimintes the routine, since, once names and addresses have been entered in a file, any or all of them can be printed onto labels (or envelopes). Some of these programs offer search facilities, usually of the 'all names in town X or county Y' variety, though some have the further refinement of searching by post-code and other features. Most can also sort the file by at least one field (usually name), and in some cases by city, post-code or keywords (assigned by the user). Many mailing programs are designed to link with word processing software, so that standard letters and forms can be addressed automatically. This, incidentally, is one area where North American software does not travel well: UK postcodes will not fit into fields designed for US zip codes.

Film and other media bookings can be handled by one or two programs which are available for microcomputers. They are actually intended for use by the media suppliers, but could be used in any organization, such as a library, which not only lends its own media, but also hires them from a third party. One program (called, with great originality, Film Bookings) can

handle 850 films per floppy disk and 250 customers. As well as sea
and sorting, it will produce daily lists of films due for return and
associated statistics. Any library involved in this activity on a large scal
could find such software very useful in ensuring accurate and comprehensive records.

Sections and departments within an oranization must often maintain an
inventory of all equipment and furniture, usually so that a check can be
made on the location of valuable items, and libraries are no exception, since
they frequently contain expensive equipment which has to be recorded. A
typical inventory will contain details of the make and model, plus serial
number(s), location and date of purchase/installation. There may also be
space for a record of maintenance and maintenance agreements, together
perhaps with information on cost and depreciation.

Inventories can be maintained easily on word processing software,
particularly if they are subject to alteration and amendment at more or less
regular intervals. The additional capabilities of DBMS would probably not
be needed, although for a multisite library it can be useful to be able to list
all equipment in each location, particularly if there is a lot of such
equipment. Listing by date of purchase will give an indication of equipment
that may be due for replacement or that is out of warranty and in need of a
maintenance agreement.

An alternative, of course, is to use an inventory program and one is
available specifically for audiovisual equipment. AV Equipment Inventory
is an inexpensive program ($30) which records details of equipment,
including locations, source of funding, supplier etc. It offers several sorting
and listing options so that various approaches to the inventory are possible.

A task often carried out with reluctance in many libraries is stock-taking,
which may be done on a more or less regular basis. Pikes Peak Library
overcame many of the problems associated with stock-taking when it used
portable TRS-Model 100 microcomputers equipped with bar code readers
(all stock carried bar codes for the circulation control system). By reading
the codes on each volume on the shelves and merging this information with
the circulation control records stored on the main computer, the library was
able to ascertain which volumes were missing from stock with very little
effort: the inventory of 300 000 volumes was carried out with a labour cost
of less than $700 in a few days [3].

The University of Sussex carried out a major re-shelving exercise in 1984,
and used a BBC Micro with the Ultracalc spreadsheet program to plan the
movement of stock so that adequate space could be left to accommodate
future growth. It was possible to make provision in each area for different
growth rates, so that the best use was made of available shelving without
wasted or unused space [4].

A network of 23 libraries in Illinois, anxious to implement a collection,
development and resource sharing programme, realized that, as a first step,
they had to assess the degree to which the various collections overlapped

In a test project, a program was developed to run
eekends which could compress the records downloaded
abase into a coded format. Random records were then
des for these records compared with the test database to
hich matched. Unique records were transferred to a
but where duplication occurred, only one record and a
put onto the master file. This is an example of the way
omputer can analyse a very large collection (with four
million online records), though it should be noted that this was a test run
intended to ascertain the accuracy of the system for use with the full
database [5].

Information professionals in smaller organizations may often feel that,
from the management point of view, they are limited in what they can do:
most of their time is spent simply running the unit on a day-to-day basis and
it is difficult for them to apply any sophisticated management techniques
which may help them in their work. It is the purpose of this section to show
how the microcomputer can help in this, and an excellent example has been
provided by Linköping University's Laboratory of Library and Information
Science (LIBLAB). Here, using interlibrary lending as an application,
LIBLAB have indicated how microcomputer-based flowcharting can help
library staff accurately to describe often complex routines in an effort to
improve those routines [6]. The work at LIBLAB is particularly significant,
since it recognizes the need for such management tools to be used by library
staff who have little or no programming experience — an undoubted fact,
at present!

6.2.2 Statistics

The amount of statistical information maintained by a library will vary,
often depending on the size of the library, on how much statistical data are
needed and not least on how well the librarian can handle the data!
Expertise may range from adding weekly loans figures and producing the
occasional graph to complex operations on patterns of library use,
distribution of users etc.

Generally speaking, there are three types of statistics software available
to the librarian: the 'true' statistics programs, business statistics software
and spreadsheets. Their use can improve the quality of the presentations
which the librarian invariably has to make when applying for increased
funding, staffing etc., and can also provide additional information which
may reveal a new aspect of the library service.

There are, first of all, the true statistics programs which will carry out all,
or most of, the standard statistical operations such as means, medians, chi-
squared test, regression analysis and so on. They may be too sophisticated
for many areas of library work (and for many librarians), since they often

assume a knowledge of statistics such that the user understands the significance of these operations. However, they can be used by those who have that knowledge in analyses of user populations, book usage patterns, and similar large-scale projects. The business statistics packages tend to be less demanding, as they are aimed at a population which is not expected to have that expertise readily available.

Statistical data can also be stored and manipulated with the spreadsheet programs considered below, though these may be more limited in the form of output possible.

Features to look for when selecting a program are fairly self-evident. It must cope with the range of data to be analysed and carry out all the required operations. It will also be necessary to assess the level of knowledge required to operate the program and to be clear whether any special peripherals are needed. If the printer cannot cope with the graphic output from the program, additional devices such as a graph plotter may be required. A very basic point will be to ensure that, if graphs, charts etc. are needed in printed form, they can be passed easily ('dumped') from the screen to the printer. The use of colour invariably facilitates interpretation of the output, but obviously requires a printer capable of handling colour.

Consideration must also be given to the form in which the figures will be presented. A simple tabular format may be sufficient for most purposes, but it is often useful (and more interesting) to present the data as graphs, bar charts, pie charts etc., and this could apply particularly if the figures are to be incorporated into annual reports or other documents. Fig. 6.2 illustrates the output possible from software of this kind. The pie charts, graphs and bar charts were produced using Grafix software on a Sirus 1. Fig. 6.2a shows how the ratio of staff to student loans has changed over a 4-year period. Figs 6.2b and 2c are two presentations of the same data and by the same program: it is simply necessary to state which presentation is required. The figures given (for Computer Room use) could just as easily relate to the number of users in the library at given times during the day.

As was suggested above, very sophisticated statistical analyses can be produced with this software, and the interested librarian can be advised to consider these pacakges carefully, since their use may enable him or her to improve significantly the quality and range of information available. The more advanced techniques are presented in Simpson's standard work on statistics for librarians [7].

Microcomputer-based systems have been used with more general software to analyse the results of surveys conducted by, or relevant to library and information services. For example, British Columbia Library Association's Newspapers Committee developed a plan for a province-programme of newspaper acquisition, preservation and bibliographic control. In order to assess the contemporary situation in the province, the committee surveyed all newspaper collections in some three hundred organizations, and analysed the results using PFS : File and PFS : Report software on an Apple IIe [8].

More relevant to our current theme of the management and administration of libraries is the analysis of research interests of faculty staff which was carried out at Arizona State University Library [9].

Again using PFS : File and PFS : Report, the library has automated its index of faculty profile cards, cards which detail the teaching, professional and research interests of members of staff. Information on these cards was derived from a questionnaire, and was used in collection building, orientation of new staff and, of course, as an aid to subject specialists in providing new information to the appropriate lecturers. The manual file, however, was of limited use, particularly for new library staff, since it had only two sequences, of lecturer's name and department, so it was difficult, for example, to determine which department could be concerned with a particular problem, and thus to direct new information to that department.

The new database included a field for keywords associated with the record for each individual, and a printed index to this list was created. Printed reports were necessary because a microcomputer was not available at the reference desk where the subject specialists worked. An IBM XT is now provided in the library and the system is being re-created using dBase III: the opportunity has been taken to provide two new fields relating to language ability and consultancy work. Use of a hard disk has eliminated the need to segment the profiles of the faculty staff.

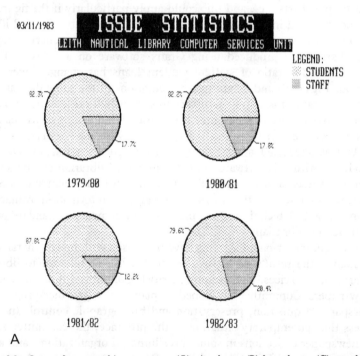

Figure 6.2 Output from graphics program: (A) pie charts; (B) bar charts; (C) graph.

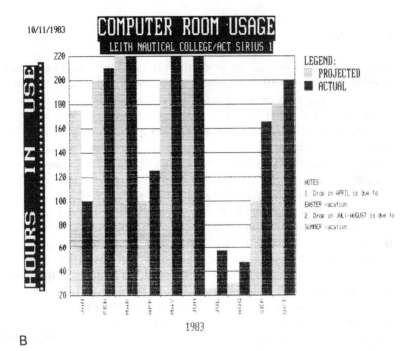

B

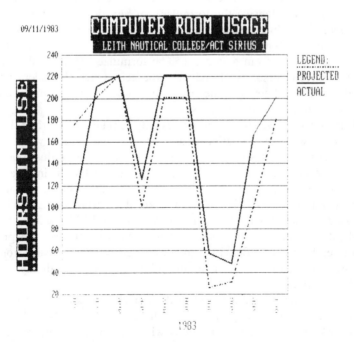

C

6.2.3   Finance

Perhaps of more overall value to the librarian, though more limited in graphic output, is the spreadsheet, or financial modelling program. The range available runs in price from £30 to £800. Certain features can be regarded as standard; others are usually found on the more expensive programs. Since some of these features are perhaps only of use when the program is being used to model very large (company) budgets, the points that are considered here are those thought to be of most relevance to libraries.

Spreadsheet programs consist of a matrix of boxes or 'cells', into which the user enters data or formulae. The maximum number of cells is determined by the program, but may be restricted by the available RAM; however, the software will indicate the minimum RAM capacity needed. A cell is defined by vertical and horizontal coordinates (usually represented by a letter and a number) which are based on the columns and rows set up by the user. Since the number of cells is finite, more rows means fewer columns and vice versa, though the reduction is rarely significant, since programs will typically handle several thousand cells.

Column width determines how big a number can be entered in each cell, and a maximum will be stated. The cells can contain words, data or formulae which act on data elsewhere on the sheet, and a further point to consider is how extensive the formulae can be: ideally, they should allow every operation which will be needed, and most programs provide a very wide range. It should be possible in a formula to use data that are themselves derived from a formula. The formulae are normally 'invisible' until the screen cursor is placed over the cell. Once the calculations are carried out, the cell contains the answer derived from the formula, although the formula remains for future use.

All spreadsheets will print out data exactly as they are recorded, but some will also allow the presentation of graphs, bar charts etc., which may be more effective. If the spreadsheet itself is not capable of this, one way in which it can be done is to use a graphics program which is integrated with the spreadsheet. For example, BEEBPLOT (an inexpensive graphics program for the BBC Micro) can take data from BEEBCALC, the spreadsheet, and present it as a histogram or graph. These two programs also illustrate what can be done with inexpensive software: the programs cost £24 each, but BEEBCALC provides a facility often missing from more expensive programs, in that column widths can be individually varied to suit their contents.

A more significant development of the last two years has been the arrival of integrated business programs such as Lotus 1–2–3, Symphony, Framework, etc. These are programs which combine a database management system, word processor and spreadsheet in one package. Earlier criticism that the constitutent parts of such programs, taken individually, were not very powerful or sophisticated, have been answered by the most recent software of this kind. Here, all the modules contained in the package are of a sufficiently high standard to ensure that there is no loss of performance in any application. Their main advantage, of course, lies in the ability to transfer information from one module to another as required. Thus, when preparing the annual report on the word processor, it is a simple task, involving a few keystrokes, to call up the spreadsheet software which shows annual acquisitions rate, loans records, etc. and to incorporate them into the report. Similarly, records from the database management system can be incorporated into a reading list or bibliography with text added.

There have been few reports on the use of such integrated software by libraries and information services for business work, though some libraries have used the software in related ways. For example, the use of Lotus 1–2–3 to maintain statistics on the use made of the library reference service has been described by Corbett [10], while the library of the University of Arkansas also uses Lotus 1–2–3 for a file of information on online databases [11]. The file records the main details of each database used by the library, and the user can consult the file to select the best database to use for any given search.

The uses of spreadsheets in a library are various. The most obvious will be in recording expenditure, but as suggested above, they can also analyse loans in various ways. Fig. 6.3 shows how a spreadsheet can be used to record expenditure on books: the reader can no doubt think of other features which could be added if relevant. Spreadsheets are usually large enough to record all areas of spending on one sheet, and thus provide an overall picture of the budget. Used like this, spreadsheets simply replace manual systems and offer the opportunity to do more analyses than would otherwise be feasible [12].

However, spreadsheets have a particular value when used for modelling ('what if?' operations). Suppose that the spreadsheet includes every element in the annual estimate — salaries, repairs, heating etc. Formulae would be used to express any and all relationships between data. It is then possible to work out automatically (and instantly) the effect of a 5% salary increase, plus a 10% rise in heating costs on the estimate and to make suitable adjustments. If the data for loans included, say, ratios of loans to students and loans to stock, the impact of a 10% increase in student numbers could be calculated, indicating perhaps how great an increase in stock would be needed to maintain those ratios. Used in this way, spreadsheets are also an aid to library planning, though naturally they will only be as good as the (intelligent) estimates used in the 'what if?' operations. However, it is always possible to add real data as they become available so that predictions made in this way can be corrected.

Relevant statistical applications of spreadsheets include: analysis of user

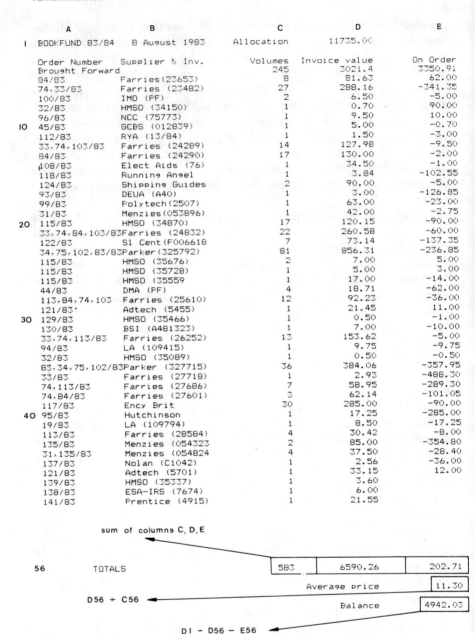

	A	B	C	D	E
1	BOOKFUND 83/84	8 August 1983	Allocation	11735.00	
	Order Number	Supplier & Inv.	Volumes	Invoice value	On Order
	Brought Forward		245	3021.4	3350.91
	84/83	Farries(23653)	8	81.63	62.00
	74,33/83	Farries (23482)	27	288.16	-341.35
	100/83	IMO (PF)	2	6.50	-5.00
	32/83	HMSO (34150)	1	0.70	90.00
	96/83	NCC (75773)	1	9.50	10.00
10	45/83	GCBS (012839)	1	5.00	-0.70
	112/83	RYA (13/84)	1	1.50	-3.00
	33,74,103/83	Farries (24289)	14	127.98	-9.50
	84/83	Farries (24290)	17	130.00	-2.00
	108/83	Elect Aids (76)	1	34.50	-1.00
	118/83	Running Angel	1	3.84	-102.55
	124/83	Shipping Guides	2	90.00	-5.00
	93/83	DEUA (A40)	1	3.00	-126.85
	99/83	Polytech(2507)	1	63.00	-23.00
	31/83	Menzies(053896)	1	42.00	-2.75
20	115/83	HMSO (34870)	17	120.15	-90.00
	33,74,84,103/83	Farries (24832)	22	260.58	-60.00
	122/83	Sl Cent(F006618	7	73.14	-137.35
	34,75,102,83/83	Parker(325792)	81	856.31	-236.85
	115/83	HMSO (35676)	2	7.00	5.00
	115/83	HMSO (35728)	1	5.00	3.00
	115/83	HMSO (35559	1	17.00	-14.00
	44/83	DMA (PF)	4	18.71	-62.00
	113,84,74,103	Farries (25610)	12	92.23	-36.00
	121/83'	Adtech (5455)	1	21.45	11.00
30	129/83	HMSO (35466)	1	0.50	-1.00
	130/83	BSI (A481323)	1	7.00	-10.00
	33,74,113/83	Farries (26252)	13	153.62	-5.00
	94/83	LA (109415)	1	9.75	-9.75
	32/83	HMSO (35089)	1	0.50	-0.50
	83,34,75,102/83	Parker (327715)	36	384.06	-357.95
	33/83	Farries (27718)	1	2.93	-488.30
	74,113/83	Farries (27686)	7	58.95	-289.30
	74,84/83	Farries (27601)	3	62.14	-101.05
	117/83	Ency Brit	30	285.00	-90.00
40	95/83	Hutchinson	1	17.25	-285.00
	19/83	LA (109794)	1	8.50	-17.25
	113/83	Farries (28584)	4	30.42	-8.00
	135/83	Menzies (054323	2	85.00	-354.80
	31,135/83	Menzies (054824	4	37.50	-28.40
	137/83	Nolan (C1042)	1	2.56	-36.00
	121/83	Adtech (5701)	1	33.15	12.00
	139/83	HMSO (35337)	1	3.60	
	138/83	ESA-IRS (7674)	1	6.00	
	141/83	Prentice (4915)	1	21.55	

sum of columns C, D, E

| 56 | TOTALS | | 583 | 6590.26 | 202.71 |

Average price 11.30

D56 ÷ C56

Balance 4942.03

D1 – D56 – E56

Figure 6.3 Spreadsheet software used for a book fund.

population, library use patterns, extent and distribution of reference enquiries etc. It should always be remembered, however, that the data still have to be collected and it is important to assess the value of any such analyses for the library service: data should not be collected for their own sake!

Most spreadsheet programs offer a report generator which will allow the insertion of additional text, will re-arrange the sheet, automatically add page numbers, and so on. In addition, it will be possible to view different parts of the spreadsheet on the screen, often by placing two parts side by side. This allows the operator to compare parts of the sheet which are separated by a large space.

6.2.4 Other applications

In order to indicate how versatile the microcomputer can be with the right software (and to demonstrate the novelty and ingenuity of some librarians!), we would mention two similar applications of Apple microcomputers. Carnegie-Mellon University Library uses an Apple Macintosh with its MacPaint program to produce a wide range of informational, instructional and promotional signs and guides. MacPaint has the facility to store regularly-used symbols, text or graphics, so the library has designed a number for various purposes. Text and further images can be added as required, and MacPaint offers a range of fonts for printing, along with patterns and shading for greater effect. Signs and other products can be made in a few minutes to a very high standard, and can, of course, be 'stored' on disk should they be required again [13].

A more homely approach is demonstrated by the work of an American preparatory school which uses software called the Print Shop on an Apple IIe to design and produce a range of promotional material such as greetings cards, public signs, labels, invitations, and so on [14]. The Print Shop has a basic range of symbols, which can be augmented by a further 120 graphic signs.

Approaches like this, we would suggest, indicate that the possibilities of using the microcomputer in the more routine areas of library and information work are limited only by the imagination, but that the results may often be an improvement in the image of the library, as well as an extension of the service provided.

6.3 ELECTRONIC MAIL AND TELETEX

Up to this point, we have simply considered the microcomputer as a means of automating existing in-house practices for the sake of speed and, in some cases, to extend the range of possible operations. This, however, falls short of exploiting the full potential of the microcomputer to revolutionize the way in which business documents, memoranda, reports etc. are produced and disseminated. For example, we still entrust the delivery of documents to a system which relies ultimately on a human being manually transporting those documents to their destination — a situation probably comparable to travelling in a horse-drawn Concorde!

Electronic mail, the associated bulletin board systems (BBS) and Teletex offer the prospect of electronic document and text *delivery* as well as the electronic document *production* we have already discussed. Text can be composed on a microcomputer and then sent over telephone lines to another computer, where it is stored in the addressee's 'mailbox'. The addressee looks in his mailbox at intervals and can read the material he has been sent: the document may never appear as words on paper, and replies can be sent in the same way. The alternative involves sending messages direct to the addressee's microcomputer rather than to a set of mailboxes on a central computer.

The difference between the two systems can be illustrated by analogy with a set of letterboxes located in the entrance to an apartment block, with one box for each resident. Post is delivered to the individual boxes, but residents must check each morning to see if anything has been delivered. By contrast, someone living in a house has his letters delivered directly to his door.

Electronic mail is widespread in North America, but in the UK it was limited until 1983 by British Telecom's monopoly of telecommunications. Individual companies could use electronic mail facilities, but only to transmit information within the company. Now that this monopoly has ended, the technology is being employed on a much wider scale.

6.3.1 The equipment and its operation

Electronic mail and Teletex can be transmitted using a variety of equipment: the terminal can be a dedicated teletype device or a workstation which carries out a variety of functions, and which has its own data storage system. Which is used will depend on in-house policy and, inevitably, on the equipment already available when an electronic mail system is introduced. However, a multifunction terminal is to be recommended and the microcomputer now has everything to offer in this respect. Not only does it provide local information retrieval (in the library sense), but it is also capable of serving as a word processor, an intelligent terminal to online data bases and an electronic mail and Teletex terminal. The point was made when we discussed word processing: generally speaking, libraries can be recommended to use a suitable microcomputer with any necessary ancillary equipment for all these functions. This avoids a plethora of hardware and makes training easier, since operators will already be familiar with the nucleus of the hardware and will only require training as and when new functions are added.

It will, however, be important to consider the cumulative costs of the additional hardware and software needed and the amount of work involved in each activity. There may come a point when it is more cost-effective to use dedicated equipment.

For anyone involved with online searching, the equipment needed for electronic mail will be familiar: in addition to the microcomputer itself (which is the terminal), an acoustic coupler or modem will be needed. Acoustic couplers are cheaper than modems but usually receive and transmit data at 300 baud, which is approximately equal to 30 characters per second. A modem, on the other hand, can transmit data at much higher speeds and can incorporate automatic dialling. Modems are connected directly to the telephone line, so they are less susceptible to line noise, which can corrupt messages.

A still cheaper alternative which is a compromise between these two is the 1200/75 acoustic coupler. This will receive data at 1200 baud, but only sends at 75 baud. This slow sending rate is not normally a problem, since this type of acoustic coupler is only used in those situations where the operator sends a few keystrokes, e.g. to call up page numbers on Prestel: it would not really be feasible to use a 1200/75 acoustic coupler for electronic mail that involves anything larger in the way of text.

In addition to the acoustic coupler or modem, a software package will be needed in order to control the microcomputer while mail is being sent or received: effectively, this software converts the microcomputer into an intelligent terminal. There are a number of such packages available for many of the standard business systems.

It will, of course, be necessary to subscribe to the communications service and to pay any charges levied for using it, plus the cost of the telephone 'call'.

Sending data means dialling up the central computer and (usually) following a menu of choices through to the electronic mail facility, at which point the message is entered, preceded by the 'address' to which it is being sent. (It seems almost unnecessary to state that the person or organization to which the message is going must also subscribe!)

Using a microcomputer means that messages, documents etc. can be composed offline and saved on disk for editing and correction: this avoids incurring connection charges until everything is ready — and also means that the slow typist is not penalized! Text is then loaded from disk and, on entering the system, is sent to the mailbox. This has all the advantages offered by online search assistance (see Section 4.3).

Receiving messages requires the user to check the mailbox (each subscriber is allocated a confidential box that only he or she can access) and viewing any messages. In most cases, the user will be told that a message is waiting when he or she logs on. Messages can be read on the screen (if they are short) or saved on disk for later examination offline.

The system described so far utilizes a central computer which actually contains the mailboxes, just as an online host holds the data base. The central computer operates under software which controls the storage and handling of data and text, and also ensures that the necessary communications protocols are adhered to.

The alternative approach is *direct* communication between individual microcomputers over telephone lines. In the UK this is largely contingent upon the development of the Teletex system, which began in 1983. Using Teletex, a microcomputer or word processor terminal will have its own software to control the electronic mail system and will be able to send direct to another microcomputer, where the message will be stored either on disk or in RAM. Eventually, it will be possible to use both the telephone network and the Packet-Switching System (PSS) for Teletex to both UK and overseas addresses.

Direct communication means that it will no longer be necessary to check a mailbox located elsewhere. It will also offer an improvement in central computer arrangements, in that messages can be received while the microcomputer is being used for some other task, i.e. it will be a 'background' activity. This constitutes the essential difference between electronic mail and Teletex. The former requires a central computer to control the entire mail system, including communications protocols and the mailboxes, while Teletex operates between terminals in much the same way as the present telex system (though some Teletex terminals will be capable of sending messages to a number of terminals).

The Teletex system will require either a dedicated terminal or an existing terminal of some type (microcomputer, word processor etc.) which is enhanced by Teletex software. Dedicated terminals are planned by a number of companies in consultation with British Telecom, while microcomputer and other equipment manufacturers are investigating conversion packages for their products. Manufacture of terminals is independent of British Telecom, but the latter has produced a set of guidelines and standards which terminals will have to meet in order to be connected to either the telephone network or PSS. Note that for once standards have been drawn up *before* production of equipment started! Manufacturers will be free to provide any level of facilities on their equipment, provided that the minimum requirements for Teletex are met. These include a complete office typewriter character set, some editing and correction facilities and a document log that indicates deliveries etc. British Telecom recommend that a minimum storage of 32 K is needed, and terminals should be able to transmit an A4 page (approximately 1500 characters) in about 10 seconds. Plessey are planning a 16-bit micro-computer which can be used as a Teletex terminal, while Ferranti have developed a Teletex adaptor which will connect any device with a V24 (i.e.

RS232C) interface to the Teletex network. Many business microcomputers are provided with this port, because it is needed for telecommunications generally.

British Telecom have set up a Teletex Marketing Section which can provide details of the service and the necessary equipment, while a useful study of the whole system of electronic mail includes figures which suggest that even at the peak rate, Teletex on PSS will be considerably cheaper than first class post. A ten-page document sent via Teletex will cost almost one-quarter of the first class postage — and, of course, delivery will be (almost) instantaneous [15].

6.3.2 The potential for libraries

The potential of electronic mail and Teletex for libraries and information services is no doubt obvious, particularly if a system is established between branches, departmental libraries, cooperative groups etc. Instead of a number of telephone calls (for an inter-library loan request, for example), it is possible to put one message into the system which can be delivered to all, or a selection of, the mailboxes available, or direct to a terminal, simply by heading the single message with the names of those to whom it must be delivered. An alternative is to have distribution lists stored: it is then simply a case of heading the message with the name of the distribution list, so that the system will deliver to everyone on that list.

Givens [16] has described how electronic mail within Montana has improved the handling of 2000 loan requests per month: the author claims that the system (which uses both a local network and Tymnet) has taken less than 2 years to pay for itself in terms of time and money saved.

While most libraries can use electronic mail for such applications as inter-library loans, there is also the potential to extend the information service by posting information on an electronic bulletin board [17]. In the UK this has already been done to a limited extent by public libraries using Prestel. A BBS can be 'open' at times when the library is closed and can provide a range of useful quick reference information.

Should a library decide to use an electronic mail system, then it will largely be a case of accepting the facilities offered by the system. However, there is a great deal to investigate should a group of libraries decide to establish their own system [18].

Mailbox security will obviously be vital, and this includes not only limiting access to the addressee, but also detecting if a message has been lost and notifying the sender, preventing confidential material from being printed and perhaps limiting even the display of some material to certain terminals (e.g. salaries information can only be seen in the salaries section).

It should be possible to provide a synopsis of messages waiting in a mailbox, so that users do not have to read every one to decide on priorities

169

or on which messages deal with the same subject, while separate filing of messages that have been dealt with ensures that the 'in-tray' does not become too full.

Even if the system is initially set up simply to cope with short messages, there will come a time when its value for transmitting long documents (draft reports for comment etc.) will be appreciated. The system should therefore be able to hold such lengthy documents (sub-divided if necessary) and it will be particularly valuable if documents like this can be prepared offline on a word processor before they are transferred to the mail: recipients should similarly be able to store them on disk for offline study.

Finally, to allow for even further expansion, it should be possible to link the mail system with other systems through 'gateways'. These other systems could be operated nationally (Prestel) or by other cooperative groups in the area.

Along with local area networks (see Section 5.11), electronic mail and Teletex offer many possibilities, both for housekeeping and information retrieval. One point must be made, however. The success of their operation will depend to a very large extent on the people who use them: there will not be a lot of point in all this instantaneous transfer of text and information if users forget to check their mailboxes!

REFERENCES

1. Armstrong, C.J. and Guy, R.F. Microcomputers or word processors in the library?, *Reprographics Quarterly*, **14**(3), 98–103, 1981.
2. Castle, W.I., The use of simulation as a decision support aid, *Technicalities*, **1**(7), 12–14, 1981.
3. Dowlin, K.E. and Hawley, B.G., The use of portable microcomputers for library inventory, *Microcomputers for Information Management*, **11**, 67–73, 1984.
4. Peasegood, A. and Stone, P., The model library: planning reshelving on a spreadsheet, *Library Micromation News*, (5), 2, 1984.
5. Potter, W.G. Modelling collection overlap on a microcomputer, *Information Technology and Libraries*, **2**(4), 400–407, 1983.
6. Marklund, K., Dimensional flowcharting to improve library performance, *Microcomputers for Information Management*, **2**(2), 113–128, 1985.
7. Simpson, I.S., *Basic Statistics for Librarians*, 2nd edn, Bingley, 1983.
8. Romaniuk, E., Analysis of survey results using a microcomputer, *Information Technology and Libraries*, **4**(3), 233–236, 1985.
9. Borovansky, V.T. and Machovec, G.S., Microcomputer-based faculty profile, *Information Technology and Libraries*, **4**(12), 300–305, 1985.
10. Corbett, P.K., Automating reference department functions via an electronic spreadsheet, *Medical Reference Service Quarterly*, **3**(3), 85–88, 1984.
11. Bailey, A.S., Creating and maintaining a database/databank comparison system with Lotus 1–2–3 on a (most of the time) IBM compatible micro, *Online*, **9**(2), 86–92, 1985.
12. Strazdon, M.E., A library application of the Apple Visicalc program, *Drexel Library Quarterly*, **17**(1), 75–86, 1981.

13. Diskin, J.A. and Fitzgerald, P., Library signage: applications for the Apple Macintsoch and MacPaint, *Library Hitech*, **2**(4), 71–77, 1984.
14. Everhart, N. and Hartz, C., Creating graphics with 'The Print Shop', *Library Journal*, **110**(8), 118–120, 1985.
15. Price, S.G., *Preparing for Teletex*, NCC Publications, 1982.
16. Givens, B., Micros and interlibrary loans in Montana, *Access: Microcomputers in Libraries*, **2** (3), 5–7, 24, 1982.
17. Dewey, P.R., Dear ABBS: marketing, maintenance and suggestions, *Small Computers in Libraries*, **2**(9), 1–3, 1982.
18. Welch, J.A. and Wilson, P.A., *Electronic Mail Systems: A Practical Evaluation Guide*, NCC Publications, 1981.

7

The microcomputer as a
library resource

While the emphasis of this book is on the use of the microcomputer for library routines, some consideration should be given to the provision of microcomputers and software as part of the library service. In many cases, this may be the librarian's first contact with the microcomputer, as programs are requested as teaching and learning aids, along with all the other non-book materials which libraries now stock. It seems unnecessary to rehearse all the arguments about libraries storing and providing material other than books: these have all been considered in the past in relation to tape-slide sets, video recordings etc. Few would now consider it strange that a library does provide such material, and computer software need be no exception to this. Microcomputer software and the associated hardware can be regarded as simply another form of non-book material, to be stored and exploited in the same way as all library materials. Having said that, however, software and hardware do pose some unique problems for the library.

7.1 HARDWARE

The problems of selecting microcomputer hardware are considered in Chapter 9, and the points made there are also relevant to the choice of hardware of library users. In many academic libraries, there may not be a choice, as the parent organization may have standardized on a particular make, but this is not universally true.

If there is no policy of standardization, the librarian will be free to choose any suitable system within the budget allocation. Naturally, the opinions of staff should be sought as well, and these should not be limited to the staff of computing or mathematics sections, valuable though their comments will be. As with any computer application, the available software must be the principal determining factor in any choice: there will be little point in buying an otherwise excellent microcomputer if the educational software available for it is not suitable for the potential users, or if the range of programs is very limited.

As is indicated in Chapter 9, the choice of operating system and programming language will be complicated by the fact that there are numerous types and versions of both, although it is suggested there that the CP/M operating system (for 8-bit microcomputers) and the BASIC programming language will almost certainly be required.

However, for 16-bit systems, the choice of operating system is less clear, and it will also be necessary to consider if other languages will be useful (for both 8- and 16-bit systems). Pascal and Forth are growing in popularity as general-purpose languages, while Logo has particular applications in education since it is an interactive language. If these languages are available, they will extend the range of software that can be used.

The storage of microcomputer hardware should pose few problems beyond those associated with any item of valuable and (relatively) delicate equipment. Security will be important, and there are various ways in which microcomputers can be permanently or semi-permanently fixed to furnishings, including adhesive pads or anchoring bolts with special keys. Chapter 9 also considers the overall ergonomics of hardware design and the environment in which the system will operate. Factors such as lighting and seating will have to be considered when installing microcomputers, and while they are virtually silent in operation, the use of the keyboard may produce some noise which other users will find irritating.

Although microcomputers are relatively robust, they do not take kindly to frequent moves from one location to another, particularly on wheeled trollies. The vibration may cause the chips to work loose over a period of time, and if they have to be pushed back into their sockets, it is very easy to bend or break one of the 'legs.'

Dust is an enemy of microcomputers as it is with any piece of electrical apparatus, and a dust cover costing a few pounds is a worthwhile purchase. Disk drives and disks are particularly susceptible to damage by dust and airborne particles (see Fig. 9.8), and drives should be kept away from windows, air and heating vents and similar sources of air-borne contamination. The regular use of a head cleaning kit is advisable.

Whether or not a maintenance contract is taken out after the guarantee expires will be a matter for in-house policy, but the cost of maintenance contracts (which can be 10% of the total purchase price) will have to be included in estimates. A contract is to be recommended, however, in view of the regular and varied use which will be made of the hardware by users of varying degrees of experience!

7.2 SOFTWARE

If only one make of microcomputer is provided within the library, this will simplify the choice of software so far as operating system and programming language are concerned. Those libraries that provide several different makes will have to consider how far to provide the same (or very similar) programs in versions for each system. This has proved to be a particular problem, for example, in the libraries of colleges of education, which provide software for student teachers to use during teaching practice. Since the hardware used in the schools can vary, the college libraries have to consider how far they duplicate provision of the same program in order to cater for some or all of the makes and models that the student teacher may encounter. This will be largely a matter of individual policy, although the move towards standardization within a given education authority may ease the problem.

The problem appears in another form for those public libraries which lend software, since they then have to consider the range of microcomputers which their borrowers could be using — a range potentially as large as the number of available systems! In practice, of course, it will be possible to limit the range to the most popular makes of home or personal computers. The names of popular systems can be determined from 'league tables' which appear frequently in microcomputing journals, while local variations can be obtained from a questionnaire to library users, examination of enquiries for software or from local computer retail stores, which may be willing to provide information on the systems they have found to be most popular.

What kind of software is provided will also be the subject of an in-house policy. Within educational institutions, this will largely be determined by the subjects taught. However, both educational and public libraries will have to consider the provision of other kinds of software, and a glance at any microcomputing journal will show the wide range that is available.

Not every microcomputer will have this variety of software, but very popular makes of home computer have a considerable number of programs on every conceivable subject. Other than the criterion of compatibility with the hardware, selection can be based on the well-established principles of book selection, including assistance from journal software reviews.

The question of whether libraries should provide games software will no doubt be raised at intervals. However, if libraries can provide recreational reading and video recordings of popular films, there seems little justification for not supplying Space Invaders and Pac Man in some at least of their endless variations.

Most of this software is available only on cassette tape and as such should pose few problems in terms of handling and storage which have not already been encountered with audio cassette tapes and other magnetic media. They should be protected from strong magnetic fields and always kept in their containers when not in use. Disks are more delicate, and as has already been suggested, dust is a major problem (see also Section 9.2.3).

One factor, however, will have to be considered by libraries. It is axiomatic that backup copies of software are made and stored safely, so that, should anything happen to the cassette or disk, the program is not lost. This is standard practice in business applications, where a backup copy may be provided by the supplier.

Should libraries, then, make master copies of software which they lend and simply make another loan copy if anything goes wrong? It would seem advisable, but how often do libraries keep backup copies of the *books* they stock? If a book is damaged, it is either repaired or replaced, and borrowers are often required to pay for replacement copies. Software suppliers may object to the pratice of making master copies for this purpose, but it is so much easier to damage a cassette or disk that libraries could be faced with frequent replacement of software. However, if users are required to make good the cost of damaged software, the only extra cost is that of the time spent in reordering and reprocessing the replacement copy.

The situation is complicated further by the fact that a few software suppliers have stated that their software cannot be loaned by libraries. The suppliers fear, with some justification, that their software will be copied and that they will therefore lose revenue; in other words, this is precisely the same argument as has been applied to the copying of music recordings borrowed from a library. An amendment to the Copyright Act of 1956 has now placed computer software within the Act, thus removing an area of doubt which existed for some time. The proviso made by some suppliers that their software cannot be loaned may also be prompted by the fear that they will lose revenue because microcomputer users will borrow software rather than buy it. This fear was expressed by publishers and booksellers when the first lending libraries were established and by and large it has proved to be unfounded: indeed, some publishers and booksellers rely heavily on libary purchases, and libraries often make the claim that they encourage book-buying. If this parallel holds for software — and this has yet to be established — the suppliers may have little to fear from library provision of software. It is in everyone's interest to ensure that abuses are kept under control. If suppliers are forced out of business, there will be less software to lend and prices will rise with the lack of competition. If suppliers refuse to sell programs to libraries, they could be losing a substantial number of sales. It is to be hoped that a satisfactory compromise can be reached as soon as possible: there may even be a case to be made for a Public Lending Right for software, which will assure the suppliers of some income from the loan of their programs. One writer has already examined the problem of libraries paying 'royalties' to software suppliers, as software lending libraries already do [1].

For the library that does supply software, one unique problem can arise. It is relatively easy for anyone with programming experience to change a program, perhaps because he or she thinks it works better that way, and to record that change on the disk or cassette. While both of these can have 'write-protect' facilities, these are easily removed: in the case of a disk, for example, it is simply an adhesive label which covers a notch on the envelope. The next person to borrow the program may then find that it does not work properly, or it does not respond as the documentation and instructions say it should.

How to prevent such changes will be a matter of some concern. It will be impossible to check every program on return, and the only simple way may be to use write protect labels which will immediately indicate whether they have been removed or tampered with. This will suggest that the program has been changed, and only those disks and cassettes showing such signs will have to be checked.

A final point to consider is one which few librarians would expect to be a problem. The *Anglo-American Cataloguing Rules*, 2nd edition (AACR2), are intended 'as a basis for cataloguing commonly collected materials of all kinds and library materials yet unknown' [2], and Chapter 9 of AACR2 provides the rules for cataloguing 'machine-readable datafiles'. It is to this that the cataloguer is referred by the index from 'computer programs'. Datafiles, however, are not programs, and Chapter 9 does not provide for many of the elements which will be needed in the description of a program. For example, there is no direct provision for a description of the hardware needed for a program or the language used, although Rule 9.7B10 does provide for a description which could include these elements.

```
BISHOP, Peter


    AMC simulation system
Walton-on-Thames : Nelson, 1982
1 program file on disk  (Commodore Basic 4.0) + 1
user guide book (102p).  Version 3.0   Book
numbered : ISBN 0-17-431265-2
Mode of use : Commodore Pet 4032   ISBN 0-17-431294-6


001.64   IN LIBRARY OFFICE
```

Figure 7.1 Catalogue entry for microcomputer software.

Chapter 9 is not entirely without value for software, however, and a little thought will show that it is possible to include the elements which are not covered by the rules. As an example, Fig. 7.1 illustrates a possible entry for a microcomputer program which contains sufficient detail for the prospective user. Templeton has described [3] possible cataloguing rules for microcomputer software as part of a British Library R&D Department Project and other writers have commented on the problems of applying AACR2 to computer software and proposed solutions [4].

A number of libraries have now begun to supply microcomputer software as part of their lending service. Apart from the obvious one of cost, few major problems have been reported, it seems. Staff have to develop some familiarity with the hardware (if hardware is also provided within the library), but in many cases, the provision of software has often encouraged greater use of the library by a range of age groups — use is not entirely restricted to the young! [5–8].

REFERENCES

1. Marshall, P., The strange case of 'software lending right', *Library Association Record*, **85**(7/8), 269, 1983.
2. Anglo-American Cataloguing Rules, 2nd edn, p.1, Library Association, 1978.
3. Templeton, R. and Witten, A., A Study of Cataloguing Computer Software: Applying AACR to Microcomputer Programs, LIR Report No. 28, British Library, 1984 (0–7123–3041–0).
4. Intner, S., Problems and solutions in descriptive cataloguing of microcomputer software, *Cataloguing and Classification Quarterly*, 5(3), 49–56, 1985.
5. Batt, C., Lending computer software, *Library Micromation News*, (4), 5–6, 1984.
6. Dewey, P.R., *Public Access Microcomputers: A Handbook for Librarians*, Knowledge Industry, 1984 (0–86729–086–2).
7. Ebrahim, H., Bedfordshire County Library microcomputer project, *Program*, **19**(2), 150–159, 1985.
8. Marchbank, A.M., Libraries and micros, *SLA News*, (181), 13–18, 1984.

8
Selection of software

Once the librarian has examined the applications which are to be automated and has established precisely what is required for each application, it is time to look at the available software. A glance at any of the microcomputing journals will show the range of software which is available for practically every purpose: the librarian will therefore be faced with the task of matching requirements with this range. We cannot pretend that it will always be an easy task, but it is an important aspect of the whole process, because to choose the wrong software will only cause frustration and disappointment, two emotions which are usually followed in short order by the abandonment of the whole process!

Applications software is distinguished from *systems* software by virtue of being designed for specific tasks and to produce specific task-related output. There is a view that applications programs do the 'useful' work, because it is they that manipulate data and text to produce the information needed by the business or library: this is akin to saying that the engine is the useful part of a car. Obviously it is necessary (indeed, vital), but to create a comfortable means of transport, a number of other parts must work together.

Though usually dedicated to a single task, the software is capable of many specific in-house applications, provided that these fall within the overall capabilities of the program. Thus, there are programs to store and retrieve records in a file, but those records can relate to bibliographic information or periodicals subscriptions. Similarly, a spreadsheet will manipulate figures with user-set formulae: the figures can be the library bookfund or issue statistics.

The available applications software which is relevant to the library world can be divided for our purposes into housekeeping and information retrieval software. The former includes word processing, finance and statistics, while the latter area can be handled by the numerous DBMS or file handlers, or one of the growing number of programs specifically designed for almost every library application (see Appendix 1).

From the various studies of the use by libraries of microcomputers [1–3], we know that they were using them for practically every library routine imaginable. All three surveys showed that word processing was the most popular application, while Burton [1] and Rowbottom [2] also indicate that most libraries were using commercial software. Other popular applications include online searching, automation of circulation control and serials control, use of the microcomputer for statistical records, catalogues and non-bibliographic databases. Naturally, the popular applications varied with the type of library: the smaller academic library was prepared to establish a microcomputer-based online catalogue, but this was impracticable for large public libraries, where databases of local and community information were more in demand.

A large number of applications programs were reported by Burton and by Rowbottom, including many DBMS programs. This is not entirely surprising, since, as we saw in Chapter 5, this type of program can be used for a wide range of routines, and is not restricted to (bibliographic) information retrieval. The programs listed (Compsoft DMS, Petaid, Cromemco DBMS and DB Master) are standard packages which, though not 'true' DBMS, have considerable flexibility for single file applications. The next most popular program, Visicalc, is a spreadsheet (see Section 6.2) which has become a model of its kind — it is said to have been responsible for the sale of more Apple microcomputers than almost any other factor! Burton's survey found a total of 24 different applications programs in use, the bulk of which were DBMS.

Before looking at the problems of selecting applications programs, however, it is instructive to consider those areas of library work for which the microcomputer — indeed, any form of computer — is not suitable, for such areas certainly exist and it is as well to be aware of them in order to avoid unnecessary effort from the outset.

Unsuitable routines can be identified (in principle at least) from a consideration of the basic characteristics of the computer. Crudely put, a computer is a device which can store large quantities of data (numeric or textual) and can manipulate that data in many ways and with great speed and accuracy. Manipulation of textual records includes sorting as required, specific or general searches of the file and printing or displaying the results. To restate what is now a well-known fact, computers are good at routine and repetitive operations on large quantities of data that would be prohibitive or time-consuming to attempt manually. They can also be used as an effective substitute for manual effort which can then be redirected towards areas which are less amenable to automation, and in particular to work involving intuitive or heuristic thought (reference enquiries etc.), which are based more on professional experience and expertise.

In the first edition of this book, we mentioned at this point that artificial intelligence could soon be a factor in the library use of microcomputers. This has, in the interim, proved to be entirely accurate. There are now a number of BLR&D-funded projects into the application of expert systems to library and information work, including a project to develop an expert system for reference work at the Central Information Services of the University of London and an investigation of expert systems for classification at the Department of Information Science, University of Strathclyde [4]. In addition, work has been carried out into cataloguing [5, 6], and, of course, much has been written about the potential of artificial intelligence to assist in information retrieval using textual analysis, relevance and other techniques [7]. None of these has, at the time of writing, reached the stage of being used in a working context on a day-to-day basis, but this will, no doubt, occur. It is also difficult, at this stage, to indicate how much of this will be microcomputer-based, though the projects cited also use expert systems on microcomputers, if only as 'test beds'.

Returning to the capabilities of computers, it follows, then, that an application is unsuitable if it fails to make use of the computer's capabilities and thus effect a good return on the investment in time and effort which is needed for the initial data entry — to say nothing of the preliminary systems analysis etc. (see Chapter 10).

There are two broad categories of application which, judged by these criteria, are unsuitable for operation on a microcomputer: those that consist entirely of data entry and those that, although they may be large files, are subject to such infrequent amendment that the initial data entry task would not be balanced by any saving in time or effort for some considerable time. In this last case, the microcomputer is effectively being used only as a substitute for the typewriter.

In the first category, the prime example is that of serials receipt, i.e. the checking-in of new journal issues as they arrive in the library. Manual systems are perfectly adequate for recording part numbers received and noting missing issues, which is all that is involved. Note, however, that this is true only of serials receipt considered in isolation: if serials control generally is automated, serials receipt should be included in the total system (see Section 5.1).

The second category could include a subject index to a collection of reports or similar documents which are filed by report number as the commonest form of entry point. If new reports are issued very infrequently, the index will need to be amended equally infrequently in order to produce an up-to-date version. Maintaining an index like this on 5 × 3" cards or sheaf slips is a relatively minor manual task: automation would produce minimal savings over a long period, while setting up the file in the first place would be a major task.

If, however, there was a perceived value in providing online access to the index, in sorting it into different sequences, or in extending the service by sending departments a copy of the index, this could tip the scales in favour of automation. A more likely instance of this type would be a union catalogue of periodical holdings.

Such a catalogue might also have relatively infrequent amendments (as new journals were added and old ones discontinued). However, it would also be distributed to all the participating libraries, which means that the updated manual file would have to be retyped and duplicated. If the file was automated, amendments could be made as they occur, or they could be 'batched', and the microcomputer could sort the entire amended file and print it far more quickly than a human typist could.

The difference between the two cases lies only in the need to *distribute* a printed version, but the ability of microcomputer printers to 'retype' the entire amended file at speeds of 100 characters per second and more makes the task considerably easier, leaving typing staff free to concentrate on other work. Table 8.1 summarizes the manual and the automated approaches to a file like this: the turning point in favour of automation is reached quite quickly.

Table 8.1 Comparison of file maintenance operations

		Manual		Automatic
	1.	Type index cards	1.	Keyboard data into data base
	2.	Sort cards	2.	Machine sort cards
	3.	File cards	3.	Print complete file
Multiple copies				
	4.	Type list from cards	4.	Duplicate list from 3
	5.	Duplicate list		
Online access				
	6.	Type copies of cards	5.	Machine search
	7.	Sort cards		
	8.	File in sequences		

The corollary to this, of course, is that the software may be incompatible with the routine. In many cases, this can be a case of using too elaborate a program for the particular application. Trevelyan and Rowat [8] have investigated the use of seven kinds of systems software for six library routines, including circulation control, acquisitions and cataloguing. It should be noted that they consider file handlers and DBMS to be systems software, rather than applications programs. Strictly speaking, this is perfectly accurate, but it must be said that microcomputer terminology tends to be less precise than that of the mainframe world. Programs which, in mainframe terms, are file handlers are frequently called DBMS, for example, and in microcomputing there is a tendency to regard DBMS as applications software.

By defining the requirements of each activity and utilizing data from five different types and sizes of library, Trevelyan and Rowat attempted to indicate the feasibility of using the programs under study for a given task in a library of a given size. While the comparison of all five libraries is not maintained throughout the report, the authors draw some useful conclusions about using these programs for the routines studied.

For example, DBMS is not considered appropriate for circulation control because the record structure involved is too simple. (DBMS as defined in the report is more akin to the 'true' DBMS of the minicomputer and mainframe.) Similarly, notification (i.e. accessions lists, current awareness and bibliographies) is not a complicated enough application for DBMS, though a file handling package would be a feasible solution provided no abstracts were included. (These programs have restrictions on the field lengths.)

An important point, therefore, which arises from this research is that an analysis of a particular task may indicate that using some applications software would be a case of 'overkill', or, to use a motoring analogy, of using a Rolls-Royce to pop down to the corner shop!

These comments refer essentially to the use of 'business software' to library and information routines: they may not always be relevant to the growing numbers of library-specific programs which are now available, and which were discussed in Chapter 5.

A further important point concerns the method by which records are accessed. If fast access is required, as will be the case with circulation control, for example, sequential or indexed sequential access will be too slow, and an inverted file structure will be needed. Areas such as cataloguing, however, where 'instant' file access is less vital, will be sufficiently well served by sequential, or indexed sequential methods. (For an explanation of these terms see Section 3.3.)

In the last analysis, a microcomputer is a small computer and will be unsuitable for no other reason than the sheer size of the files involved. Even with the capacity of hard disks, the microcomputer may prove to be too slow in handling very large files, and it may be more cost-effective to implement a minicomputer or even a mainframe: a microcomputer could still serve as an intelligent terminal to the larger computer and could be used, in addition, for the 'local' processing of smaller files or sub-sets of the main files after downloading them. Improvements are, however, being made all the time: the dividing line between microcomputer and minicomputer is already blurred.

8.1   SOURCES OF INFORMATION AND SUPPLY

When investigating software, the first problem to be faced is the lack of any single, formal and comprehensive catalogue of available software which will constitute a 'one-stop' place to look. There is, at present, no true bibliographic control over software (unless it accompanies a book, in which case it should be listed in *British National Bibliography*): there are, therefore, a number of places in which details of software can be found. The same problem exists for libraries wishing to supply computer software as a lending material, and has been the subject of a BLR&D project [9]. The problem is compounded by the rapid growth of applications software.

Advertisements and reviews are, over a period of time, probably the most comprehensive (though often confusing) source of information at present. Advertisements can be followed up by a request for the suppliers' literature, which will not, of course, be totally objective, but will at least provide some information on which to base a decision. Advertising claims can be balanced by journal reviews; these are carried by most of the microcomputing journals, but their review policies cannot as yet be considered comprehensive and it would be easy to overlook a program simply because it had not been reviewed. Reviews may also have to be related to a library context, since they are often aimed at the general or business user.

The situation is not entirely hopeless, since there are now some journals dedicated to the microcomputer in the library (details can be found in the Bibliography). *Library Micromation News* is a useful source of comment on specific applications software and provides descriptions of individual implementations, written by librarians. It has also to be said that much of its value lies in its British origin (it is published from the Library Technology Centre) and so is more relevant in many ways for the British librarian. In addition, *Vine* now carries regular reports on new micro-computer software and its applications, and these reports are usually of greater length than those of *Library Micromation News*.

Microcomputers for Information Management has now proved to be a major vehicle for lengthy articles on all aspects of microcomputers in this area, and it includes advance notice of new software as well as descriptions of their use.

Small Computers in Libraries carries short but equally useful descriptions of programs and reports by librarians, as does *The Electronic Library*, though the descriptions in the latter are not always based on actual use by librarians. One point to be noted is the current domination of software from the USA and the fact that the reviews in all three journals rarely, if ever, give details of British agents for these programs (often because there are no British agents). The USA origin does not, of course, make the software unusable — microcomputers speak international languages — but obtaining them may be difficult when it is important to assess the reputation of the supplier and to obtain support for the program, as suggested below.

In addition to these, librarians often report their experiences with programs in the other professional journals, as can be seen from the Bibliography.

Micro Software Report [10] includes a large number of business and library-oriented programs and is valuable in that it refers the reader, whenever possible, to a journal review or description of the program, as well as supplying details of the supplier and a library in which the program is used. It should, however, be used cautiously: program descriptions are often taken from the supplier's literature and thus lack objectivity. However, a companion volume, *Micro Software Evaluations*, is of greater value, since it contains evaluations of programs by librarians who have actually used them. In a similar vein (and more frequently issued) is *Library Software Review*.

The *International Microcomputer Software Directory* [11] is dated in its printed form, but it is now available online through Dialog. It provides details of a very wide range of applications software (as well as educational programs) and can be searched by name, application and hardware. No reviews or evaluations are included, however, and it is not limited to library and retrieval software.

Data Courier have an online database which will hold details of some 3500 software packages for micro- and minicomputers. The intention is to help users to locate business applications software; therefore each entry contains details of operating system, hardware, price and information on the supplier. Also included is a description of the main features of the program, and it is possible to search using keywords. The *Software Catalog. Microcomputers* is a quarterly publication from Elsevier which lists available applications programs.

In the UK, the library of Aslib and the two computing organizations, National Computing Centre (NCC) and the British Computer Society, have details of available software. In the case of Aslib, this consists of suppliers' literature, backed up by an index to journal articles. NCC also carries out evaluations of applications software, though this is done by their own staff and is primarily concerned with establishing that the program does what it claims — in itself a valuable piece of information!

The Library Technology Centre now provides advice on a number of programs, and can also offer demonstrations of packages to interested librarians. Some of these demonstrations are 'one-off', in that the software is made available for a day or so only, but the Centre also has several programs (including ASSASSIN PC and InMagic) permanently available. Demonstrations can be booked at a time to suit the librarian, and expert advice and comment can also be provided.

The reader should also refer to the list of organizations in Appendix 2.

There are various sources from which the software itself can be obtained. The most obvious source of an applications program will be a supplier or agent, who, wherever possible, should be more or less local. The name and address of the supplier should be included in any review and will certainly appear in an advertisement.

The *Small Computer Program Index* is a journal which indexes the programs listed in a range of microcomputer journals. These programs are sent in by the journals' readers and they may include short sorting and searching routines which could be of use in a library. However, they often seem to contain errors (a listing should be requested from the contributor, rather than simply copied from the journal) and they may have rather limited applications. It is, after all, free software, and may be worth every penny!

Telesoftware is an inelegant word to describe programs which can be downloaded from some central computer (mainframe or mini) on to an individual's microcomputer. The UK Council for Educational Technology has investigated its potential [12] and software can be downloaded from Prestel and MicroNet 800. Much of this is free games software, with some educational programs, but there are also some priced applications programs available.

The Microelectronics Education Programme (MEP) and its Scottish counterpart, the Scottish Microelectronics Development Programme (SMDP), have compiled details of educational software which, it is planned, will be made available as telesoftware. SMDP is further ahead at present with these plans, and has a two-tier software library, programs from which are available at the cost of the media (disk or cassette). In addition, the MEP Regions are developing software libraries at which potential users can 'browse' amongst the software and its documentation before buying it. In the Capital Region (Inner London Education Authority and a number of London boroughs) this collection of software 'rotates' around the LEA teachers' centres at regular intervals. Understandably, most of the software is educational rather than applications oriented.

Details of the suppliers of the information retrieval and library software discussed in Chapters 4 and 5 will be found in Appendix 1.

8.2   WRITING IT OR BUYING IT?

Apart from donations of free software or downloading from some central computer, there are three sources of applications software:

(a) bought off-the-shelf and used with or without modification;
(b) commissioned from a software house;
(c) written in-house, either by the librarian or by available computer staff.

Program writing is a lengthy and complicated task: it is one of the reasons for the high salaries that programmers can now command. A programmer can expect to produce less than 100 lines of tested, error-free instructions (in a high-level language) in one working week: this includes all the necessary documentation. Writing in machine code takes even longer. The complex search routines and so forth required for information retrieval on large files can contain several thousand instructions and they represent many man-hours of work. This means that commissioned or in-house software will almost certainly be expensive and it will take some time to produce a 'bug-free' program, as it will have to be tested and corrected at regular intervals. This process can take several months; more if the application is particularly complex.

The advantages of such software are, of course, that it is tailor-made for the particular application and, in the case of commissioned software, there will be (or should be) a high degree of support from the supplier.

The same cannot always be said of in-house software. This may be produced by computer department staff at little or no apparent cost, but it may not be possible to get the necessary support and documentation. Too often reliance is placed on being able to telephone the programmer if a problem arises — but what happens if the programmer resigned two weeks ago and took all his notes with him?

Generally speaking, the last two options are not feasible for the librarian seeking to implement routines on a microcomputer, though they have been used by some librarians [13, 14]. In fact, a number of librarians have written *short* programs for specific library routines, and are using them successfully, and the librarian interested in writing programs can consult Hunter's useful book [15].

The amount of programming required for complex tailor-made software can be reduced considerably by the use of a 'programmable' DBMS such as dBase II.

Off-the-shelf software, on the other hand, is readily available for many library routines, and it can be up and running immediately. It will not, of course, be tailor-made, but for the office practices of the library this may not be a problem, while for information retrieval it should still be possible to obtain a very close match of software and requirements, such is the range of programs available (see Chapter 4). Where the two do not match, the librarian should be flexible enough to consider whether the existing library routines could be adapted to the program. While this is not always an ideal solution, it has been known to result in an improved service!

A further possibility is the use of a 'program generator', though to date there are no reports of their use in libraries. Program generators permit the non-programmer to create applications programs using simple natural language instructions which are then coded *by the program* into the programming language, in order to create the applications package. Its advantages are claimed to be that the application can be totally customized, since the operator determines from the start what the program must do. Program generators do not, however, remove the need for a thorough systems analysis prior to automation — indeed, they make it even more necessary, since they utilize a flow-chart approach to the problem and prompt the user with questions on the application. The user must, therefore, know precisely what is needed before starting.

8.3 ASSESSMENT OF SOFTWARE

At some stage, the librarian will be in a position to examine closely a number of programs that are likely candidates for purchase. The software should be approached with an open mind, and the librarian should endeavour to 'translate' examples given in advertisements and literature into information retrieval and library terms. For example, if the software can search for 'all employees in Manchester who speak French and are less than 40 years old', it is likely that it will also handle typical Boolean searches for bibliographic records. There may, however, have to be a 'trade-off' between the facilities of two or more programs, in which the relative importance of these facilities for specific applications will have to be weighed.

A regular feature of the microcomputing journals is the summary or state-of-the-art report, which considers the general requirements of a particular type of program (DBMS, spreadsheet, word processor etc.) and then lists a selection of the available programs, showing how each matches up to these requirements: this is usually done with the aid of a chart. These articles are particularly useful, in that they can indicate to the inexperienced user exactly what to look for in a program, especially if a number of such reports are studied.

Their form of presentation can be adopted, and at an early stage it should be possible to draw up a chart of the necessary features of the required program, indicating in some way those that are essential and those that would simply be useful to have. The chart will, of course, differ for each type of program, but this approach will ensure that a uniform assessment of each program is arrived at, as well as making it easier to compare programs and trade-off features where necessary.

Chapter 4 considers the facilities required for information retrieval, while Chapters 5 and 6 look at those needed for library and housekeeping applications. As an indication of the kind of chart which can be constructed, Appendix 8.1 gives a summary of the points made in those chapters. Beaumont has presented a similar set of charts for DBMS [16], while Trevelyan and Rowat [17] detail the facilities of sort/merge packages, text editors, report writers and file handlers, as well as DBMS. A more detailed series of checklists is contained in a lengthy study of software selection by Perry [18].

It will also be useful to include in these assessments some information about the hardware on which each program will run. Although hardware is the last link in the process (see Chapter 9), it must be considered in essence at least: the necessary system may be too expensive, not easily available etc. and this information will add to the total picture.

Appendix 8.1 is given as a suggestion only, and it can be adapted to suit particular circumstances. Some users may prefer to have a separate chart for each program, though this can make the comparison of a number of programs difficult, unless a summary chart is also constructed.

In addition to these software-specific criteria, there are a number of general points which must be considered during the assessment process.

8.3.1 The supplier

Some thought must be given to the supplier of the program(s). What, for example, is his reputation among those who have bought software from him in the past? A reputable supplier will readily provide names of former customers who may be contacted for their opinions on service, support and maintenance. It will obviously be necessary to establish with the supplier precisely what level of support will be offered and at what price. Do not, incidentally, expect too much in this respect: very inexpensive programs may well have little or no after-sales service beyond a backup copy of the disk, but it should still be possible to telephone for advice, particularly if things go wrong. In all other cases, the support will probably include advice, free back-up copies, free or reduced cost updates and possibly some degree of operator training. However, a comprehensive service will be an additional cost: it is not unknown to pay up to one-third of the purchase price per year for support.

As with hardware (see Chapter 9), a software supplier should be reasonably local, so that it is convenient to visit his premises or for him to come to the library: this also minimizes the cost of telephone calls. It will be useful if the supplier can come to the site where the program will be used as he can then see more readily the precise context in which the program will operate. This will improve communications generally, particularly if the supplier is unaware of the often unique requirements of a library or information service.

If the supplier provides training in the use of the program, it will also be more useful if this is carried out in the library if at all possible, though this may involve an additional charge. In this way, the program can be applied to specific tasks and the training will be more relevant. Remember, however, that training will probably only be available for the more expensive programs: it would hardly be economical for a supplier to provide a one day course for a £30 program!

8.3.2 Software demonstrations

Demonstrations are a very useful way of assessing the potential of a program and suppliers should be willing and able to give such demonstrations. However, they do have their limitations.

Normally, they will not be using very large files of data, and so it will only be possible to estimate how well the program will handle typical library files for searching, indexing and the like. However, it should be possible to assess how 'user-friendly' the program is (see below) and the overall ease with which the program can be used.

It will be more useful to visit users of the software to see it in operation. While this may not be precisely the same application, it will still be a 'real' situation, handling 'real' data, and it will give a more accurate picture than a simple showroom demonstration, though this latter will be a first step in eliminating anything obviously unsuitable.

Ideally, the prospective buyer should see the program in use in a library context, and two directories of applications may provide some help.

Burton has included a directory of users in his survey of applications in academic libraries: this lists the software in use by some 70 libraries [19] and similar information is available from the Library Technology Centre at the Polytechnic of Central London which, as we have already suggested, can provide demonstrations of a range of programs.

Another alternative is to buy a demonstration disk, if one is available. This too will be limited in the amount of data which it can handle, but it does provide an opportunity to study the program at leisure and in the appropriate context. The price of the demonstration disk is relatively modest and is normally deducted from the full purchase price: it could be worth the outlay to find, at an early stage, that the program is unsuitable.

8.3.3 Documentation

The documentation that comes with a program should be examined carefully. This is the operations manual for the software and it should be clear and concise: if it is not, there could be many problems and much frustration, since it will be the only immediate source of information on running the program. Ideally, it should provide step-by-step guidance for the non-technical, first-time user as well as serving as a reference manual for the experienced operator. This will normally require two separate sections, since to combine the two approaches will only baffle one and frustrate the other. Fig. 8.1 shows the documentation of Cardbox: it can be seen that it includes a tutorial and a quick guide as well as a complete reference manual.

Like demonstration disks, it is often possible to buy the documentation separately, and this again will be money well spent, since it will be an opportunity to assess both the program and the operating instructions.

8.3.4 User-friendliness

This is a much overworked phrase which has been interpreted in different ways by software houses. It refers not only to the way in which instructions

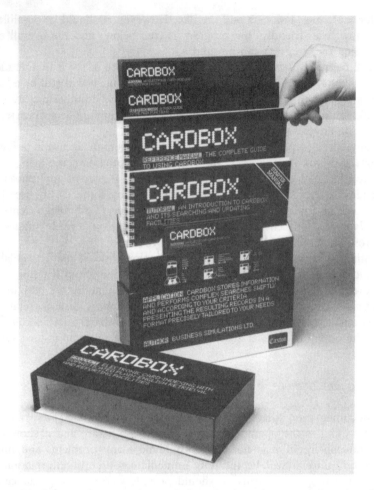

Figure 8.1 Software documentation: note the use of a reference card, an introductory tutorial and a complete reference manual (courtesy of Caxton Software).

on the screen are presented, but also to the total interaction of the operator and the program. In summary, user-friendliness relates to:

(a) screen presentation of operating instructions;
(b) error prevention and data recovery;
(c) information on what is happening;
(d) confirmation of action to be taken.

Instructions should be clear and unambiguous, and they should proceed in a logical manner. Consistency is also important: the same symbol, mnemonic or instruction should always be used for one operation, and the language employed should be as natural as possible. Mnemonics used for the sake of speed and simplicity (i.e. single key operation) should be obvious ones or truly mnemonic, i.e. capable of being remembered. They should also be unique: one program known to the authors uses the letter 'n' as both 'no' and 'next' in successive instructions. Fig. 8.2 illustrates the use of mnemonics as instructions.

An approach often adopted is the 'menu', a list of alternatives which are selected simply by pressing the appropriate key, which may be a number or a mnemonic letter. This is probably still the best overall approach, since it presents on the screen all the possible options at any stage and shows how to implement them, but even menus can vary in 'friendliness'. In some cases, all that is displayed is a list of options with numbers, while others may expand this with instructions such as 'Press "a" to view the author index'.

While a well-constructed menu will leave little or no room for error, menus can be a source of frustration for the experienced user who knows what to do. He or she has to plod through the menu each time, and so it is useful if two levels of operation can be provided which cater for both the novice and the tyro, enabling the latter to 'jump' straight to the required option. An experienced-user level may make greater use of abbreviations and mnemonics.

```
CARDBOX(U)      File = A:BOOKS.FIL      PRINT
Level  1 - RECORD 1 OF 4
```

Author: Rudyard Kipling	
Illustrator: J. Lockwood Kipling, W.H. Drake	Language:
Title: The Jungle Book	
Publisher: Macmillan	Date: 1961
Subjects: Children's fiction.	
Comments: Popular version of children's classic	

```
Enter command:
   MAsk; SElect, INclude, EXclude; HIstory, BAck, CLear; LIstindex;
ADd, DUplicate, EDit, DElete; REad, WRite; FOrmat, PRint; SAve, QUit
LIST:   ^R=1st  ^C=last  ^A=back  ^F=fwd    ENTRY:   ^X=erase ^H=backspace
```

Figure 8.2 Use of mnemonics and abbreviated commands in software. Λ = control key (courtesy of Caxton Software).

If a program receives an instruction for which it is not programmed, or the wrong kind of data is entered, it will do one of two things: either it will display some message which alerts the operator to the mistake and offers the opportunity to re-enter the correct data, or it will 'crash', which is the computer equivalent of a nervous breakdown! The former is the better procedure, though it does require additional programming. In addition, programmers may not always anticipate all the mistakes which can be made, and so crashes occur anyway, though under more limited circumstances.

If a crash does occur, it should be possible to retrieve the files as they were at the start of the session *and* most of the data which were entered prior to the crash. Otherwise, it will be necessary to establish just where data recording stopped and then re-enter everything. As we have said, in an ideal situation, there will be no crashes, but an alternative will be to indicate which errors will cause a crash, so that operators can take care.

A program should always tell the operator what it is doing once an instruction has been given: there is nothing more nerve-wracking than to enter a command and have the screen go totally blank! 'Did I press the correct key?', 'Did I press it hard enough?', 'Have I lost an entire morning's work?' are the questions which can go through the operator's mind at a time like this! At the very least, there should be a screen message of the 'please wait' variety: better still is a (brief) statement of what the program is doing (e.g. 'record being written to disk') which also confirms that the correct instruction has been given.

Related to this is an opportunity for the operator to confirm that what has been entered is correct. This can relate to the data just entered (i.e. are there any typing errors or missing fields?) and it should be possible to make corrections. The program should also ask for confirmation that an instruction is correct and this is particularly important if records are being deleted from a file.

Finally, though not obviously a user-friendly option, it will increase confidence in a program if security can be built-in to records and data files, so that unauthorized users are prevented from seeing and changing records. This will clearly be important with an online catalogue or similar index, but could apply to memoranda, reports etc.

Security in microcomputer software is generally very basic, if it exists at all. Password protection may be possible, but this usually prevents access to an entire file, and the user may also want to prevent access to particular records. It does exist in some programs (MicroSeed and MDBS III are examples) and other programs are available with security levels that can range from preventing file access to limiting access to parts of records, with or without the ability to amend records.

8.3.5 Software integration

The ability to use data files with more than one program offers considerable flexibility, particularly for printed output. If integration of this kind is available, it means that only one data file need be set up, and the data (records) can be used in various ways by various programs. The alternative is to enter the data for each application, a time-consuming task which does much to negate any savings brought about by the use of the computer in the first place. The most common such link between different software packages is between DBMS and word processing software, such that records set up under DBMS can be extracted and used with an appropriate word processing package to add more text (an introduction to a bibliography, for example). This allows the production of more professional output, which can enhance the library's image. The more powerful DBMS provide a similar facility, in that they are multifile systems, capable of accessing various files in response to an enquiry (see Chapter 4).

Similar links can be found between word processors and spreadsheet programs, so that statistical or financial data can be inserted into reports with ease. There are also links between word processors and mailing list programs which will add names and addresses to standard letters.

Integration of this type is more likely with software from the same 'family', e.g. Datastar and Wordstar, though some programs are now advertised as able to link with well-established software such as Wordstar and Wordcraft. If the programming skills are available, it may even be possible to write a short interfacing program to do this.

A number of contemporary hardware systems now come with software 'bundled', that is, incorporated with the system and included in the overall price. The type of program supplied can vary from one maker to another, but usually includes word processing, spreadsheet and DBMS, all of which are integrated. (A graphics package is also a common provision in bundled software.) Established files can therefore be used by each program as required, though it should be noted that, as a generalization, this bundled software may not always be as powerful or as sophisticated as separately available packages. However, they do provide a starting point for applications, and libraries should seriously consider whether they need all the facilities provided by some programs.

We have already noted in Chapter 5 the development of integrated library-specific software, which operates on the same general principle, with the added bonus of being available in modular form, so that modules can be bought as and when they are needed.

A development of some significance is the fully integrated package supplied on disk (i.e. not as 'bundled software' built into a particular computer). The most widespread examples are Lotus 1-2-3 and Symphony. Programs like these actually consist of three programs in one, usually a DBMS or file handler, a word processor and a spreadsheet (see Chapter 6). All three can use the same files, and it is a relatively simple matter to switch from one program to another, in order, for example, to insert graphics and statistics into a report. But the concept has been adopted by a number of software houses and the capabilities are improving rapidly.

REFERENCES

1. Burton, P.F., Microcomputer Applications in Academic Libraries (LIR No. 16), BLR&D, 1983.
2. Singleton, A., Information Technology in Industrial Information Services: A Survey of What is Available and How it is Used (BLR&D Report No. 5714), Chapter 2, University of Leicester Primary Communications Research Centre, 1982.
3. Rowbottom, M., Use of microcomputers in public libraries, *Library Micromation News*, (6), 11–16, 1984.
4. Burton, P.F., Expert systems for classification, in, Proceedings of the Joint LAITG/LIRG Conference on Expert Systems, November 1985. Taylor Graham, 1986.
5. Davies, R. and James, B., Towards an expert system for cataloguing: some experiments based on AACR2, *Program*, 18(4), 283–297, 1984.
6. Hjerrpe, R. and Olander, B., Artificial intelligence and cataloguing: building expert systems for simple choice of access points for entries. Results and revelations. LIBLAB, Linkoping University, 1985 (LiU-LIBLAB-R : 1985 : 1).
7. See, for example, *Informatics 7*: Intelligent Information Retrieval. Proceedings of a Conference held by the Aslib Informatics Group and the Information Retrieval Group of the British Computer Society, March 1983. Edited by Kevin P. Jones. Aslib, 1983.
8. Trevelyan, A. and Rowat, M., An Investigation of the Use of Systems Programs in Library Applications of Microcomputers (LIR No. 12), British Library, 1983.
9. Tagg, W. and Templeton, R., Computer Software: Supplying It and Finding It (LIR No. 10), British Library, 1983.
10. Nolan, J.M. (Ed.), *Micro Software Report*, Nolan Information Management Services (annual).
11. *International Microcomputer Software Directory*, *Imprint Software* (annual).
12. Brown, M., PRESTEL and education II: a Viewdata telesoftware system for education, 4th International Online Information Meeting, December 1980, 115–118.
13. Lomas, T., Programs in the college library, *CoFHE Bulletin*, (33), 7–8, 1982.
14. Nightingale, R.A., The use of a microcomputer for information retrieval and other purposes in the engineering departments of BP International Ltd, *Journal of Information Science*, 4(4), 149–154, 1982.
15. Hunter, E., *The ABC of BASIC: An Introduction to Programming for Librarians*, Bingley, 1982.
16. Beaumont, J., Data base management systems (DBMSs), in, Beaumont, J. and Kreuger, D. (Eds.), *Microcomputers in Libraries: How Useful are They?*, Canadian Library Association, 1983.
17. Trevelyan and Rowat, *op. cit.*
18. Perry, W.E., *Microcomputer Selection Guide*, QED Information Sciences, 1983.
19. Burton, *op. cit.*, Appendix B.

APPENDIX 8.1: CHECKLISTS FOR SOFTWARE SELECTION

Information retrieval software

Maximum record size
Maximum file size per disk
Maximum number of fields
Variable length fields
Search facilities:
    Maximum number of terms per search
    Logical operators
    Qualifiers (e.g. $<$ $>$, $=$, Range)
    'Wild card'
Sort facilities
    Multiple sorting
    Merging sub-sets
    Depth
Print formats
    Full record
    Label
    Report generator
Amend record format
Stored searches
Program utilities
    Back-up
    Directory
    File copy
Block transfer of records
Block delete of records
Support contract
Hardware
    Operating system
    Cost
    Local availability

Spreadsheet software

Maximum number of cells
Maximum column width
Formulae
Speed
RAM required
Graphics output
Report generator
Split screen
Support contract

Word processing software

Right and left margins
Line spacing
Justification
Page size
Page numbering
Headers
Single word deletion
Block deletion
Text transfer
Search and replace
Paging
Mathematics
Record merging
Spelling check
Concurrent printing
Underlining
Enhanced printing
Support contract

9
Selecting the hardware

In an ideal situation, microcomputer hardware will be the last element in the selection process. Generally accepted practice is that the requirements of a particular application will determine the software needed and the software will, in turn, determine the microcomputer system (the hardware) on which it will operate. To choose the hardware first is to place an unnecessary restriction on the programs that can be used and thus on the ways in which an application can be automated.

However, even when the accepted practice is followed, the range of software and hardware is such that the librarian may still be faced with a choice of system hardware: each system will utilize the program(s) chosen, but will also offer other features of varying usefulness for the individual library. The situation is directly analogous to choosing a car even when the required engine size, fuel consumption etc. have been determined. The final choice (of microcomputer and of car) will be determined by these other features in conjunction with those which it has been determined the system *must* offer. It would, of course, be naive to assume that cost will not be a major factor (indeed, it may be *the* factor) in selecting hardware: however, hardware costs in an area of rapid technical development are notoriously unstable. Generally speaking, prices of microcomputer systems are falling: certainly it is true that a given sum will now buy much more than was the case even one year ago, and this seems to be a trend which will continue for some time to come.

The consumer can also benefit from the fierce competition between manufacturers and suppliers which has lowered the price of many systems or has produced long-term 'special offers' of free software and the like. Within the 'more for the money' category are microcomputers with much larger RAM capacities, greater disk storage and occasionally some options which are included at no extra cost. As an example of this trend, we can quote the case of the Commodore Pet of 1979/80 and the Apricot xi of 1985/86 (see Fig. 9.1).

The Pet in 1979 cost approximately £1900 for a system containing 32 K

Figure 9.1 *Top* Apricot XEN (courtesy of Apricot Computers). *Bottom* IBM PC/AT (courtesy of IBM (Australia) Pty).

RAM, microcomputer, 340 K dual disk drive and a dot matrix printer. In 1986, it is possible to buy an Apricot xi with 512 K RAM and 1.4 Mb dual disk drives for approximately £2300. The price of Apricot is only £400 greater than that of the Pet, although there is a 16-fold increase in RAM capacity, a 4-fold increase in (floppy) disk storage, and there is an easily available 10 Mb hard disk version. A good quality printer is also available for the Apricot which would still keep the total cost to less than one-third more for the Apricot. It should also be borne in mind that the Apricot is a much faster system in operation, because it is using a faster processor.

A significant factor of the last few years has been the spread of the IBM PC (see Fig. 9.1) as the *de facto* standard in business microcomputers, despite the fact that, technically, it is by no means state of the art. The significance lies in the facts that (a) a vast library of software is now available for the IBM PC and its 'big brothers', the XT and AT, and, (b) there are a growing number of IBM PC 'look alikes', 'clones' and 'compatibles' (the terms vary both in use and in meaning). Ideally, all these clones will be able to run the software originally intended for the IBM PC, but this may not always be the case, and there are degrees of compatibility which the prospective buyer has to establish: an unofficial benchmark has been the ability to run the program Flight Simulator, the demands of which are such that, if a clone can run it successfully, it can be considered a true compatible.

It also has to be said that many of the clones can outperform the IBM PC in terms of speed and processing power, and the librarian seeking a system could be advised to compare the various systems very carefully [1].

9.1 SOURCES OF INFORMATION

The most immediate and obvious source of information about available systems are the advertisements in the microcomputing journals and the manufacturer's literature, augmented by the various reviews ('benchtests') which are reported in the journals. It goes without saying that advertising claims should be treated with caution, but product literature should contain all the necessary technical information about the system, including memory (RAM) and disk capacities, input/output ports for peripherals, available software, and so on.

The benchtests in the journals are, generally speaking, more objective, though they can rarely assess long-term reliability and in most cases assume a degree of technical knowledge. Many journals use a system of 'benchmarks' to provide a concise evaluation of hardware. Benchmarks are the times taken to carry out a set of standard operations and they are comparable to the government fuel consumption figures for cars. By comparing benchmarks, it is possible to obtain an idea of the capabilities of various systems to carry out identical operations.

There are, of course, a number of journals devoted to library automation and these too will carry hardware reviews, particularly of library-specific systems. *Computer Equipment Review* (formerly *Library Computer Equipment Review*) is one such journal.

What Micro? carries a monthly list which provides basic information about almost every microcomputer on the market. The information is brief, but does indicate cost, manufacturer, processor, operating system and available options, as well as RAM size and disk capacity. This can be a useful way to draw up an initial selection list for further investigation. Similar lists can be found in other journals and in the computing yearbooks, though these last tend to be less current, of course.

It will also be worthwhile to discuss requirements with a reputable supplier, who can offer advice on a suitable choice of hardware. However, suppliers are often agents for a particular make of microcomputer and they will naturally prefer that make to others. Their advice can be complemented by the comments of system users, and a supplier should be willing to supply names and addresses of current users. User advice is particularly valuable, since it is based on actual experience in a working environment.

9.2   CRITERIA FOR SELECTION

There are a number of points about hardware systems which will influence the final selection. Broadly speaking, these relate to the CPU itself, to data storage and to other peripherals, in particular the printer. (It is assumed here that the reader has already studied Chapter 2 on the operation of a microcomputer system.)

9.2.1   The CPU

As we saw in Chapter 2, microcomputers use a variety of processors and while they are broadly similar, some processors offer advantages over others.

Two of the most widely used processors for 8-bit systems are the Z80 and the 6502, the latter being found in early Commodore products and the Apple. The Z80 is the faster of the two, although other features of the total system may reduce the impact of this speed.

Perhaps more important is the fact that the CP/M operating system is designed for the Z80 — though not all Z80-based systems use CP/M. Since CP/M is the *de facto* industry standard for 8-bit systems, with thousands of available programs, this would make the choice of a Z80-based micro-computer (with CP/M) the more obvious — which is in no way to suggest that the 6502 is inferior or suffers from a dearth of software. 6502-based systems can often be converted by the addition of boards or cards to run under CP/M, though the extra cost of the boards is a factor to consider.

However, it would be advisable now to consider, not an 8-bit system, but a 16-bit machine, since these now have an extremely large library of software, are capable of operating at faster speeds and normally can cope with much greater RAM capacities, thus allowing more powerful and sophisticated programs to be used.

While the choice of processor is relatively simple for 8-bit machines, the situation for 16-bit systems is far from clear at the time of writing. Computer experts seem to favour three processors — the Intel 8088 and 8086 and the Motorola 68000. The 8088 is used by the IBM PC and the Future X20, while the more expensive Corvus Concept and Fortune 32 : 16 utilize the 68000. The IBM AT and the Kaypro 286 use the much faster 80286 processor.

The choice of processor is perhaps an indirect one for the librarian, who will be more interested in the effects of using a particular processor and operating system, not least for peripherals.

Eight-bit and 16-bit refer to the word length that the CPU can handle; this in turn determines the size of the system's instruction set and thus its power to handle operations. The longer the word length, the greater the number of instructions that can be stored and used. Handling data is also carried out more rapidly with large word lengths. Simply put, the difference can be represented by the transfer of boxes from a warehouse to a truck: if the transfer rate is increased from 8 boxes per load to 16 boxes, the task will be completed in a shorter time.

The speed with which a processor operates is also related to the clock speed of the processor, which is essentially the factor which controls how fast the necessary signals are transmitted within the microcomputer. Clock speeds are measured in hertz (Hz), but the situation is confused in that manufacturers may use the same processor but configure it to run at different speeds. Thus, the IBM AT has a 80286 processor operating at 6 MHz, while the Tandon PCA runs the same processor at 8 MHz and is regarded as offering better performance.

The reader should note that 32-bit processors are already available for microcomputers, providing yet more processing power and speed. They are not, at the time of writing, in widespread use, but will undoubtedly spread in response to demand.

The system will obviously have to offer the language used by the chosen program(s), and it will have to be in the correct 'dialect'. The availability of other languages may offer more options for future development, but it is difficult to say at the moment which language(s) will be important —

though Pascal seems set to be one of them.

Similar remarks apply to operating systems, though CP/M can be recommended as a necessary feature for 8-bit systems if only because of the number of programs which it can handle. It is less easy to suggest an operating system for 16-bit hardware, since the situation is unclear. At the time of writing, a number of operating systems are on offer, including Microsoft's MS-DOS, and PC-DOS, which is provided in the IBM PC. As we noted above, some 16-bit systems offer a choice of operating system.

An interesting development is *Unix*, which was originally designed for minicomputers. It is now available for the 68000 processor and is of particular value for multi-user systems. Certainly, converts to Unix are enthusiastic about its potential.

The Random Access Memory (RAM) is an important consideration because, as we saw in Chapter 2, this is where the program (or program modules) and data will be temporarily stored during operation. This means, of course, that it must be large enough to hold the program and the data to be manipulated: it should be remembered that bibliographic records will take up a considerable amount of RAM. Generally speaking, 'big is beautiful', and this will allow for future developments. Off-the-shelf systems are available with 128 K, 256 K and 512 K RAM, and many others can be upgraded with add-on packs or cards. The minimum required will normally be quoted by the software supplier, but 128 K is probably the lowest acceptable level for library applications, bearing in mind the complexity of the programs which will be needed and the likely file sizes.

On a more practical level, it should be remembered that an operator will have to sit in front of a microcomputer system for quite lengthy periods, carrying out a variety of tasks. It is therefore most important to assess the overall *ergonomics* of the system to ensure that fatigue and general discomfort are reduced to a minimum. Many trade unions have established policies about the use of VDUs, in particular in order to minimize health risks, and it will be necessary to ascertain whether such a policy is in operation.

The ergonomics of a microcomputer system are complex, consisting of the overall layout of the hardware itself and the environment in which it operates [2, 3]. Users should be able to adopt a comfortable sitting position, and screen displays should be clearly visible without glare or poor focus and contrast. Screen visibility will be affected by the ambient lighting, and the screen should be positioned to avoid reflections. There is an optimum distance between the eyes and the screen, and it should be possible for the operator to 'rest' the eyes by looking past the screen at more distant objects (which should not, however, be a distraction).

In an effort to provide the greatest possible flexibility when actually using the hardware, manufacturers have produced screens which can be tilted and moved from side to side, together with detachable keyboards which can be

Figure 9.2   Detachable keyboard (courtesy of IBM (Australia) Pty).

placed in the most comfortable position. Fig. 9.2 shows an IBM system
with these features, while Fig. 9.3 illustrates an ICL Personal Computer
arrangement in which the keyboard has been placed in tailor-made furniture
at the correct level for typing, with the screen at the most comfortable
viewing height for a seated operator. Note too that the 5¼″ hard disk drive
can slide back inside the unit. Tailor-made furniture like this is readily available and is a worthwhile alternative to simply placing the hardware on a desk.

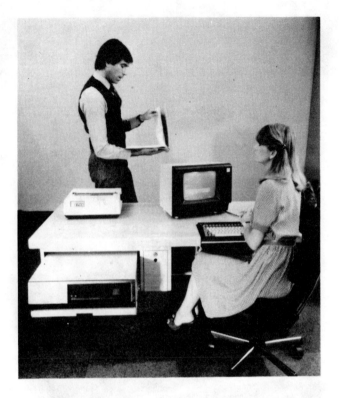

Figure 9.3 Use of specialized furniture (courtesy of ICL Ltd).

Screen displays can often be improved by attaching a polarizing filter to eliminate glare and reflections, and to improve contrast. Though they can be expensive, such filters are useful when it would be difficult or expensive to provide a better lighting environment. The screens are easy to attach and remove.

The keyboard should be clearly laid out and easy to read, without distracting reflections from overhead lights. Any special keys should be clearly marked, so that they are not touched accidentally, and clearly understood mnemonics or similar devices should be used: it may be necessary to allow for operators who make infrequent use of the system and who cannot, therefore, develop a familiarity with its idiosyncracies. A point worth noting is that keyboards may well differ in some respects from those of standard typewriters: this will affect touch typists in particular. Some systems have special function keys which can be programmed by the operator in order to simplify operations.

Floppy disk drives are now usually integrated with the VDU (in Fig. 9.2 they can be seen on the right) and this at least has eliminated some of the stretching to insert new disks which was necessary with separate disk drive. This arrangement also takes up less horizontal space.

Screen-based manipulation of data and many aspects of keyboarding have been greatly assisted by the introduction, a few years ago, of the 'mouse', a small, hand-held device which converts movements of the hand on the desk-top into signals upon which the microcomputer can act. These can include selecting options from a menu of commands, indicating which operation is to be carried out, and so on. A mouse attached to an IBM AT is shown in the operator's right hand in Fig. 9.4, but 'mice' are now available for a wide range of microcomputers and associated software.

Figure 9.4 Using a mouse to select icons.

One use of the mouse is in free-hand drawing, but it also improves drastically the way in which data can be manipulated once they have been keyboarded into a file. The microcomputer displays a range of small symbols known as 'icons' which are 'keyed' to resident programs: the symbols can be seen on the screen in Fig 9.4. Using the mouse, it is possible to indicate text, data or a record: the mouse is simply moved about the desk-top to produce corresponding movements of a pointer on the screen. The mouse is then moved from the highlighted data etc. to the desired program symbol and the data (or record) is transferred to the control of the program. The transfer of data etc. is effected by pressing the raised bar on the top of the mouse, rather like pressing the carriage return on a keyboard.

Reviewers have praised the ease with which a mouse can be used and its simplicity: it does not even have to be lifted to the screen as a light pen must be. However, the desk-top does have to be kept clear of foreign bodies such as paper clips!

A number of other facilities are now standard features of business microcomputers, although it must again be stressed that their overall value will depend largely on the needs of the particular library and its applications in both the short and long term.

It is possible, for example, to purchase optional extras such as bar-code readers, joysticks and paddles (usually only necessary for games), sound and speech synthesizers and graph plotters. The last-mentioned will obviously be useful in statistical presentations, while bar-code readers will be required for circulation control (see Section 5.1). Options such as these are available from both the original manufacturer and from the numerous suppliers who may or may not be licensed or in some way 'approved' by the manufacturer. There will normally be a greater safeguard in terms of quality and the ability to match with the original equipment if approved products are used.

An RS232C port will be needed if *telecommunications* facilities with minicomputers and mainframes are necessary or desirable. This will allow data to be sent over the communication lines and it must naturally be possible to set the appropriate baud rates and parity. Telecommunications like this can also be used for electronic mail systems, which are described in Section 6.3. Most recent products provide an RS232C port, together with other ports which can be used for other peripherals.

Multi-user systems as a standard feature tend to be found on more expensive equipment, although it is possible to buy a multi-user facility for many of the remaining microcomputers.

Multi-user systems allow a number of microcomputers to share common (and often expensive) peripherals such as disk drives and printers (see Fig. 9.5). In theory, each 'workstation' behaves as if it alone were connected to the peripheral, calling data from disks etc. Problems can occur when a number of users are connected at one time (just as with online systems) and there must be provision to prevent an operator changing a record or file while someone else is working with it (record and file locking). A multi-user system will require hard disks, since floppies wil not provide the storage capacity needed.

Some of the more expensive systems are designed as multi-user systems, and their specification will indicate the maximum number of users possible. The Rair Black Box, for example, is designed to provide up to eight workstations with simultaneous access to a maximum of 76 Mb of hard disk storage, and each workstation can have its own printer. The microcomputer itself includes the workstation ports required: the work-stations are VDUs with keyboards and interface controllers which plug in to these ports. All the processing is handled by the microcomputer.

As an indication of costs involved, the microcomputer costs £4500, and each workstation costs approximately £863. Similar systems include the Altos 986 (9 users), Torch 700 (8 users) and Systime's S600 (5 users).

Figure 9.5   Multi-user system (courtesy of HM Systems Ltd).

The possibilities of a multi-user system within a library are great, since it means that workstations could be located for use by both library staff and users, the latter accessing the catalogue and similar 'public' indexes. However, thought will have to be given to the number of workstations required: allowing for staff use, eight stations may not be sufficient for a large library and there will be a limit on the maximum distance between stations and the central computer. While a multi-user system may be useful in a smaller library, larger libraries occupying a number of floors or with multiple sites will have to consider a local area network (see Sections 2.3 and 5.11) — and may, in fact, be too big for microcomputer-based automation, although microcomputers could be used as intelligent terminals to a mainframe or minicomputer (see Section 4.3).

It has been assumed here that the microcomputer is being chosen to run a variety of software for a variety of applications. If, however, only one program is currently under investigation, it will also be of value to establish for the future which *programs* will also run on a particular system. The availability of software will add to the attraction of a given microcomputer system by allowing for future developments in the library.

9.2.2 Data storage

Record files and programs can be stored on floppy disks (5¼" or 8") or hard (Winchester) disks, while smaller microfloppies of around 3" diameter are also popular. Most microcomputers for business use have hard disks available as add-on options or as an integral part of the system, but it will be important to check that hard disk is available, if one is not bought with the system. Floppy disks can hold between 100 000 and 1 500 000 characters, depending on the system, and it will be necessary to assess if this will be enough for any one file (a rule of thumb is to allow 1 Mb of storage for each 1000 bibliographic records: this will usually allow enough space for indexes, etc., which can occupy as much space as the records). If it is not, files will have to be spread over two or more disks, and it may not be convenient to divide the file in this way.

Floppy disk drives will usually have to be dual, unless the program can be loaded in its entirety into RAM, otherwise the program disk will run in one drive with a data disk in the second. The available drive capacity for data will therefore be 50% of the drive's stated capacity, which is also measured in kilobytes. Hard disks can have capacities of from 5 Mb to over 100 Mb, and they are faster and cheaper per byte of data stored. They are a necessity for multi-user systems, networks, and, of course, for large files.

A further and very important consideration is the backup system. Making backup copies of data and program disks is vital and should be done on a regular basis. Exactly how often will depend largely on the amount of use of the data disk: one that is used daily should be backed-up daily. If this is done, should anything happen to the master disk, only one day's data will be lost and have to be re-entered.

Backing-up floppy disks is straightforward and simply involves making a copy on another floppy disk: the program may even prompt for this and contain a sub-routine that carries this out, a process taking only a few minutes. It would hardly be economical to backup a hard disk with another hard disk (though this is probably the best solution), so there are two alternatives available. One uses floppy disks; this is the cheaper method, but it can be a lengthy process requiring a large number of disks. A more expensive but less cumbersome method is to use a tape streamer, which copies the data onto a high quality magnetic tape. Tape streamers can be 'built-in' to the hard disk unit, making the backup process almost automatic. Some attempts have been made to use video tape, but the results have been poor, with data losses and corruption.

Bubble memories are slowly becoming available for microcomputers. These offer the opportunity for large-scale, *permanent* data storage within the CPU, rather than on an external device. Data that are entered create magnetic 'bubbles' within a magnetic material: the presence or absence of a bubble represents a binary one or zero respectively. Bubble memory is the subject of much research at present and it remains to be seen just how much data storage they will provide, and at what cost.

Microdisks or microfloppies are available for a wide range of business microcomputers, and though in the early days after their introduction they held less data than did the standard 5¼" floppies, they have improved considerably, and can now compete with the larger size in terms of storage capacity. They are also more robust than standard floppies, since they are enclosed in a rigid plastic envelope.

9.2.3   Care of disks

One of the advantages of the microcomputer over larger installations is the fact that it does not have to be housed in a special environment, which can be expensive to provide and maintain. Microcomputers can sit on a desk in a normal office environment and function perfectly well.

This does not mean, however, that proper care is not needed, and this applies particularly to disks and disk drives. Some thought must be given *before* the equipment arrives to protecting disks from the worst excesses of the office. They should never be exposed to the magnetic fields which can be generated by a variety of devices, including fluorescent desk lights, fans

What can cause contamination of diskettes?

Any material can change the contact between the drive head and the diskette surface. It takes only a minute particle to affect data transfer and cause errors. The diagram below illustrates the most common causes of data loss.

As you can see from the illustration, just about anything is large enough to interrupt the head's contact with the diskette surface. Remember, *any* separation of the head and diskette surface can result in loss of data. Besides dry contaminants, any liquid that is spilled on the recording surface will affect its performance.

Figure 9.6   The effect of airborne contaminants on floppy disks (courtesy of Verbatim Ltd).

and even piezo-electric lighters! Library security systems, it appears, do not affect disks that are taken through in the normal way, though the disks should not be placed in or near the checkout unit or left close to the exit barriers.

A great source of trouble is airborne contamination such as dust and smoke. This can be trapped on the surface of the disks, thus breaking the contact of the reading head with the magnetic surface, with consequent data loss. Fig. 9.6 illustrates dramatically the relative sizes of these contaminants. Disks should be kept in a closed container when not in use, and drives should be located away from dusty areas: they should not be placed below or in front of air and central heating ducts or windows. As with all electrical equipment, liquids should be kept well away — the usual culprit in this case is the cup of coffee placed on top of the drive unit!

It is possible to buy disk cleaning kits which, used as instructed, will ensure that the reading head is kept free of contaminants which could cause data loss.

9.2.4 Printers

Despite continued assurances about the arrival of the paperless society, it remains a fact that most people want to see information down in black and white. It is, after all, a habit of several centuries' standing and until the electronic storage and transmission of information is as widespread as that of paper-based systems, it will continue to be necessary in many cases to print out in some form the information stored on the microcomputer.

Printers can be attached to all microcomputers, and there are four types currently available: *daisy wheel, dot matrix, thermal,* and *ink jet.*

Daisy wheel printers have a series of petals radiating from a hub and each petal is embossed with a character (see Fig. 9.7). Output is indistinguishable from that of a quality typewriter, and different typefaces can be used, though this usually means stopping in the middle of a text to change the wheel first. Daisy wheels tend to print more slowly than matrix printers, though they are still capable of respectable speeds, and they tend to be more expensive. The quality of print, however, makes them a necessity for many library publications (bulletins, catalogue cards etc.). The design of the print wheels is such that it is possible to have large character sets on one wheel: the Qume wheel in the illustration has all that is needed to print in up to ten languages.

Dot matrix printers have a matrix or 'grid' of pins which are pushed against the ribbon by solenoids in response to CPU signals: the pins create the shape of the letter. They are described in terms of the number of pins in the matrix, usually 7×7 or 9×7. The more pins there are, the closer they are together and the more solid the image. More pins will also allow for the

Figure 9.7 A daisy wheel print head with 130 characters
(courtesy of Qume (UK) Ltd).

'true descenders' on letters such as 'p' and 'y', the descender being that part
going below the line. Print without descenders can be confusing to a
typesetter or typist, who may have difficulty in distinguishing upper and
lower case when there are no descenders.

Some dot matrix printers can operate at two speeds, one very fast for
rough work, drafting etc. and a slower speed for the final product. They are
slower because they actually print each character twice, the second being
slightly offset to produce a more solid image.

Many dot matrix printers are capable of producing bold and condensed
characters within a block of ordinary text, usually under software control,
so it will be necessary to ensure that the required instructions can be added
to the program. The microcomputer may also be capable of excellent graphics
which could be used in the library: it will then be necessary to ensure that
the printer can reproduce them. However, the print quality may not always
be acceptable for anything but internal documents.

Both types of printer are noisy and will have to be placed away from
public areas and/or shielded with an acoustic cover (which can be very
expensive).

Thermal printers are much quieter, but are slow and the type of paper
often used means that the image degrades with age and exposure to the
light.

Ink jet printers are now produced for microcomputer systems which have an extremely high quality print at great speed. There are also less moving parts to wear out (see Fig. 9.8). The prices of such systems are directly comparable with daisy wheel and dot matrix printers: Hewlett Packard's Think-Jet, for example, costs approximately £425. The printing speeds are also comparable at some 150 characters per second.

Figure 9.8   Qume Laser Ten printer (Courtesy of Qume (UK) Ltd).

Printers are the slowest element in a microcomputer system: the fastest and usually the most expensive are capable of some 180 characters per second (cps), while the CPU is operating in nanoseconds for each operation. This means that the microcomputer may have completed a task in a few seconds, but the operator must wait for several minutes for the results to be printed, during which time the computer is 'tied up'.

Unless such a situation is acceptable and work can be scheduled so that something else can be attended to while documents are printed, an answer to this is to insert a *character buffer* between microcomputer and printer. All printers have a buffer, usually 2 K or more. Data buffers, however, come in much larger sizes — 16 K, 24 K and 32 K are common — and they will accept that quantity of data at the speed of the computer and let it 'trickle through' to the printer at the appropriate speed, thus freeing the computer for the next task.

Some data buffers are available with an interface which will allow the microcomputer to be connected to a printer (or other peripheral) for which it does not have a suitable input/output (I/O) port.

Microcomputers communicate with other devices through input/output ports which are built-in (see Chapter 2). Three different types are found: Centronics parallel, RS232C and IEEE-488. The last of these is usually provided to allow the connection of scientific instruments. Both the Centronics parallel and RS232C ports may be provided on newer systems, not least because the former is a common port for printers, while the latter is required for data communications.

The printer must attach to one of these ports, and if it cannot do so directly, an interface must be provided. This is a situation which could arise because a particular printer is purchased on the grounds of cost, print characteristics, etc. Data buffers with interfaces can be obtained for between £150 and £250 depending on the buffer size, and if an interface is necessary, then it will be worth buying a combined buffer/interface — though it is rarely a case of two devices for the price of one!

A final point for consideration will be whether the printer is *friction feed*, as in a typewriter, or *tractor feed*. The former will be needed for single sheets of plain paper, while the latter is used for continuous listing paper which is perforated (see Fig. 9.9). In fact, many modern printers will handle both types of paper, usually by adding a tractor feed system.

9.2.5 Inexpensive systems (home/personal computers)

We cannot leave this discussion of hardware without considering the very inexpensive microcomputers now available which are normally aimed at the domestic market (though, as we shall see, there are some intermediary systems with low prices intended for the lower end of the business market). A Commodore 64 (see Fig. 9.10) retails for well under £300, though this price does not include a monitor (most inexpensive systems are designed for use with a domestic television set) or disk drive. The BBC Micro (see Fig. 9.10) is slightly more expensive, but is popular in the UK, not least as a result of Government action to place at least one in every secondary school. By way of complete contrast, however, there is the Amstrad range of microcomputers, which most experts suggest could revolutionize the small computer market (see Fig. 9.11).

Amstrad's microcomputer range comes complete with monitor and at least a cassette unit, though the more expensive models have a built-in disk drive.

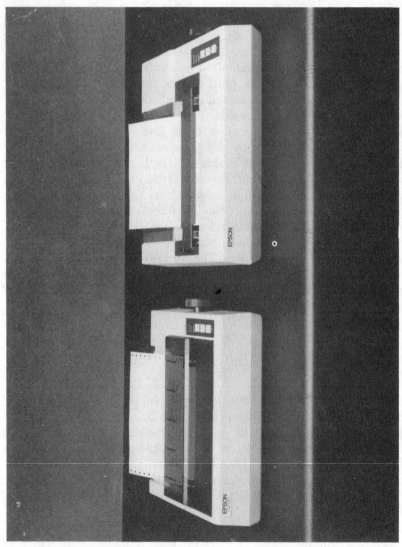

Figure 9.9　Tractor feed printer (left) and friction feed printer (right) (courtesy of Epson (UK) Ltd).

Figure 9.10 Two inexpensive systems. *Top* BBC Micro (with kind permission of Acorn Computers); *bottom* Commodore 64 (courtesy of Commodore).

Figure 9.11   Amstrad PCW 8256 and PCW8512 (Courtesy
of Amstrad Consumer Electronics plc).

In addition, software is included in the models aimed at the business market: indeed, one Amstrad model, the PCW 8256, is essentially marketed as a word processor the price of which (approximately £399) includes monitor, disk drive and printer. At the other end of the range, Amstrad have the CPC 6128 with disk drive and monitor at £299, with a wide range of business software available. The main criticism of the Amstrad systems is their use of 8-bit technology and CP/M, which is seen as dated, but it does have a large software library to call on.

The drawbacks of 'home computers' are mainly in the software, which, with the exception of certain systems such as the Commodore 64, Amstrad and, to a certain extent, the BBC Micro, tends to be of low performance, since it is aimed at the domestic, rather than the business user. Library applications will also need disk drives, rather than cassette-based storage, which is too slow.

Inexpensive computers of this type should not be dismissed totally, of course: they may have a useful role to play in training and familiarization. Given that systems such as the Amstrad are now coming on to the market, the smaller library could find them an attractive proposition for stand-alone applications such as word processing, indexes, etc.

9.2.6   Hardware suppliers and system reliability

As a final point, we shall look at the question of choosing a hardware supplier. Most of the comments about suppliers will be self-evident — which is another way of saying that the points get overlooked in the rush to buy.

It will obviously be most convenient if a local supplier can be used, since maintenance calls etc. will be attended to more quickly, but wherever the supplier is located, it will be worthwhile establishing his reputation for service and maintenance. As was suggested above, this can best be done by contacting existing customers. If the supplier is an approved agent for the hardware, this will normally be an additional point in his favour: lists of approved suppliers can be obtained from the manufacturer and often from advertisements.

Suppliers should also be able to give comprehensive instruction in the use of the hardware, perhaps including a training course. This is obviously valuable, but it will be preferable to have training done in the library, where relevant data are to hand and the supplier can get an accurate picture of how the system will be used.

It will be necessary to establish what level of after-sales service and maintenance is available and at what cost. Maintenance contracts can vary considerably: the less expensive business systems, for example, may not be covered for regular preventative maintenance calls. Sometimes it will be possible to negotiate special contracts, but how much is included will depend on the librarian's estimate of the importance of any particular application: one or two days 'downtime' on the acquisitions file may be acceptable, but most librarians will want instant attention to any faults which develop in the issue system! Maintenance contracts can cost as much as 10% of the total purchase price.

In general terms, it will be best to choose an established product which has a proven track record: again, current users can be an invaluable source of practical comment. It may not always be wise, in this instance, to rely heavily on the manufacturer's reputation: even the best have been known to issue a bad product now and then. On the other hand, good systems can come from companies who have yet to establish themselves — even Apple had to start somewhere! If a new product is selected, then the user runs the risks of all pioneers. A compromise could be to buy from an established supplier whose judgment about a new product can be relied upon.

It will pay, incidentally, to study the user's manual as much as possible: while all the technical details may not be of immediate interest, it will be easier to discuss faults, modifications and extensions with the supplier when the time comes.

9.3   THE MICROCOMPUTER MARKET

It will be evident by now that the microcomputer market is a complex place. Quite apart from a completely new vocabulary, the whole mystique of computers is still a source of bewilderment, even anxiety, to many, and there are large sections of the population who are certain that they do not need to bother because microcomputers will only affect the younger age groups — a remark that has been made by individuals in every age group over 35!

Part of the problem is that we have yet to take the computer for granted, as it were, in the same way that the car and the aeroplane are no longer a source of amazement. An awareness of this kind can only come with time and familarity: it is already obvious that the present generation of schoolchildren readily accept the microcomputer as a learning and recreational aid.

It would be impossible and pointless to try to provide details of all the microcomputers currently available: not only are there too many, but new ones appear every month — one need only look at the current issue of journals such as *Byte* or *Personal Computer World*.

Journals like these (and there are many available) are probably the best source of summary information on the wide range of microcomputers now in production: they are also able to keep pace (more or less) with the arrival of new systems, providing 'road tests' and comparisons of new products. As we have already suggested, some of the microcomputing journals carry regular lists of current systems, providing a synopsis of basic information, and the librarian wishing to survey the market could make profitable use of such facilities. As with any range of products, there will be one or two which can be described as 'the best', equivalent to the Rolls-Royce in the motoring world. It must be remembered, however, that not everyone needs a Rolls-Royce, and the aim should be to pick the system that does all that is required without wasting time and money on systems with features which will never be used.

9.4   OPTICAL AND VIDEO DISKS

Data storage for microcomputers will be raised to greater heights by the development of the video disk and particularly the digital optical disk, which can store up to 2 gigabytes, or 2 thousand million characters. Linked to a microcomputer with appropriate software, the data can be searched in much the same way as with a magnetic disk.

The principal drawback to the video disk at present is the lack of recording facilities. A solution lies in the sheer capacity of the disk: it is possible to insert codes so that the software 'ignores' obsolete data. If the unit cost can be made low enough, it is possible to 're-issue' a database at regular intervals.

This subscription basis on which optical disks are issued is currently being used by a number of producers. The entire LC MARC file has been issued on CD-ROM by Bibliofile: an annual subscription brings bi-monthly updates to the file, which can then be inserted in a CD-ROM player linked to an IBM PC. The accompanying software allows the librarian to search the file for records in a way exactly parallel to that of online searching, though the claim is that the disk system is faster, with access times of 1 second or less.

The Library of Congress has begun a programme of recording some 7 million catalogue cards on video disk [5] in order to improve retrieval, and a smaller scale project has been implemented by the National Library of Canada [6]. In 1986, the Library Association announced its intention to analyse the potential market for a CD-ROM version of the Library and Information Science Abstracts database, which would be 'published' on a subscription basis. At the time of writing, no final decision had been reached, but it seems certain that ventures like this will increase in number. At present, the user base for interactive video systems (i.e. those with software to provide sophisticated search facilities) is small, and commercial operations will be correspondingly small, until that base is widened.

A widening of the user base will be caused by the introduction of write facilities for disk players, so that users can record new information as they currently do with magnetic disks. Many observers feel that read and write capabilities will be introduced by 1986, though this remains to be seen. A major factor, of course, will be the cost of such systems, though Verbatim have mentioned an erasable disk and player at prices comparable to those of floppy disk systems.

The technology of video and optical disks (see Ch. 2) is complex [7], but the applications potential for libraries and information services is great, and will increase as the costs come down. At present, to create an optical disk requires a video tape to be made and then transferred to a master disk, from which subsequent disks are pressed. This mastering is usually done by one of the commercial manufacturers, such as Philips, and obviously the more copies which are pressed, the lower the unit cost of each disk. Figures vary, but are in the order of £6 per disk for quantities of 100 or more.

REFERENCES

1. Grosch, A.N., The IBM Personal Computer and the IBM Extended Personal Computer, *Library Technology Reports*, **20**(1), 61–84, 1984.
2. Health and Safety Executive, *Visual Display Units*, HMSO, 1983.
3. Toruk, A.G., Ergonomic considerations in microcomputing, *Microcomputers for Information Management*, **1**(3), 229–250, 1984.
4. Barrett, R., Further Developments in Optical Disc Technology (LIR Report No. 27), British Library, 1984, (0–7123–3038–0).
5. Price, J.W., Optical disks and demand printing research at the Library of Congress, *Information Services and Use*, **5**(1), 3–20, 1985.
6. Sonneman, S.S., The videodisc as a library tool, *Special Libraries*, **74**(1), 7–13, 1983.
7. Parsloe, E. (Ed.), *Interactive Video*, Sigma Technical Press, 1983.

10
Operation and management of systems

The introduction of a computer system, however small, implies some change in the organization. That change has to be carried out successfully and certain management skills are needed to ensure that this happens. In addition, we have often said in the course of this book that before any software or hardware is purchased, it is necessary to investigate very carefully the applications that are to be automated. Only then is it possible to have a clear idea of what the software and hardware must do, and thus armed to look critically at the available programs and makes of microcomputer.

It must be said that, in many cases, the purchase of a microcomputer system plus the necessary hardware will not always justify the setting up of a full project team and a detailed systems analysis. The 'project team' may only consist of the librarian and one other member of staff, but a methodical approach will still offer many benefits.

In this chapter, we will discuss the main points involved in an automation project, and then look at various aspects of the day-to-day and long-term management of an automated system. In an introductory book such as this, it is not possible to go into the fine detail of systems analysis: the reader can be referred to a number of standard textbooks on the subject, and in particular to a series of articles that looked specifically at systems analysis for the microcomputer user [1].

10.1 PROJECT MANAGEMENT

The first task is to define the project in terms of the ultimate objectives to be achieved. By defining projects in terms of goals, it is possible to organize all developments into manageable pieces, and a project can therefore be defined as an organized effort to reach a predefined goal or goals.

Often a single person is assigned to lead a project and is given responsibility for ensuring that a project is completed according to requirements, within costs and on time. The project leader has to be provided with the resources necessary to carry out the project, and this implies a measure of sympathetic understanding on the part of the parent organization. This may be assumed if it is the parent organization that sets up the project in the first place, as would happen if the librarian was asked to investigate a microcomputer-based circulation system, for example. If, however, the librarian makes the first move (and this is more likely), he will first have to convince management that the proposed automation is worthy of a formal investigation. He or she will therefore have to undertake a certain amount of preliminary investigation, possible with little assistance. Such preliminary work will normally include details of:

(a) time to be saved by automation;
(b) money to be saved by automation;
(c) possible extensions to the service;
(d) approximate costs of capital equipment;
(e) approximate running costs;
(f) overall reasons for automating (e.g. the present system can no longer cope).

These need not be presented in precise detail, but an indication will help to convince the parent body of the need to set up a project.

The purchase of a single microcomputer system, together with software to carry out a particular function could be regarded as a small project with limited demands on the expertise of qualified staff. If, on the other hand, software needs to be developed locally (see Section 8.2), the project would immediately grow in size and would require greater resources. The implications for project management, resource allocation etc. are correspondingly greater.

The use of appropriate personnel and their expertise for project development is advisable and if such expertise is not available within the organization, consultants can be brought in. The choice of project staff, including consultants, can be critical and any increase in the complexity of the project puts greater demands on project management. However, the resources devoted to a project should be related to the cost of the equipment and the anticipated benefits and savings. The low cost of some microcomputers and software may make it worthwhile minimizing the amount of expert advice obtained. Even consultants' fees are likely to be related to the size and complexity of a project, and for one involving microcomputers may be fairly low. Often it may only be necessary to obtain sound advice on which of a number of different software products to choose.

'Appropriate personnel' in this case can and should include those staff who will ultimately operate the new system and who will often be called upon to explain it to library users. They or their representatives should be involved at an early stage in discussions and investigations, so that their views on actual operating practice can be taken into account. In addition, their involvement in the planning process will go a long way towards allaying any fears over automation and will ensure that staff are aware of the reasons behind the decision to automate.

10.1.1   The phased approach

Normally it is necessary to move from the initial idea towards a realization of that idea, and one method that has been used successfully for some time in data processing applications is the phased approach. Individual techniques may differ, but the approach which we describe below has been successful in the past. The main phases of the project include the following.

The initial study: this is a fairly rapid look at the whole project to consider the overall requirements, how the system might work, any staffing implications, time-scales, and the costs and benefits. It will result in a plan for the rest of the project being drawn up, plus a detailed plan for the next phase. The final decision will be made on whether or not to carry on. If it is decided not to do so, then the minimum of resources have been devoted to the project, with minimal waste of time.

Analysis of requirements: the definition of requirements will vary in detail depending, for example, on whether a complex program has to be written. If this is the case, the definition will have to be used by the design and programming staff to build the system. If this is not the case, then the definition may be a more loosely constructed document. In either case, the planning process will be updated at the end of this phase to provide a detailed plan for the next phase and for the rest of the project. A specification of requirements will be agreed and a decision will be taken on whether or not to continue the project.

Design: at this stage, a decision will be made on how to construct the system. Possible approaches include:

(a) a custom-built system
(b) in-house development
(c) a turnkey system
(d) off-the-shelf hardware and software

Using off-the-shelf software may, of course be the only realistic choice for many libraries (see Chapter 5).

It is possible that some modifications to the earlier definition of requirements will have to be made, perhaps because of design constraints or because a particular software package seems to satisfy most, but not all, of the requirements. This feedback process may be repeated several times before a final conclusion on the best design is reached. At this stage, the planning for the project can be updated and a detailed plan for the construction phase drawn up.

The design specification, costings and forward planning will ideally be considered by a committee representing the interested parties, including those involved in maintenance and operation, and those who may require information from the system, such as auditors. Even at this stage, a decision can be made to abandon the project, based on the best available information, before committing resources to building the system itself. A plan for the construction and implementation phases will be drawn up, if it is decided to go ahead.

Construction: once construction has begun, it is unlikely (and largely undesirable) that *major* changes will be made to the requirements: any important ones will have to be made through a formal procedure. The complexity of this phase will depend on the size of the project, and particularly on whether a particular software system has to be implemented. For many microcomputer systems this stage will be rather simple: equipment will be acquired and bought-in software implemented. Precisely how simple this is will depend to a large extent on the previous planning, analysis and design phases.

The system will then have to be thoroughly tested and proved to be acceptable, while maintenance procedures will have to be investigated. There are two possible types of maintenance: that which deals with any required changes as soon as possible in order to keep the system operational, and that which simply makes necessary changes which are not, however, time-critical.

There are two ways in which the new automated system can be implemented, depending largely on the application itself. In some cases, it may be necessary to 'switch over' to the new system completely and in one move, since to try to operate a partially automated and partially manual system may prove to be confusing and liable to errors.

The alternative is, of course, to convert important or major areas of the application and to work on the remaining areas as and when it is convenient (though preferably according to a planned programme). Two systems will then operate in tandem, with the manual element gradually declining. This approach is suitable for applications that can be conveniently divided for this purpose: the catalogue, for example, could be automated on the basis of classification numbers, with entries for the most-used subjects being converted first. A further option is to make a chronological division, where feasible. In this case, a decision will be made to automate all catalogue entries for items received after a given date. It will then also be necessary to consider and plan for retrospective cataloguing (See Section 5.4.3), and this could proceed on the basis of classification numbers, as suggested above.

The size of the task, i.e. the quantity of material to be converted, will often be a major factor in any decisions. The need to run two systems in parallel (possibly for some time) will have to be balanced against the time taken to prepare all records and materials for a once-only conversion. In addition, of course, it will be necessary to arrange and implement staff training, and to prepare any operations manuals which are required (see below).

If software is bought off the shelf from a software house, the software support will be important if a serious time-critical problem occurs. For much low-priced commercial software, it will be necessary to contact the supplier in the event of a problem, but without a support contract, action may be slow or non-existent. The cost of software support — which can be as much as 10% of the purchase price per year — will have to be included in costings.

10.2   DATA SECURITY

In our context, this refers to the physical handling and copying of data disks to prevent damage to, and loss of, data, and also to the problem of access to data by staff and users. We will consider both in this section.

10.2.1   Physical security

As has been suggested elsewhere in this book, it is axiomatic that regular backup copies of data disks be taken, in order to ensure that data are not accidentally lost. Some of the techniques used to make backups are considered in Section 9.2.2. In the context of systems management, it will be necessary to develop a policy for making copies of data and to ensure that the policy is adhered to.

Generally speaking, a data disk should be backed up whenever new data are entered or existing data are amended in any way. Whether this is always feasible may depend on how quickly and easily it can be done, but it is the ideal to be aimed for, and a set period should be set aside for the procedure. It should be a matter of policy to mark clearly both master and backup copy, and both should be kept securely when not in use, preferably in different locations. Both locations, however, should be convenient ones for the operator. As a rule, everything possible should be done to make it easy to make *authorized* backup copies of data, and thus to encourage adherence to the policy.

The precise procedure for taking copies should also be established. The most straightforward method is simply to copy data onto another disk (or disks, in the case of a hard disk) and to use the same disk each time, storing it safely between backups. This method does mean that one master disk is used all the time for normal operations, while the backup is (relatively speaking) unused: to spread the wear, it may be useful to use the *copy* on the next occasion and then to back this up on the (former) master disk, thus alternating the wear on each disk. A further option is to use a third disk in a 'grandfather-father-son' arrangement, which also doubles the data security.

Although with modern disks wear and tear is not normally a significant problem, one way in which to reduce it even further is to employ, where appropriate, one disk for each day of the week, labelling each one accordingly. Monday's disk is then copied onto Tuesday's disk, which is then used on Tuesday and copied onto Wednesday's disk, and so on. In the event of a disk failure, it is always clear which disk has the most recent data, and use is spread over five disks. This method is probably only applicable when floppy disks are used: it would scarcely be feasible with hard disks!

Storage locations for both master and backup copies should be fireproof metal containers, sited away from any source of electromagnetic fields. It may be useful to label such locations with appropriate notices, which can be obtained from computer accessory suppliers, together with similar labels for the disks themselves. Master copies of programs, for example, can be labelled as only for use in providing working copies, and it may be thought advisable to restrict access to master copies to individuals who can authorize the making of copies as required.

Security should not, however, be so complex as to discourage the making of backup copies: if it is, they will not be made, with disastrous results when the system crashes one day, as will certainly happen.

10.2.2   Security of access to data

It may be necessary to restrict access to files or parts of records for various reasons which will depend largely on the nature of the file. Some information may be confidential (personnel records, for example), in which case access will be restricted to those whose job it is to administer those records. At the other extreme are 'public' records which everyone may *access*, but where it is necessary to prevent unauthorized *amendments*. The library catalogue is perhaps the best example: users and staff alike will be able to consult catalogue entries, but only library staff (and perhaps only staff in the cataloguing section) will be authorized to change, insert or delete records.

Finally, there will be records of which only part of the data could be regarded as confidential. An accessions file could be of interest to users, informing them of books on order or recently received, but it may be thought necessary to prevent users from seeing the ordering details (supplier, order number, budget heading etc.).

The security aspects of library files are complex, as we can see (some are covered by the Data Protection Act), and it will be necessary to have clearly defined policies on who is authorized to consult files and to make changes to them. It must, however, be said that complex security arrangements may not be possible with the less expensive programs, in which security, if it exists at all, may only consist of a password, which, once known, provides access to the whole file. Provided that passwords are kept confidential — and it is also a good policy to change them regularly — this may be sufficient.

Programs that are designed to operate open access files such as library catalogues usually contain a module for record amendment, access to which is only by password. Circulation control records can be similarly protected from unauthorized alteration.

The passwords used should be chosen with some care, in order to avoid obvious words or numbers which could easily be deduced by those with a desire to 'beat the system'. Nor should they be of a type which could be keyed accidentally. The best choice may well be a totally random one, though it must be borne in mind that authorized operators have to remember it without pasting it up on the wall beside the terminal!

It may be easy to become paranoid about security, but library files do represent a considerable investment in time and money, and it is not difficult to picture the chaos which could arise if users were free to amend catalogue entries or issue system records, quite apart from the standard confidentiality of personnel records. Perhaps the major problems will be accidental access and the malicious attempt to cause confusion: the first can be prevented with little difficulty, and the latter can be deterred sufficiently with relatively standard methods which do not make life difficult for authorized personnel.

10.3   CARE AND MAINTENANCE OF HARDWARE

Some of the major points concerning care of hardware, particularly disk drives, were considered in Chapter 9.

Microcomputers are complex electronic devices and should be treated accordingly. Liquids should be kept well away, and they should be sited so that they are not exposed to dust and other airborne contamination. Static electricity and electromagnetic fields can destroy data held on disks and displayed on screens. If static is a problem, it can usually be cured by the use of an anti-static mat and regular applications of anti-static sprays, both available from accessory suppliers. Disk reading heads can be cleaned using special kits also easily obtained.

To ensure the best working environment for operators, it may be worthwhile purchasing computer desks which will ensure that keyboards and screens are at the optimum height. These desks are available in various configurations, some capable of holding a printer and working documents.

Common causes of data loss and system crashes are fluctuations in the power supply (spikes and surges). The voltages used in microcomputers are so low that even the smallest fluctuation in power supply can affect them, and so it is possible to install between the computer and the power supply a control box that suppresses any surges and ensures a steady and accurate supply to the computer and its peripherals. Also worthy of consideration is a battery-powered backup supply. This will cut in automatically should the mains supply fail and so ensure that there is no data loss. The system can be closed down properly, and since the backup can operate for some hours, it may even be possible to go on working. The batteries are recharged when the power supply is restored.

Precisely how far care and maintenance of the system is taken can depend on the nature of the applications involved. In some cases (the issue system, for example) even the shortest breakdown will be unacceptable, while in other areas, it may be possible to tolerate a 'downtime' of hours or even one or two days. The library will scarcely grind to a halt if the acquisitions file is unavailable for a day!

Adequate training will help to minimize faults and damage. Operators should know about the correct handling of disks, for example, including storage when not in use.

The design of microcomputers is such that very little preventative maintenance is possible or necessary, other than that suggested above. The moving parts (disks, reading heads, the keyboard) are usually described as having a life of so many operations. In the case of disks, this can be millions of revolutions, keyboards will be tested to millions of depressions, and print heads similarly will be capable of producing several million characters before failure.

To rectify failures, the librarian has two choices. Either qualified in-house staff can be used or a maintenance contract can be taken out with the supplier once the guarantee expires (normally after the first year).

10.4   DOCUMENTATION OF OPERATIONS

While both the software and the hardware will (or should) come with appropriate documentation, i.e. manuals on their operation, it will be necessary to draw up operating instructions for the staff who will be using the new automated system. These do not have to duplicate the supplier's documentation, except where absolutely necessary, but they do have to cover all day-to-day operations as they relate to the specific library.

Ideally, such instructions should be drawn up as far in advance as possible and distributed to all the relevant staff *before* the new system is operational. This will give staff time to assimilate the instructions, to clarify any points of uncertainty and to gain at least a general impression of the changes that the new system will bring about. This last point is also an important factor in staff training (see below), since the introduction of any new technique will have an effect on staff morale, and it will be better to reassure staff in advance of implementation of the system.

One important function of the operating instructions will be to clarify any new terms or phrases which the system introduces, and to ensure that everyone concerned is clear about their meanings: that way, a great deal of confusion can be avoided from the start!

Operating instructions will apply the system documentation to the specific operations needed in the library. Naturally, relevant examples from daily practice should be used. They will have to be detailed and proceed in a step-by-step manner through each operation or routine, so that staff can follow the routine easily. No doubt, in time, experienced staff will be able to dispense with large parts of the instructions, but they should be retained, not only for new staff, but also for reference use by the experienced staff.

While the operating instructions must be regarded as authoritative, they should not be seen as sacrosanct tablets of stone. Once the system is 'up and running', day-to-day experience will rapidly find any faults that might exist, and may well indicate a better way of doing things. While there is a fine line between a genuine improvement and non-constructive criticism stemming from an understandable dislike or fear of the system, there should be a feedback mechanism whereby improvements and constructive comment can be assessed and implemented — and, of course, incorporated in the operating instructions.

In order that this feedback can operate, it will be useful to define an introductory period during which the new system may be regarded as settling in (also known as the 'shake-down period'). During this time operations will be carefully monitored and improvements made through the feedback system will be adopted. It will, therefore, be a disturbing time for staff, as practices may be changed at intervals, just as they were getting used to them. The shake-down period should therefore be clearly defined, and staff should be encouraged not simply to accept the new system 'warts and all', but actively to study what they are doing. They will then be playing a constructive part in the development of the system and will be aware that their opinions are regarded as valuable.

The whole process of drawing up the operating instructions and modifying parts of them may be the responsibility of one person or a number of section heads, depending on the sizes of the library and the application(s). In the latter case particularly, there should be a clear line of communication between staff operating the system and those above them, so that comments and instructions flow freely. Ideally, it should be the responsibility of one person actually to prepare and distribute the operating instructions and any amendments. This will ensure a standard presentation which will make the instructions easier to follow. Equally, it means that there is a single person to whom feedback should be addressed, though it will be that person's responsibility in turn to ensure that comments etc. are passed on to the appropriate individual. Properly handled, this should not lead to any undue delay, though the individual will have to be given both the time and the authority necessary for the position.

While smaller libraries, or those implementing only one or two applications, may not need to go to such lengths, the general principle remains valid: clear documentation with a feedback mechanism for the adoption of constructive suggestions.

An over-riding concern should be to prevent any outbreak of the well-known syndrome of 'blaming it on the computer', 'it' being any fault, mistake or delay that occurs. Other than mechanical breakdown, faults and errors in computers are usually caused by human beings. Outbreaks of this syndrome are best prevented by open communications and the active involvement of all concerned, together with a clear presentation of day-to-day procedures.

10.5 TRAINING

One way in which to prevent this problem of 'blaming it on the computer' arising is through proper training of staff. Obviously, staff will have to be instructed in the use of the new system, be it word processing or a full-scale circulation system, but the training should extend to developing an understanding of why things are done this way and how they will contribute to greater efficiency, time saving and an improved library service.

Training given by the software and hardware suppliers will tend, by its very nature, to be at a general level, and in-house training will have to cover all the specific aspects relevant to the library. The precise approach may vary, depending on the application. A word processing program is best learned in use, once the overall procedures have been mastered. Staff using it should be encouraged to experiment and practise with it, and all due allowance should be made for mistakes (in the early days at least!). It may even be a good idea to hold on to the typewriter for some time, just in case!

This will not always be suitable for large-scale routines such as circulation control or an online catalogue. Since staff should be fully acquainted with the operation of such systems before they are implemented this will mean (a) that those carrying out the training must be well-versed in its operation beforehand, and (b) that some time will have to be set aside for regular training sessions — with all that that entails for the continued running of the library.

A change-over date should be established, but this should not be regarded as fixed, since the progress of training may indicate that it should be put back or brought forward.

Training should cover all the relevant operations in a logical order, and there should be an opportunity for staff to practise each operation as it is taught or demonstrated. The training period will also provide a further and early opportunity to assess the success of the proposed method of operating the new system, and any feedback from staff should be studied carefully before preparing the operating instructions.

It will be useful if practical training can be preceded by a consideration of why it was felt necessary to automate the particular routine. This need not be lengthy, since staff should have been involved from an early stage in the investigations in automated systems. However, some time may have elapsed between the initial investigation and the arrival of the hardware and software, and a repetition of the 'philosophy' will be a useful reminder, as well as necessary background for any new staff. It will also help to focus attention on the training and to provide a basis from which useful comment can be made.

REFERENCE

1. Antill, L., Secrets of systems analysis, *Personal Computer World*, 3(9), in 11 parts, 1980.

Appendix 1: Software for information retrieval and library applications

This is a list of the software available at the time of writing for information retrieval and for various library routines. It should not be regarded as definitive, since new software is being developed and introduced at regular intervals, and some programs may have been missed (the authors would be happy to learn of any software not included here). The list does not include the innumerable business programs which can also be used in libraries and which are considered in Chapters 3–6, but further details of such software can be obtained from the sources discussed in Chapter 8.

Each entry contains, as far as possible, details of the hardware on which the program runs, the name and address of a supplier and an indication of the cost. Where they are given, prices do not include VAT or the cost of carriage, postage etc, and the full price should obviously be checked with the supplier at the time of investigation.

Further details of software for library and information retrieval applications can be found in Hilary Gates' directory of microcomputer software, and the directory of text retrieval software published by the Institute of Information Scientists, both of which are listed in the Bibliography to this work.

INTEGRATED SYSTEMS

ADLIB-2
Lipman Management Resources Ltd, 54–70 Moorbridge Road, Maidenhead, Berks SL6 8BN. Unix-based systems. 7 modules in integrated package.

Bookshelf
Logical Choice Ltd, 3 Newtec Place, 66–72 Magdalen Road, Oxford OX4 1RE. PICK operating system. Suite of 5 modules for library housekeeping, available in various configurations for 1–3 users up to 64 users.

CALM (Computer Aided Library Management)
Pyramid Computer Systems Ltd, 9 Church Street, Reading, Berks RG1 2SB. From £7000 (including hardware). IBM XT and AT and compatibles, Televideo PM-16. Integrated software packages with 5 modules.

Ocelot
Oriel Computers Ltd, 1–5 West Street, Chipping Norton, Oxfordshire OX7 5LY. MS-DOS or PC-DOS. Less than £2000 per module. Suite of modules for catalogues, circulation control, acquisitions.

SAILS (Swets Automated Independent Library System)
Swets (UK) Ltd, Cranbook House, 287–291 Banbury Road, Oxford OX2 2JQ. Integrated set of modules (acquisitions, cataloguing, serials control, circulation control) designed for mainframe operation, but can be used with microcomputers as front-end terminals.

INFORMATION RETRIEVAL

Aquila
Kent Barlow Information Associates, 250 Kings Road, London SW3 5UE. CP/M (5¼ or 8″ disks): £310. Can also be interfaced with some commercial databases; interface modules are extra.

ASSASSIN-PC
MGS Computing Services, 132/133 Fairlie Rd, Slough, Berks SL1 4PY. Intertec Superbrain (with 10 Mb hard disk); IBM PC. Program derived from ASSASSIN minicomputer software; price includes all hardware.

BRS Search
BRS Europe, 26 Little Portland St, London W1N 5AF. 16-bit systems with UNIX.

Bibliotek
Scientific Software Products, 3171 Donald Ave., Indianapolis, Indiana 46224. Apple II and IIe; $195.

Eagle
Kent Barlow Information Associates, 250 Kings Rd, London SW3 5UE. RM 380Z, Apple II, CP/M, 16-bit systems. Uses the Common Command Language for searching.

Finder
Aaron/Smith Associates, Inc., Suite 518, 1422 West Peachtree Street NW., Atlanta, Georgia 30309. IBM PC and compatibles and TRS Model 11 or 12. Full text retrieval system.

Golden Retriever
Capital Systems Group Inc., 11301 Rockville Pike, Kensington, Maryland 20895. CP/M, IBM PC, TRS-80 Model II; $1800.

Information Systems Design, 23 Arthur Road, Erdington, Birmingham B24 9EX. Apricot range of microcomputers. £295. Can be bought integrated with Circ (see Circulation Control below).

InMagic
Head Computers Ltd, Oxted Mill, Spring Lane, Oxted RH8 9PB. CP/M and CP/M-86; £420 (CP/M), £780 (CP/M-86). Will also run on MS-DOS. There is an extra charge for DataStar interface.

KWIRS
Norman Paton, 21 Airyhall Gdns, Aberdeen AB1 7QL. Apple II; £28 plus £18 for Search module.

Librarian
Eurotec Consultants, 143 Hythe Hill, Colchester, Essex CO1 2NF. CP/M and CP/M-86; £450–£950.

Library Mate
Geosystems Inc., 802 E. Grand River, Williamston, MI 48895. Apple II, IIe, II Plus, III; £179.95. General-purpose data base management system with keyword retrieval capabilities.

Literature Search
Systemics Ltd, 21–23 The Bridge, Harrow, Middlesex HA3 5AG. Apple II and Apple III; £60 and £75.

Mikro-Polydoc
Norsk Senter for Informattikk, Forskingveien 1, Oslo 3, Norway. CP/M; Norwegian Kroner 15 000.

MicroCAIRS
RTZ Computer Services Ltd, 1 Redcliff Street, Bristol BS99 7JS. Many 16-bit microcomputers with minimum 10 Mb hard disk.

Micro-STATUS
AERE, Marketing & Sales, Building 329, Harwell, Oxfordshire OX11 0RA. Fortune 32 : 16, IBM PC.

Mirabilis
Central Information Services, University of London, Senate House, Malet St, London WC1E 7HU. CP/M (56 K RAM minimum); £250. A development of the FIRS program.

PRIMATE
Institute for Scientific Information, 132 High St, Uxbridge, Middlesex UB8 1DP. A complete hardware/software system, also capable of word processing and accessing online data bases.

Rasmus
Dudley Evans Computers Ltd, Archer House, 15 Market Square, Ely CB7 4NP. CP/M-86; £500.

SCIMATE
CITECH Ltd, PO Box 5, Ickenham, Middlesex UB10 8AF.

STAR
Cuadra Associates, 2001 Wilshire Blvd, Santa Monica, California 90403. Alpha Microsystems AM-100. A complete hardware/software system which, with special modules, can produce KWIC indexes and magnetic tapes for photocomposition.

Strix
Delta Design & Graphics, The Old Stud Farm House, Ossington Lane, Sutton on Trent, Neward. Southwest Technical Products S/09; £950 (£1045 with retrieval software for microfilm reader). Includes facilities for retrieval of documents stored on microfilm.

ACQUISITIONS

Bookline
Blackwell's Technical Services, Beaver House, Hythe Bridge St, Oxford OX1 2ET.
DEC Professional 350; £13857 (£16857 with PEARL: see Serials Control).
Hardware software package with 5 Mb hard disk. Can interface with Blackwell's
Bookfile, though user is not required to use Blackwell as supplier.

UNIFACE Order Production
Tacoma Public Library, 1102 Tacoma Avenue South, Tacoma, Washington 98402.
'Hardware independent'; $250. Can be used with BITS communications interface to
capture MARC records for use in acquisitions.

ADMINISTRATION

AV Equipment Inventory.
Media Center Factory, PO Box 13536, Greensboro, NC 27405. Apple II, II Plus;
IIe, TRS-80 I, III, IV; $30. Maintains details and locations of equipment.

Art Print Inventory
Media Center Factory, PO Box 13536, Greensboro, NC 27405. Apple II, II Plus,
IIe, TRS-80 I, III, IV; $20. Designed to keep track of art prints or art works:
includes details of subject.

Rangefinder
University of Rhode Island, Kingston, Rhode Island. Apple II Plus. Calculates the
shelf space available in library stacks based on an average size for each new book
added.

BIBLIOGRAPHIES

Bibliography Compiler
Libraries & Learning Inc., 210 5th Ave., New York NY 10010. Apple, Commodore
Pet, TRS-80; $20. Cassette-based system which stores bibliographies for printing
and updating. Available for other systems at 25% extra.

Bibliography Writer
Library Software Co., PO Box 23897, Pleasant Hill, California CA 94523. Apple II
Plus, TRS-80 Model III.

CATALOGUING AND CATALOGUE CARD PRODUCTION

AV Catalog Writer
Library Software Co., PO Box 23897, Pleasant Hill, California CA 94523. Prints a catalogue of the media held.

Avcat
Computer Business Systems, 1707 View St, Myrtle Point, OR 97458. TRS-80 (with 64 K RAM); $175. Produces catalogue cards for audio visual media.

Card
Capital Systems Group Inc., 11301 Rockville Pike, Kensington, MA 20895. TRS-80 and CP/M; $300. Prints catalogue cards to AACR2 format, including adding punctuation etc. Also available for AACR1.

Card Datalog
Data Trek Inc., 121 W.E. St, Encinitas, CA 92024. CP/M, Altos; $200.

Catalogue and Retrieval System
G + G Software, Old Cider House, Golant, Fowey, Cornwall. North Star Horizon (with 15 Mb hard disk); £750. System in use at Mid-Cornwall College of FE.

Computer Cat
Colorado Computer Systems Inc., 3005 West 74th Ave., Westminster, Colorado 80030. Apple II Plus and hard disk. A multi-user version is also available.

MITINET/retro
Information Transfer Inc., 502 Leonard St, Madison, WI 53711. Apple IIe, II Plus; $85. Supports retrospective conversion to MARC format records, using COM catalogue ($90) or existing COM union catalogue.

Telemarc
Gaylord Bros, PO Box 4901, Syracuse NY 13221. Apple II Plus, TRS-80. For catalogue card production with automatic indentation and punctuation.

CIRCULATION CONTROL

Apple Circ II and III
CTI Library Systems, 1455 South State St, Orem, Utah 84057. Apple II and Apple III (with hard disk); $1500, $3500.

Circ
Information Systems Design, 23 Arthur Road, Erdington, Birmingham B24 9EX. Apricot range of microcomputers. £995. Can be bought in integrated system with 'i' package for information retrieval (see Information Retrieval above).

College Library Accession System Software
G + G Software, Old Cider House, Golant, Fowey, Cornwall. North Star Horizon; £750.

Gaylord System 100
Gaylord Brothers Inc., Box 4901, Syracuse, NY 13221. Apple II; $2500.

Nonesuch Circulation System
Ringgold Management Systems, Box 368, Beaverton, Oregon 97075. 64 K RAM
and hard disk needed.

Overdue Book Checker
Media Center Factory, PO Box 13536, Greensboro, NC 27405. Apple II, II Plus,
IIe, TRS-80 I, III, IV; $50. Described as suitable for small- to medium-sized
libraries.

Telepen
SB Electronic Systems, Arden Grove, Harpenden, Herts AL5 4SL. Intelligent data
collection terminals with bar-code readers. Codestar terminal can be used at branch
locations.

INDEXING

Bookdex
Capital Systems Group Inc., 11301 Rockville Pike, Kensington, Maryland 20895.
TRS-80 Model II, CP/M, IBM PC; $450. Produces 'ready to publish' indexes from
page proofs (i.e. back-of-book indexing).

Documate Plus
Ortho Code Corp., PO Box 6191, Albany, California CA 94706. CP/M; $125. An
indexing program for documents prepared on a word processor. 'See' and 'see also'
references can be inserted.

Inforonics
Inforonics Inc., 550 Newtown Rd., Littleton, MA 04160. Produces keyword lists to
documents and text.

Macrex
H & D Colvert, 38 Rochester Road, London NW1 9JJ. CP/M systems and a range
of 16-bit microcomputers. £190. For back of book indexing.

Newsdex
Capital Systems Group Inc., 11301 Rockville Pike, Kensington, Maryland 20895.
TRS-80 Model II, CP/M, IBM PC; $450. Produces indexes to newspapers and
journals, including 'see' and 'see also' references.

Permdex
A. Yerkey, School of Information and Library Studies, State University, Buffalo
NY 14620. Software uses a simplified version of the PRECIS approach to indexing.

Poppytime Index Build
Poppytime Ltd, 40 Triton Square, London NW1 3HG. IBM PC, Sirius and Xerox 820. £950. System to build indexes to documents; contains word processing module which can be used separately.

ONLINE SEARCH ASSISTANCE

Astra Financial Journal
NEC Information Systems, Lexington, Maryland. NEC Astra Business System. Interface to Dow Jones News/Retrieval database via Telenet or Tymnet. Automatic dial-up, log-on and downloading. Downloaded data can be manipulated with word processing software

BITS (Boeing Intelligent Terminal System)
Boeing Computer Services, PO Box 24346, Seattle, WA 98124. 'Hardware independent'; $300. Intelligent terminal software with additional modules for text processing, graphics and spreadsheet applications.

Connect
Learned Information (Europe) Ltd, Besselsleigh Road, Abingdon, Oxford OX13 6LG. MS-DOS, PC-DOS and CP/M systems. £195.

CORTEX
British Library Bibliographic Services Division, 2 Sheraton St, London WC1V 0BE. Zenith Z-100, CP/M. Used to download records from MARC files for local editing.

DataLink
CL Systems Inc., 81 Norwood Ave., Newtonville, Massachusetts 02160. Offers assistance in accessing both CLSI-based files and selected IAC databases, using the latter's SEARCH HELPER. Searches are formulated on a microcomputer.

Headline
Head Computers, Oxted Mill, Spring Lane, Oxted, Surrey RH8 9PB. CP/M and CP/M-86, MS-DOS; £120.

HeadForm
Head Computers, Oxted Mill, Spring Lane, Oxted, Surrey RH8 9PB. £125. CP/M and MS-DOS systems. Format conversion software for copy data from one program to another. Will also handle downloaded records from online databases.

Liaison
CAPTEC Ltd, 3 St James' Terrace, Malahide, Co. Dublin. IBM PC, Sanyo 555 and other MS-DOS microcomputers. £280.

Micro Search
ERIC Clearing House, 130 Huntingdon Hall, Syracuse University Syracuse, NY 13210. Apple II Plus. A subscription includes floppy disks with subsets of the ERIC data base.

OL'SAM (Online Search Assistance Machine)
Franklin Institute Research Laboratory, 20th & Race Streets, Philadelphia PA 19103. North Star Horizon; $995. Complete hardware/software package available at $7500.

Sci-Mate
ISI, 3501 Market St, University Science Center, Philadelphia, PA 19104. CP/M, Apple II, IBM PC, TRS-80 Model II, Vector 3 & 4; $440. Search assistance for Dialog, BRS, ISI and Medline. Optional Personal Data Manager ($540) allows user to set up own data base of retrieved references.

Swift
Kent Barlow Information Associates, 250 Kings Rd, London SW3 5UE. Cifer 2684, Superbrain, Sirius; £225. An enhanced version (Magpie) is planned for the IBM PC which will also link with Aquila (see above).

Userlink
Userlink Systems Ltd, Mansion House Chambers, High Street, Stockport, Cheshire SK1 1EG. MS-DOS, PC-DOS and CP/M-86. Range of programs includes Assist, Information Transfer (uses artificial intelligence techniques) and Userlink Junior (for log-on procedure).

SERIALS CONTROL

Checkmate
Capital Systems Group Inc., 11301 Rockville Pike, Kensington, Maryland 20895. TRS-80, CP/M, IBM PC; $2500.

Magazine File
Media Center Factory, PO Box 13536, Greensboro, NC 27405, Apple II, II PLus, IIe, TRS-80 I, II, IV; $25. Allows for most operations except details of holdings and circulation lists.

Microcomputerized Periodical Management System
Avery International Research Center, 325 North Altadena Drive, Pasadena CA 91107. Apple IIe. Will handle up to 600 periodicals.

MicroLinx Check-in
Faxon Company Inc., 15 Southwest Park, Westwood, MA 02090. IBM XT or AT. Pricing options available. Also has bar code check-in facilities and a CD-ROM player and disk available.

OCLC SC350 Serials Control Module
OCLC Europe Ltd, Lloyds Bank Chambers, 75 Edmund Street, Birmingham B3 3HA. IBM PC and M300 Workstation. Links with OCLC online serials database.

PC-SMS (Serials Management System)
Dawson Serials Management Services, Cannon House, Folkestone, Kent CT19 5EE. IBM PC or compatibles. £1500 ('for those who place a significant proportion of orders through Dawson Subscription Agency') plus approx. £450 for database and communication software. Online option also available.

PEARL
Blackwell Technical Services, Beaver House, Hythe Bridge St, Oxford OX1 2ET. DEC Professional 350; £13857 (£16857 with Bookline: see Acquisitions). Hardware/software package including 5 Mb hard disk. Can be interfaced with Blackwell's periodicals network.

Appendix 2: Organizations

This is a list of the principal organizations involved in the use of microcomputers for information retrieval and in libraries. Further information is also available from the Library Association's Bibliographic and Information Systems Officer.

Advisory Unit for Computer Based Education (AUCBE)
19 St Albans Road, Hatfield, Herts AL10 0HU. AUCBE was initially responsible for the development of the program MicroQUERY. It is also investigating telesoftware and the use of the microcomputer in school libraries in the region.

Aslib (The Association for Information Management)
26–27 Boswell Street, London WC1N 3JE. Aslib's library has details of software suitable for information retrieval etc. Its research department is involved with the SIR project in schools.

British Computer Society
Information Officer, IEEE Library, Savoy Place, London. The Librarian offers an information service to BCS members.

Council for Educational Technology
3 Devonshire Street, London W1N 2BA. CET is closely involved in the development of telesoftware using PRESTEL.

Institute of Information Scientists
Special Interest Group on Computerized Information Management. The SIG organizes regular meetings, workshops etc. on word processing and microcomputers, many of which are later reported in its newsletter.

Library Technology Centre
Polytechnic of Central London, 309 Regent Street, London W1R 8AL. The Centre was opened in November 1982 and is funded jointly by the Department of Trade and Industry and the Britih Library. It is currently investigating library applications of local area networks, and provides demonstrations and advice.

Library Association
Verina Horsnell, Bibliographic and Information Systems Officer, 7 Ridgmount Street, London WC1E 7AE. The Officer is responsible for, among other things, activities connected with microcomputers, and maintains a list of contacts. There is also a New Technology Group of the Library Association.

National Computing Centre
Oxford Road, Manchester M1 7ED, (Microcomputer Centre, 11 New Fetter Lane,

London EC4A 1PU). NCC has investigated many aspects of micros and publishes a number of relevant books. The Microcomputer Centre offers advice and consultancy on the selection of hardware.

Scottish Council for Educational Technology
Dowan Hill, 74 Victoria Crescent Road, Glasgow G12 9JN. Like CET, SCET is involved in the development of telesoftware.

Appendix 3: An example of information retrieval using the FIRS system

The example of a microcomputer information retrieval system shown below uses the FIRS system from the University of London Central Information Service.

The application shown is an online search request management system, operating on a Cifer 2684 microcomputer under CP/M.

Each request for an online search is entered into the microcomputer and can be stored for future use. It is valuable to see, for example, if similar searches have been carried out in the past. A number of other questions can be put to the system to provide management information. The mode of operation of the system is essentially the same as a mainframe information retrieval system.

1. CREATION OF A DATA BASE

A) **FCREATE** (*bold terms are entered at keyboard*)
         ★ ★ FIRS ★ ★ file creation and compaction program

Copyright (C) 1980, 1981 CIS, University of London.
Unauthorised copying is illegal.

★ ★ FIRS ★ ★ system serial number : CF 042

CREATE or COMPACT : **CREATE**
         ★ ★ FIRS ★ ★ file creation program

Insert disc to receive new file in drive B – press 'return' when ready, (or <ESC> to abort) :
Is it a new disc? – Y/N : **N**
The FIRS files on the disc in drive B are:

SLOG   .FRS LOG   .FRS (*other existing files on disk*)

Do not use an existing FIRS file name

A file name consists of up to eight letters and/or digits.
The system will insert the appropriate suffixes (.FRS, .KEY etc).

File name : **USERS**   *(data base to be called 'USERS')*
Number of fields per record (1 – 15) : **13**

Field names:

Maximum length is 16 characters. They may contain any characters, including spaces. Any or all fields may be nameless (just key <RTN>).
If a field has a name, the name must be at least two characters in length.

Name of field 1 : **SRCH. NO.**
Name of field 2 : **STATUS**
Name of field 3 : **DATE**   *(fields in the data base)*
Name of field 4 : **REQUESTOR**
Name of field 5 : **ADDRESS**
Name of field 6 : **TELEPHONE**
Name of field 7 : **TYPE OF ENQUIRER**
Name of field 8 : **AUTHORISED BY**
Name of field 9 : **ALTERNATIVE ADDR**
Name of field 10 : **PAYMENT METHOD**
Name of field 11 : **SEARCH STRATEGY**
Name of field 12 : **HOSTS:DATABASES**
Name of field 13 : **NOTES**

Please confirm –

Field 1 is SRCH. NO.
Field 2 is STATUS
Field 3 is DATE
Field 4 is REQUESTOR
Field 5 is ADDRESS
Field 6 is TELEPHONE
Field 7 is TYPE OF ENQUIRER
Field 8 is AUTHORISED BY
Field 9 is ALTERNATIVE ADDR
Field 10 is PAYMENT METHOD
Field 11 is SEARCH STRATEGY
Field 12 is HOSTS:DATABASES
Field 13 is NOTES

Please confirm – Y/N : **Y**   *(enter details of how fields*
                                                are to be indexed)
Which fields are to be indexed?

For each field which is to be indexed you will be asked whether it is to be indexed as NAME, as ENTRY or by TEXT WORDS.

Refer to manual for further details – if in doubt choose TEXT WORDS

Is field 1 SRCH. NO. to be indexed? – Y/N : **Y**
Is this field to be indexed as 'NAME' (N), 'ENTRY' (E) or by TEXT WORDS (W) : **E**
Is field 2 STATUS to be indexed? – Y/N : **Y**
Is this field to be indexed as 'NAME' (N), 'ENTRY' (E) or by TEXT WORDS (W) : **E**

Is field 3 DATE to be indexed? – Y/N : **Y**
Is this field to be indexed as 'NAME' (N), 'ENTRY' (E) or by TEXT WORDS (W) : **E**
Is field 4 REQUESTOR to be indexed? – Y/N : **Y**
Is this field to be indexed as 'NAME' (N), 'ENTRY' (E) or by TEXT WORDS (W) : **E**
Is field 5 ADDRESS to be indexed? – Y/N : **Y**
Is this field to be indexed as 'NAME' (N), 'ENTRY' (E) or by TEXT WORDS (W) : **W**
Is field 6 TELEPHONE to be indexed? – Y/N : **N**
Is field 7 TYPE OF ENQUIRER to be indexed? – Y/N : **Y**
Is this field to be indexed as 'NAME' (N), 'ENTRY' (E) or by TEXT WORDS (W) : **E**
Is field 8 AUTHORISED BY to be indexed? – Y/N : **Y**
Is this field to be indexed as 'NAME' (N), 'ENTRY' (E) or by TEXT WORDS (W) : **E**
Is field 9 ALTERNATIVE ADDR to be indexed? – Y/N : **Y**
Is this field to be indexed as 'NAME' (N), 'ENTRY' (E) or by TEXT WORDS (W) : **W**
Is field 10 PAYMENT METHOD to be indexed? – Y/N : **Y**
Is this field to be indexed as 'NAME' (N), 'ENTRY' (E) or by TEXT WORDS (W) : **E**
Is field 11 SEARCH STRATEGY to be indexed? – Y/N : **Y**
Is this field to be indexed as 'NAME' (N), 'ENTRY' (E) or by TEXT WORDS (W) : **W**
Is field 12 HOSTS:DATABASES to be indexed? – Y/N : **Y**
Is this field to be indexed as 'NAME' (N), 'ENTRY' (E) or by TEXT WORDS (W) : **W**
Is field 13 NOTES to be indexed? – Y/N : **N**

Please confirm –

Field 1 SRCH. NO. is to be indexed as ENTRY
Field 2 STATUS is to be indexed as ENTRY
Field 3 DATE is to be indexed as ENTRY
Field 4 REQUESTOR is to be indexed as ENTRY
Field 5 ADDRESS is to be indexed as TEXT WORDS
Field 6 TELEPHONE is not indexed
Field 7 TYPE OF ENQUIRER is to be indexed as ENTRY
Field 8 AUTHORISED BY is to be indexed as ENTRY
Field 9 ALTERNATIVE ADDR is to be indexed as TEXT WORDS
Field 10 PAYMENT METHOD is to be indexed as ENTRY
Field 11 SEARCH STRATEGY is to be indexed as TEXT WORDS
Field 12 HOSTS:DATABASES is to be indexed as TEXT WORDS
Field 13 NOTES not indexed

2. ENTER DATA RECORDS INTO DATA BASE

A) **FTEXT** (*enter data base maintenance program*)

* * FIRS * * Information retrieval system

Copyright (C) 1980, 1981, 1982 CIS, University of London.
Unauthorised copying is illegal.

* * FIRS * * system serial number : CF 042

Data entry and editing program

Which disc drive are the files on – A or B : B

The FIRS files on this disc are –   *(This is the new data base)*

SLOG   .FRS LOG   .FRS USERS   .FRS

Filename (or (ESC)) : USERS

File USERS found

Field 1 is 'SRCH. NO.'
Field 2 is 'STATUS'
Field 3 is 'DATE'
Field 4 is 'REQUESTOR'
Field 5 is 'ADDRESS'
Field 6 is 'TELEPHONE'
Field 7 is 'TYPE OF ENQUIRER'
Field 8 is 'AUTHORISED BY'
Field 9 is 'ALTERNATIVE ADDR'
Field 10 is 'PAYMENT METHOD'
Field 11 is 'SEARCH STRATEGY'
Field 12 is 'HOSTS:DATABASES'
Field 13 is 'NOTES'

There are 0 records in the file
Length of file : 3 blocks

(any key to continue)

Options –		
	Read	R
	Write	W
	Edit	E
	Change files	C
	Index	I
	Search	S
	Append	A
	Exit the system	X

245

Choice : **W**
*Write – please confirm – Y/N : **Y**

Type H for help, or <RETURN> to continue : (*Enter first record*)
*(1)
SRCH. NO. : **0001**
STATUS : **0** (*0* = ongoing)
DATE : **830823**
REQUESTOR : **BLOGGS, A**
ADDRESS : **PHYSICS**
TELEPHONE : **2378**
TYPE OF ENQUIRER : **PG** (*PG* = *postgraduate*)
AUTHORISED BY : **SMITH, DR B**
ALTERNATIVE ADDR :
PAYMENT METHOD : **DE**
SEARCH STRATEGY : **LASERS INFRA RED RAMAN**
HOSTS-DATABASES : **DIALOG INSPEC INFOLINE CHEMICAL ABSTRACTS**
NOTES : **SEND ACCOUNT TO SUPERVISOR**
  ('R' for rewrite, <ESC>, any **other key** to continue)
*(2)
SRCH. NO. : **0002**
STATUS : **C** (*C* = complete)
DATE : **830825**
REQUESTOR : **JONES, E.F.**
ADDRESS : **ECONOMICS**
TELEPHONE : **2856**
TYPE OF ENQUIRER : **ST** (*ST* = Staff)
AUTHORISED BY : **WHITE, PROF. E.F.**
ALTERNATIVE ADDR : **POLITICS**
PAYMENT METHOD : **RG**
SEARCH STRATEGY : **RELATIONS UNITED KINGDOM ARGENTINA FALKLAND ISLANDS**
HOSTS:DATABASES : **DATASTAR ECONOMIC ABSTRACTS INTERNATIONAL DIALOG PAIS**
NOTES : 75 **ONLINE P   FFLINE PRINTS AWAITED**   (*typing error*)
  ('**R**' for rewrite, <ESC>, any other key to continue)
* *(2)
SRCH. NO. : **0002**   (*Go through record to correct 'NOTES' field*)
STATUS : C
DATE : 830825
REQUESTOR : JONES, E.F.
ADDRESS : ECONOMICS
TELEPHONE : 2856
TYPE OF ENQUIRER : ST
AUTHORISED BY : WHITE, PROF. E.F.
ALTERNATIVE ADDR : POLITICS
PAYMENT : RG
SEARCH STRATEGY : RELATIONS UNITED KINGDOM ARGENTINA FALKLAND ISLANDS
HOSTS:DATABASES : DATASTAR ECONOMIC ABSTRACTS INTERNATIONAL DIALOG PAIS
NOTES : **75 OFFLINE PRINTS AWAITED, INVOICE TO RESEARCH**

GRANT 123456   (*correct field*)
('R' for rewrite, <ESC>, any **other key** to continue)
*(3)
SRCH. NO. : **0003**
STATUS : **B**   (*new record*)
DATE : **830821**
REQUESTOR : **JONES, E.F.**
ADDRESS : **ECONOMICS**
TELEPHONE : **2856**
TYPE OF ENQUIRER : **ST**
AUTHORISED BY : **HARRIS, PROF. D**
ALTERNATIVE ADDR : **ECONOMICS**
PAYMENT METHOD : **DE**
SEARCH STRATEGY : **MONETARY POLICY INFLATION UNEMPLOYMENT**
HOSTS:DATABASES : **DATASTAR ECONOMICS ABSTRACTS INTERNATIONAL**
NOTES : **COST £25.23**
('R' for rewrite, <ESC>, any other key to continue)

Options –		
	Read	R
	Write	W
	Edit	E
	Change files	C
	Index	I
	Search	S
	Append	A
	Exit the system	X

Choice : **I**
*Index – please confirm – Y/N : **Y**   (*now index records, i.e.*
                                                create inverted index)

Loading indexing program

★ ★ FIRS ★ ★ Indexing program

Copyright (C) 1980, 1981, 1982 CIS, University of London.
Unauthorised copying is illegal.

★ ★ FIRS ★ ★ system serial number : CF 042

Please indicate diagnostic display required – full, partial or none
Enter F,P or N : **P**
Which disc drive is the file on – A or B : **B**
Remove system disc from drive A, insert spare disc
Press (return) when ready

The FIRS files on this disc are –

SLOG   .FRS LOG   .FRS USERS   .FRS

FILENAME : **USERS**

File USERS found

There are 3 records in the file.

Records edited since last index run :   0
Records deleted since last index run :   0

New records written :   3

Generate complete index – please confirm – Y/N : **Y**
  (memory 16996 bytes.)

* (B)
* Sorting (55 words).
* Sorted.

* Merging – pass 1
  (memory 13248 bytes.)
* 1 0001 (1)
* 2 0002 (1)
* 3 0003 (1)
* 4 830821 (1)
* 5 830823 (1)
* 6 830825 (1)
* 7 ABSTACTS (1)
* 8 ABSTRACTS (2)
* 9 ARGENTINA (1)
* 10 B (1)
* 11 BLOGGS A (1)
* 12 C (1)
* 13 CHEMICAL (1)
* 14 DATASTAR (2)
* 15 DE (2)
* 16 DIALOG (2)
* 17 ECONOMIC (1)
* 18 ECONOMICS (2)
* 19 FALKLAND (1)
* 20 HARRIS PROF D (1)
* 21 INFLATION (1)
* 22 INFOLINE (1)
* 23 INFRA (1)
* 24 INSPEC (1)
* 25 INTERNATIONAL (2)
* 26 ISLANDS (1)
* 27 JONES E F (2)
* 28 KINGDOM (1)
* 29 LASERS (1)
* 30 MONETARY (1)
* 31 O (1)
* 32 PAIS (1)
* 33 PG (1)
* 34 PHYSICS (1)
* 35 POLICY (1)

* 36 POLITICS (1)
* 37 RAMAN (1)
* 38 RED (1)
* 39 RELATIONS (1)
* 40 RG (1)
* 41 SMITH DR B (1)
* 42 ST (2)
* 43 UNEMPLOYMENT (1)
* 44 UNITED (1)
* 45 WHITE PROF E F (1)
* End of merge.   45 words in index.

* Copying main index
* Copy complete
* Copying postings file
  (1 blocks)
Output postings : 53
* Copy complete

Indexing complete

3. SEARCHING THE DATA BASE

A) **FSEARCH** (*enter this to call up search program*)

★ ★ FIRS ★ ★ Search program

Copyright (C) 1980, 1981, 1982 CIS, University of London Unauthorised copying is illegal.

Which disc drive is the file on – A or B : **B**

The FIRS files on this disc are –

SLOG   .FRS LOG   .FRS USERS   .FRS

FILENAME (or <ESC>) : **USERS**

File USERS   found

Field 1 SRCH. NO. is indexed as 'entry'.
Field 2 STATUS is indexed as 'entry'.
Field 3 DATE is indexed as 'entry'.
Field 4 REQUESTOR is indexed as 'entry'.
Field 5 ADDRESS is indexed as text words.
Field 6 TELEPHONE is not indexed.
Field 7 TYPE OF ENQUIRER is indexed as 'entry'.
Field 8 AUTHORISED BY is indexed as 'entry'.
Field 9 ALTERNATIVE ADDR is indexed as text words.
Field 10 PAYMENT METHOD is indexed as 'entry'.

Field 11 SEARCH STRATEGY is indexed as text words.
Field 12 HOSTS:DATABASES is indexed as text words.
Field 13 NOTES is not indexed.
There are 3 records in the file

Index contains 45 terms

* **S LASER:** (*search for the word 'LASER' but truncated on the right, colon is the truncation symbol*)
* Searching

LASERS (1)   (*one record found*)

* Total LASER: 1

Total : S1 : LASER : (1)

* **P**   (*Enter 'P' to see the record*)
Set number : **1**
The options are Print All (P) or Display (D)

'P' will print postings, in reverse order.
'D' will display one record at a time and await a further command.

Enter 'P' or 'D' : **D**
*(1)
0001
0
830823

BLOGGS, A   (*record displayed*)
PHYSICS
2378
PG
SMITH, DR B
DE

LASERS INFRA RED RAMAN
DIALOG INSPEC INFOLINE CHEMICAL ABSTRACTS
SEND ACCOUNT TO SUPERVISOR
    ('K' to keep, <ESC>, or any **other key** to continue)

* **S JONES-E-F\RE**(*searching for 'E.F.JONES' as a 'REQUESTOR'*)

* *Searching*

JONES E F   (2)

Total : S8 : JONES-E-F\RE   (2) (2 records found)

* **P**
Set number : **8**
The options are Print All (P) or Display (D)

'P' will print postings, in reverse order.
'D' will display one record at a time and await a further command.

Enter 'P' or 'D' : **D**
★ (3)
0003
B
830821
JONES, E.F.
ECONOMICS
2856
ST
HARRIS, PROF. D
ECONOMICS
DE
MONETARY POLICY INFLATION UNEMPLOYMENT
DATASTAR ECONOMICS ABSTACTS INTERNATIONAL
COST #25.23
   ('K' to keep, <ESC>, or any other key to continue)
★ (2)
0002
C
830825
JONES, E.F.
ECONOMICS
2856
ST
WHITE, PROF. E.F.
POLITICS
RG
RELATIONS UNITED KINGDOM ARGENTINA FALKLAND ISLANDS
DATASTAR ECONOMIC ABSTRACTS INTERNATIONAL DIALOG PAIS
75 OFFLINE PRINTS AWAITED, INVOICE TO RESEARCH GRANT 123456
   ('K' to keep, <ESC>, or any other key to continue)

★ **S C**＼ST   *(searching for all 'completed' searches)*
               ('C' in the 'ST' or 'STATUS' field)
★ Searching

C   (1)

Total : S9 : C＼ST (1)

★ P
Set number : **9**
The options are Print All (P) or Display (D)

'P' will print postings, in reverse order.
'D' will display one record at a time and await a further command.

Enter 'P' or 'D' : **D**
★(2)
0002

C
830825
JONES, E.F.
ECONOMICS
2856
ST
WHITE, PROF. E.F.
POLITICS
RG
RELATIONS UNITED KINGDOM ARGENTINA FALKLAND ISLANDS
DATASTAR ECONOMIC ABSTRACTS INTERNATIONAL DIALOG PAIS
75 OFFLINE PRINTS AWAITED, INVOICE TO RESEARCH GRANT 123456
  ('K' to keep, <ESC>, or any other key to continue(

* S FALKLAND AND ISLANDS   (*search for FALKLAND' together with 'ISLANDS'*)

* Searching

FALKLAND   (1)

ISLANDS   (1)

Total : S10 : FALKLAND and ISLANDS (1)

* P
Set number : **10**
The options are Print All (P) or Display (D)

'P' will print postings, in reverse order.
'D' will display one record at a time and await a further command.

Enter 'P' or 'D' : **D**
*(2)
0002
C
830825
JONES, E.F.
ECONOMICS
2856
ST
WHITE, PROF. E.F.
POLITICS
RG
RELATIONS UNITED KINGDOM ARGENTINA FALKLAND ISLANDS
DATASTAR ECONOMIC ABSTRACTS INTERNATIONAL DIALOG PAIS
75 OFFLINE PRINTS AWAITED, INVOICE TO RESEARCH GRANT 123456
  'K' to keep, <ESC>; or only other key to continue)

* C (*enter 'C' to exit from the retrieval program*)
Close – please confirm – Y/N : **Y**

Bibliography

(Note: This bibliography is largely restricted to the most recent references of the past two to three years. A full bibliography is maintained by one of the authors (PFB) and, in its complete version, contains over 650 references. The complete bibliography has been published by Gower Publishing Ltd, to whom thanks are due for permission to publish these extracts.)

SOURCES OF INFORMATION

Burton, P.F., *Microcomputers in Libraries and Information Services: An Annotated Bibliography*. Gower, 1986 (ISBN 0–566–03540–5).

Gates, H., *A Directory of Library and Information Retrieval Software for Microcomputers*. Gower, 1985 (ISBN 0–566–03531–6).

Hamilton, C.D., Kimberley, R. and Smith, C.H., *Text Retrieval: A Directory of Software*. Gower, 1985 (ISBN 0–566–03527–8).

Micro software evaluations. Edited by J.M. Nolan. Nolan Information Management Services, 1984 (ISBN 0–915995–03–4).

Pratt, A.D., Microcomputers in libraries, in, *Annual Review of Information Science and Technology*, Vol. 19, 1984. Knowledge Industry, 1984 (ISBN 0–86729–093–5), pp.247–269.

SURVEYS

Avallone, S., The trial by error phase. *Library Journal*, **110**(8), 96–99, 1985.

Batt, C., Microcomputers in UK public libraries: a review of current trends. *Program*, **19**(1), 39–47, 1985.

Burton, P.F., *Microcomputer applications in academic libraries*. British Library, 1983 (LIR Report No. 16) (ISBN 0–7123–3021–6).

Petrie, J.H., Microcomputers in Australian libraries and information services. *Program*, **19**(1), 20–28, 1985.

Rowbottom, M., Use of microcomputers in public libraries. *Library Micromation News*, (6), 11–16, 1984.

Yates-Mercer, P.A. and Bracegirdle, A.A.S., Word processing in information services. *Aslib Proceedings*, **36**(4), 187–198, 1984.

GENERAL GUIDES TO SELECTING MICROCOMPUTER SYSTEMS

The application of mini- and micro-computers in information, documentation and libraries: proceedings of the International Conference . . . Tel-Aviv, Israel, 13–18 March 1983. Edited by Carl Keren and Linda Perlmutter. North Holland, 1983 (ISBN 0–444–86767–8).

Armstrong, C.J. and Guy, R.F., Microcomputers or word processors in the library? *Reprographics Quarterly*, **14**(3), 98–103, 1981.

Cost estimates for integrated micro-systems, *Library Systems Newsletter*, **4**(6), 41–43, 1984.

Costa, B. and Costa, M., *A Micro Handbook for Small Libraries and Media Centers*. Libraries Unlimited, 1983 (ISBN 0–87287–354–4).

Falk, H., *Personal Computers for Libraries*. Learned Information, 1985 (ISBN 0–938734–10–5).

Fredenburg, A.M. and Pugh, W.J., Help in choosing microcomputer software and hardware: an update. *Online*, **10**(2), 38–54, 1986.

Gates, H., Factors to consider in choosing a microcomputer for library housekeeping and information retrieval in a small library: experience in the Cairns Library. *Program*, **18**(2), 111–123, 1984.

Gillman, P.L., Microcomputers in special libraries: a means to an end? *Electronic Library*, **2**(3), 197–203, 1984.

Grosch, A.N., Configuring a professional microcomputer for information processing. *Microcomputers for Information Management*, **1**(1), 15–29, 1984.

Kesner, R.M. and Jones, C.H., *Microcomputer Applications in Libraries: A Management Tool for the 1980s and Beyond*. Aldwych Press, 1984 (ISBN 0–86172–039–3).

Leggate, P. and Dyer, H., The microcomputer in the library: 1. Introduction. *Electronic Library*, **3**(3), 200–209, 1985.

Leggate, P. and Dyer, H., The microcomputer in the library: 2. Hardware and operating systems. *Electronic Library*, **3**(4), 260–274, 1985.

Mazursky, A.D., Corporate policies for effective microcomputer use. *Journal of Information Systems Management*, **1**(3), 82–84, 1984.

Megna, R.J., Solving big problems with small computers. *Museum News*, **62**(1), 61–66, 1983.

Microcomputers for Libraries: Product Review and Procurement Guide. James E. Rush Associates, 1984 (ISBN 0–912803–09–6).

Microcomputers in Museums. Edited by Richard B. Light and D. Andrew Roberts. Museum Documentation Association, 1984 (MDA Occasional Paper 7) (ISBN 0–905963–50–4).

Rush, J.E., Evaluation of integrated online library systems: minis and micros. Parts 1 and 2, in, 2nd National Conference on Integrated Online Library Systems, 1984, pp.306–323.

Seidmann, A. and Arbel, A., Microcomputer selection process for organizational information management. *Information and Management*, **7**(6), 317–329, 1984.

Walton, R.A., Microcomputers: *A Planning and Implementation Guide for Librarians and Information Professionals*. Oryx Press, 1983 (ISBN 0–89774–097–1).

Woods, L.A. and Pope, N.F., *The Librarian's Guide to Microcomputer Technology and Applications*. Knowledge Industry (for the American Society for Information Science), 1983 (ISBN 0–87629–045–5).

SOFTWARE

(For software intended for specific applications, see the application).

Armstrong, C.J., Micro-automation — the problems of selection. *Electronic Library*, **2**(3), 165–174, 1984.

Bookshelf: an integrated, modular package for the smaller library.) *Vine*, (54), 37–38, 1984.

Burton, P.F. and Gates, H., Library software for microcomputers. *Program*, **19**(1), 1–19, 1985.

Chen, C-c. and Hu, C., A statistical profile of micro-based software. *Microcomputers for Information Management*, **1**(3), 199–214, 1984.

Dyer, H., CALM: computer aided library management. *Electronic Library*, **3**(4), 242–248, 1985.

Hunter, E.J., *The ABC of BASIC: An Introduction to Programming for Librarians*. Bingley, 1982 (ISBN 0–85157–355–X).

Manson, P., Housekeeping systems for small libraries. *Library Micromation News*, (7), 11–16, 1985.

Pegg, N., Micro Library: an integrated system for small to medium sized libraries. *Vine*, (59), 26–34, 1985.

Tenopir, C., Identification and evaluation of software for microcomputer-based in-house databases. *Information Technology and Libraries*, **3**(1), 21–34, 1984.

Trevelyan, A. and Rowat, M., *An investigation of the use of systems programs in library applications of microcomputers*. British Library, 1983 (LIR Report No. 12) (ISBN 0–7213–3017–8).

HARDWARE

Davis, C.H., Portable micros: potential for information management. *Microcomputers for Information Management*, **1**(1), 57–65, 1984.

Goldstein, C.M., Storage technology: present and future. *Microcomputers for Information Management*, **1**(2), 79–93, 1984.

Mason, R.M., Current and future microcomputer capabilities: selecting the hardware. *Microcomputers for Information Management*, **1**(1), 1–13, 1984.

Torok, A.G., Ergonomic considerations in microcomputing. *Microcomputers for Information Management*, **1**(3), 229–250, 1984.

PROVISION OF MICROCOMPUTERS FOR PUBLIC USE, AND 'COMPUTER LITERACY'

Batt, C., Lending computer software. *Library Micromation News*, (4), 5–6, 1984.

Baughman, S., Software collection management. *Education Libraries*, **9**(1/2), 17, 30, 1984.

Dewey, P.R., *Public Access Microcomputers: A Handbook for Librarians*. Knowledge Indusry, 1984 (ISBN 0–86729–086–2).

Ebrahim, H., Bedfordshire County Library microcomputer project. *Program*, **19**(2), 150–159, 1985.

Freeman, S., The 'Apple Corps' at St. Louis. *Library Journal*, **110**(8), 110–112, 1985.

Geddes, G., How an education college library uses computer software. *Library Association Record*, **86**(10), 425–427, 1984.

Horne, D.L., Teaching microcomputer applications in the library. *Bulletin of ASIS*, **12**(1), 23–25, 1985.

Intner, S.S., Problems and solutions in descriptive cataloging of microcomputer software. *Cataloging and Classification Quarterly*, **5**(3), 49–56, 1985.

Lytle, S.S. and Hall, H.W., Software, libraries, and the copyright law. *Library Journal*, **110**(12), 33–39, 1985.

Marchbank, A.M., Libraries and micros. *SLA News*, (181), 13–18, 1984.

Marshall, P., The strange case of 'software lending right'. *Library Association Record*, **85**(7/8), 269, 1983.

Rose, P.E., Microcomputers: one library's approach. *Online*, **8**(1), 30–32, 1984.

Smisek, T., Circulating software: a practical approach. *Library Journal*, **110**(8), 108–109, 1985.

Strong, G.E. and Gibson, L., Adult computer literacy: the California State Library commitment. *Microcomputers for Information Management*, **1**(2), 143–153, 1984.

Tagg, W. and Templeton, R., *Computer software: supplying it and finding it.* British Library, 1983 (LIR Report No. 10) (ISBN 0–7123–3014–3).

Templeton, R. 'Public domain' software. *Aslib Proceedings*, **35**(11/12), 440–443, 1983.

Templeton, R. and Witten, A., *Study of cataloguing computer software: applying AACR2 to microcomputer programs.* British Library, 1984 (LIR Report No. 28) (ISBN 0–7123–3041–0).

MICROCOMPUTERS IN SCHOOL LIBRARIES

Cullen, P., Are we ready for the micro? *Audiovisual Librarian*, **10**(1), 30–33, 1984.

Gilman, J.A., *Information technology and the school library resource centre: the microcomputer as resourcerer's apprentice.* Council for Educational Technology, 1983 (ISBN 0–86184–098–4).

Microcomputer Information for School Media Centers. Edited by N.W. Thomason, Scarecrow Press, 1985 (ISBN 0–8108–1769–1).

School Libraries Group. *The microelectronics revolution and its implications for the school library.* School Libraries Group, 1981.

Smith, L. and Swigger, K., Microcomputers in school library media centers. *Drexel Library Quarterly*, **20**(1), 7–15, 1984.

ADMINISTRATION

Ben-Shir, R., Fast Inter Library Loans and Statistics: the second, enhanced release. *Library Software Review*, **4**(3), 132–138, 1985.

Borovansky, V.T. and Machovec, G.S., Microcomputer-based faculty profile. *Information Technology and Libraries*, **4**(4), 300–305, 1985.

Corbett, P.K., Automating reference department functions via an electronic spreadsheet. *Medical Reference Services Quarterly*, **3**(3), 85–88, 1984.

Desroches, R.A. and Rudd, M., Shelf space management: a microcomputer application. *Information Technology and Libraries*, **2**(2), 187–189, 1983.

Diskin, J.A. and FitzGerald, P., Library signage: applications for the Apple Mackintosh and MacPaint. *Library Hi-Tech*, **2**(4), 71–77, 1984.

Dowlin, K.E. and Hawley, B.G., The use of portable microcomputers for library inventory. *Microcomputers for Information Management*, **1**(1), 67–73, 1984.

Ede, S.J. and Wheatley, M.L., The use of microcomputers in interlibrary lending. *Interlending and Document Supply*, **13**(3), 63–70, 1985.

Evans, E.A., Microcomputers: an interlibrary loan application. *Special Libraries*, **75**(1), 17–27, 1984.

Everhart, N. and Hartz, C., Creating graphics with 'The Print Shop'. *Library Journal*, **110**(8), 118–120, 1985.

Gadsden, S.R. and Adams, R.J., *The administration of interlending by microcomputer*. British Library, 1984 (LIR Report No. 30).

Marklund, K., Dimensional flowcharting to improve library performance. *Microcomputers for Information Management*, **2**(2), 113–128, 1985.

Neill, C., Callaway, A. and Algermissen, V., Creation of a book order management system using a microcomputer and a DBMS. *Library Software Review*, **4**(2), 71–78, 1985.

Peasegood, A. and Stone, P., The model library: planning reshelving on a spreadsheet. *Library Micromation News*, (5), 2, 1984.

Pistorius, J.M. and Smith, J.W., Microcomputer application in a library for document ordering and delivery. *Electronic Library*, **3**(4), 290–295, 1985.

Potter, W.G., Modelling collection overlap on a microcomputer. *Information Technology and Libraries*, **2**(4), 400–407, 1983.

Pritcher, P.N., Integrating microcomputers and the information professional: strategies for training information managers to use the PC. *Online*, **9**(2), 15–22, 1985.

Romaniuk, E., Analysis of survey results using a microcomputer. *Information Technology and Libraries*, **4**(3), 233–236, 1985.

Shaw, D.S., Visicalc and the library acquisitions budget, in, *Online 83 Conference Proceedings*, 10–12 October 1983, pp.266–270.

Smith, D.E., Create: customized reference statistics programs. *American Libraries*, **15**(3), 179, 1984.

Stancil, I. and Harmeyer, K., A microcomputer application in information services evaluation, in, *National Online Meeting*, New York 12–14 April 1983, pp.523–528.

Witters, M., Interlibrary loans with a micro: clean and quick. *Online*, **8**(6), 53–61, 1984.

CATALOGUES

Bocher, R., MITINET/Retro in Wisconsin libraries. *Information Technology and Libraries*, **3**(3), 267–274, 1984.

Burton, P.F., Review of existing microcomputer systems for online access, in, *Online public access to library files: conference proceedings*. The proceedings of a conference held at the University of Bath, 3–5 September 1984. Edited by Janet Kinsella. Elsevier, 1985 (ISBN 0–946395–18–7), pp.27–44.

Cheng, C-C., Microcomputer-based user interface. *Information Technology and Libraries*, 4(4), 346–351, 1985.

Drake, V. and Smith, M.P., Retrospective conversion with REMARC at Johns Hopkins University. *Information Technology and Libraries*, 3(3), 282–286, 1984.

Duke, J.K., NAF Card: a microcomputer-based reference card generator. *Technical Services Quarterly*, 1(4), 73–82, 1984.

Lundeen, G. and Tenopir, C., Microcomputer-based library catalog software. *Microcomputers for Information Management*, 1(3), 215–228, 1984.

McNamara, F., OCLC's Cataloging Micro Enhancer software. *Library Software Review*, 4(4), 193–195, 1985.

Pemberton, J.E., Cataloguing on a micro with LIBRARIAN. *Library Micromation News*, (3), 7–14, 1984.

Rowlands, J., CARDS: a program to print multiple catalogue cards. *Library Micromation News*, (8), 10–11, 1985.

Schaub, J., CD-ROM for public access catalogs. *Library Hi-Tech*, 3(3), 7–13, 1985.

Stone, P., Pendlebury, J., Lewis, M. and Lee, S., Soft reading lists in Sussex. *Library Micromation News*, (5), 15–16, 1984.

Taylor, D., An online catalogue and issue system for smaller college libraries. *Library Micromation News*, (5), 14–15, 1984.

Taylor, D., Progress with G&G Software: an update on Harper Adams Agricultural College library's computerisation programme. *Library Micromation News*, (8), 3–6, 1985.

Turock, B.J. and Shelton, H., Online catalog in the small public library: enhanced subject access via microcomputer, in *5th National Online meeting*, 1984, pp.405–411.

CIRCULATION CONTROL

Clark, A.J., Choosing a microcomputer-based circulation system for the College of Librarianship Wales Library. *Program*, 20(1), 39–49, 1986.

Evans, P.W., Barcodes, readers and printers for library applications. *Program*, 17(3), 160–171, 1983.

Evans, P. and Palmer, D., Biblio-Tech systems for college size libraries. *Vine*, (57), 13–19, 1984.

Millar, P. and Cochrane, J., Administration of a reserve collection at Paisley College using dBase II. *Program*, 19(3), 262–270, 1985.

Rees, H., An online system for college libraries. *Vine*, (50), 42–46, 1983.

Thomason, N.W., *Circulation Systems for School Library Media Centers: Manual to Microcomputer*. Libraries Unlimited, 1985 (ISBN 0–87287–370–6).

Wood, L.R., An online microcomputer-based system at the University of Aston Library. *Program*, 18(1), 66–82, 1984.

Wood, L.R., A circulation control system on an ACT Apricot. *Vine*, (57), 4–12, 1984.

INDEXING

Batty, D., Microcomputers in index language design and development. *Microcomputers for Information Management*, 1(4), 303–312, 1984.

Bennett, J., Indexing The Scotsman. *SLA News*, (179), 5–7, 1984.

Faulkner, R.W., dBase III and newspaper indexing. *Library Software Review*, 4(5), 280–284, 1985.

Flower, E. and Menchen, G., A simple newspaper index using dBase II. *Small Computers in Libraries*, 4(10), 6–8, 1984.

Harter, S.P., Authex: printed index production. *Online Review*, 9(6), 451–453, 1985.

Orna, E., Using a micro to help in thesaurus construction. *MDA Information*, 8(3), 66–72, 1984.

Raper, R., The business of computer-aided indexing. *The Indexer*, 14(2), 118–119, 1984.

Tomaselli, M.F., Microcomputer-based indexing and abstracting. *The Indexer*, 14(1), 30–34, 1984.

Yerkey, A.N., A preserved context indexing system for microcomputers: PERMDEX. *Information Processing & Management*, 19(3), 165–171, 1983.

INFORMATION RETRIEVAL: GENERAL CONSIDERATIONS

Hjerppe, R., What artificial intelligence can, could, and can't, do for libraries and information services, in *7th International Online Information Meeting*, December 1983, pp.7–25.

MacDonald, J.S., *Bibliographic databases on microcomputers: a series of demonstrations for staff and research students in the humanities*. British Library, 1984 (BLR&D Report No. 5844).

Rowbottom, M., First steps in choosing information retrieval packages. *Library Micromation News*, (4), 13–16, 1984.

Winfield, B., Document transfer by satellite. *Aslib Proceedings*, 36(4), 177–185, 1984.

INFORMATION RETRIEVAL: SPECIFIC SYSTEMS

Armstrong, C.J., The use of a commercial microcomputer database management system as the basis for bibliographic information retrieval. *Journal of Information Science*, 8(5), 197–201, 1984.

Bailey, A.S., Creating and maintaining a database/databank comparison system with Lotus 1-2-3 on a (most of the time) IBM compatible micro. *Online*, 9(2), 86–92, 1985.

Betts, F.M., Quick Search Librarian fast but frustrating. *Electronic Library*, 2(3), 153–155, 1984.

Broering, N.C., An affordable microcomputer library information system developed at Georgetown University. *Microcomputers for Information Management*, 1(4), 269–283, 1984.

Brooks, H., Mirabilis information retrieval system. *Assignation*, 1(1), 23–27, 1983.

Brunelle, B., The vendor's corner: the BRS/SEARCH System. *Software Review*, 2(4), 245–254, 1983.

Callow, M., Producing an index to legal periodicals in the Foreign and Commonwealth Office library using Cardbox. *Program*, **19**(3), 251–261, 1985.

Cohill, A., Bibliophile brings microcomputer order out of chaos. *Online*, **8**(1), 34–41, 1984.

Dover, M., Community information the PIRATE way. *Library Micromation News*, (7), 2–4, 1985.

Felten, S.Y. and van Camp, A.J., Bibliotek: the bibliographic management software. *Online*, **8**(6), 47–50, 1984.

Garten, E.D., Library Mate: database with keyword indexing. *Electronic Library*, **2**(4), 242–243, 1984.

Gillespie, J., dBase II at Nepean, Ont., Public Library. *Canadian Library Journal*, **41**(6), 339–343, 1984.

Greengrass, L., Creating a database with children. *Library Journal*, **110**(8), 113–116, 1985.

Heaton, C., Local community information: a Citizens Advice Bureau joint project. *Library Micromation News*, (8), 6–9, 1985.

Hensel, M. and Nelson, R., CDROM: dramatic key to information dissemination and use. *Electronic Library*, **2**(4), 257–259, 1984.

Institut fur Maschinelle Dokumentation. Description of the IV+V System software package. *Microcomputers for Information Management*, **1**(3), 191–197, 1984.

Kittle, P.W., Putting the medical library online: electronic bulletin boards . . . and beyond. *Online*, **9**(3), 25–30, 1985.

Koll, M.B., Noreault, T. and McGill, M.J., Enhanced retrieval techniques on microcomputer, in *5th National Online Meeting*, 1984, pp.165–170.

Lundeen, G. and Tenopir, C., Microcomputer software for in-house databases: four top packages under $2000. *Online*, **9**(5), 30–38, 1985.

Mitlin, L.R., Bibliotek: designed for handling bibliographies. *Electronic Library*, **2**(4), 239–241, 1984.

Noerr, P.L. and Noerr, K.T.B., Browse and navigate: an advance in database access methods. *Information Processing and Management*, **21**(3), 205–213, 1985.

Palmer, R.C., *dBase II: An Introduction for Information Services*. Pacific Information, 1984 (ISBN 0–913203–07–6).

Portable software packages for information handling. *UNISIST Newsletter*, **12**(1), 1–7, 1984.

Portoghese, C. and Schrader, D.B., ZyINDEX: a powerful indexing and searching package. *Electronic Library*, **3**(1), 30–33, 1985.

Portoghese, C.P. and Schrader, D.B., SIRE: information storage and searching. *Electronic Library*, **3**(5), 314–316, 1985.

Rosenberg, V., The Personal Bibliographic System: a system for creating and maintaining bibliographies. *Information Technology and Libraries*, **2**(2), 184–187, 1983.

Rosenberg, V., The Personal Bibliographic System: a 'front end' to the online library. *American Libraries*, **15**(1), 46–48, 1984.

Rowell, P.P. and Utterback, N., Scientific literature currency and organization using a microcomputer. *Online*, **8**(1), 18–21, 1984.

Schulman, J-L., Video PATSEARCH: unique solution to a unique problem. *International Journal of Micrographics & Video Technology*, **2**(1), 21–25, 1983.

Sullivan, J., Using dBase II for bibliographic files. *Online*, **9**(1), 46–51, 1985.

Tally, R., DB Master for the Apple. *Small Computers in Libraries*, **4**(3), 1–3, 1984.

Tocatlian, J. and Rose, J.B., Unesco's General Information Programme and the application of information management software for microcomputers. *Microcomputers for Information Management*, **1**(4), 257–267, 1984.

Town, W.G., Microcomputer-based graphical input and retrieval of chemical structure information, in *8th International Online Information Meeting*, December 1984, pp.29–37.

Townley, C.T., ODIN: a multifunction, multitype library microcomputer network. *Information Technology and Libraries*, **3**(2), 174–176, 1984.
Vogt, S., Seekeasy. *Electronic Library*, **2**(4), 237–238, 1984.
Yerkey, N., Ultrafile for predefined data. *Electronic Library*, **2**(4), 233–236, 1984.

INFORMATION RETRIEVAL: CASE STUDIES

Barlow, D. and Buttery, R., An integrated administration information system for National Health Service authorities, in *7th International Online Information Meeting*, December 1983, pp.435–439.
Bordwell, S., dBase II — library use of a microcomputer database management system. *Program*, **18**(2), 157–165, 1984.
Dewey, P.R. and Garber, M., Easy to use microcomputer generated 'subject guide' wall chart. *Online*, **7**(2), 32–43, 1983.
Dewey, P.R., The electronic bulletin board arrives at the public library: the North-Pulaski Library prototype. *Library Hi-Tech*, **1**(4), 13–17, 1984.
Green, K.E. and Whiting, J., Combined production of a current awareness bulletin and database on a microcomputer. *Program*, **18**(4), 298–307, 1984.
Sonneman, S.S., The videodisc as a library tool. *Special Libraries*, **74**(1), 7–13, 1983.
Thompson, G.K., The use of microcomputers in information management in organizations of the United Nations system. *Microcomputers for Information Management*, **1**(3), 177–189, 1984.

LOCAL AREA NETWORKS

Collier, M., *Local area networks: the implications for library and information science*. British Library, 1984 (LIR Report No. 19) (ISBN 0–7123–3028–39).
Copeland, J.M. and Flood, S., Users and local area networks: opportunities for information transfer. *Electronic Library*, **2**(4), 273–277, 1984.
Copeland, J. and Flood, S., Database software for a local area network. *Library Micromation News*, (5), 11–13, 1984.
Levert, V.M., Applications of local area networks of microcomputers in libraries. *Information Technology and Libraries*, **4**(1), 9–18, 1985.
Mitev, N., Microcomputer networking in libraries: a progress report. *Library Micromation News*, (5), 8–10, 1984.

ONLINE SEARCH ASSISTANCE: GENERAL CONSIDERATIONS

Atkinson, S.D. and Watkins, S.G., Managing database information. *Online*, **9**(1), 52–66, 1985.
Foster, A., Extending the electronic library by downloading: its advantages and disadvantages. *Library Association Record*, **86**(9), 358–359, 1984.

Griffiths, J-M., Microcomputers and online activities. *Bulletin of the American Society for Information Science*, **10**(4), 11–14, 1984.

Jansen, A.A.J., Problems and challenges of downloading for database producers. *Electronic Library*, **2**(1), 41–51, 1984.

Lucchetti, S.C., CAS Online: access via lower cost Tektronix terminal look-alikes. *Online*, **8**(1), 44–49, 1984.

Mortensen, E., Downloading in online searching: a review of the literature, in *8th International Online Information Meeting*, December 1984, pp.331–342.

Murr, K.R., After downloading: how to get the most out of your microcomputer, in *5th National Online Meeting*. 1984, pp.243–246.

Roberts, S.K., The intelligent online terminal. *Information Today*, **1**(4), 28–30, 1984.

Warrick, T.S., Large databases, small computers and fast modems: an attorney looks at the legal ramifications of downloading. *Online*, **8**(4), 58–70, 1984.

ONLINE SEARCH ASSISTANCE: SPECIFIC SYSTEMS

Armstrong, C.J. and Large, *J.A.*, *A microcomputer teaching package for online bibliographic searching: manual, and workbook*. British Library, 1984 (BLR&D Reports Nos. 5740 & 5741) (ISBN 0–7123–3023–2 and 0–7123–3024–0).

Arthur, A., Online searching with an Apple II micro on a local area network. *Library Micromation News*, (6), 5–8, 1984.

Bean, C.S., Softerm and its use in online searching. *Online*, **8**(5), 52–56, 1984.

Chapman, P. and Noerr, P., BLAISE CORTEX: a microprocessor system for libraries. *Information Processing & Management*, **19**(2), 77–81, 1983.

Citroen, C.L., Multiuser microcomputer-assisted access to online systems, in *7th International Online Information Meeting*, December 1983, pp.37–44.

Ensor, P. and Curtis, R.A., Search Helper: low cost online searching in an academic library. *RQ*, **23**(3), 327–331, 1984.

Grotophorst, C.W., Another method for editing downloaded files. *Online*, **8**(5), 85–93, 1984.

Klausmeier, J., Microsearch: ERIC's approach to the downloading dilemma, in *5th National Online Meeting*, 1984, pp.149–154.

Kolner, S., The IBM PC as an online search machine. Part 1: anatomy for searchers. *Online*, **9**(1), 37–42, 1985.

Kolner, S., The IBM PC as an online search machine. Part 2: physiology for searchers. *Online*, **9**(2), 39–46, 1985.

Kolner, S., The IBM PC as an online search machine. Part 3: introduction to software. *Online*, **9**(3), 44–50, 1985.

Kolner, S., The IBM PC as an online search machine. Part 4: telecommunications and CROSSTALK XVI. *Online*, **9**(4), 27–34, 1985.

Levy, L.R., Gateway software: is it for you? *Online*, **8**(6), 67–79, 1984.

Marcus, R.S., An experimental comparison of the effectiveness of computers and humans as search intermediaries. *Journal of the American Society for Information Science*, **34**(6), 381–404, 1983.

Marcus, R.S., Computer-assisted search planning and evaluation, in *Proceedings of the 46th ASIS Annual Meeting*, 1983, Vol. 20, pp.19–21.

Miller, R., Designing your own low cost front-end software. *Online*, **9**(2), 94–98, 1985.

Mullen, A., Moller, E. and Blunck, M., Applications of PC 350 (DEC) for online searching, evaluation and upgrading of results from patent and literature files, in *8th International Online Information Meeting*, December 1984, pp.305–320.

Nevins, K., Microcomputers in the mainframe environment, in *8th International Online Information Meeting*, December 1984, pp.321–330.

Pratt, G.E.C., Using the microcomputer to simplify database access: designing interfaces to complex files. *Journal of Information Science*, **10**(3), 131–138, 1985.

Ryan, P.S., User friendly systems: the problem, the process, the progress at MGH Health Sciences Libraries, in *8th International Online Information Meeting*, December 1984, pp.5–11.

Stigleman, S., Instantcom: for online communications. *Online Review*, **8**(6), 539–542, 1984.

Tenopir, C., Dialog's Knowledge Index and BRS/After Dark: database searching on personal computers. *Library Journal*, **108**(3), 471–474, 1983.

Toliver, D.E., OL'SAM: an intelligent front-end for bibliographic information retrieval. *Information Technology and Libraries*, **1**(4), 317–326, 1982.

Wales, J.L., Using a microcomputer to access bibliographic databases: experience with Userlink software in the ICI Organics Division Information and Library Services Unit. *Program*, **18**(3), 247–257, 1984.

Williams, P.W., A model for an expert system for automated information retrieval, in *8th International Online Information Meeting*, December 984, pp.139–149.

Williams, P.W., Intelligent access to remote computer systems. *Library and Information Research News*, **8**(2), 5–10, 1985.

SERIALS CONTROL

Carney, R., InfoTrac: an inhouse computer-access system. *Library Hi-Tech*, **3**(2), 91–94, 1985.

Gadikian, R., Development of a periodicals list in dBase II. *Library Software Review*, **4**(3), 139–142, 1985.

Holmquist, L.J., Periodical management at the Apple Computer Library. *Database*, **7**(4), 31–35, 1984.

Schmidt, N.P., Choosing an automated serials control system. *Serials Librarian*, **9**(1), 65–86, 1984.

Serials control from OCLC Europe. *Vine*, (60), 40–46, 1985.

Vogel, J.T. and Burns, L.W., Serials management by microcomputer: the potential of DBMS. *Online*, **8**(3), 68–70, 1984.

PROFESSIONAL EDUCATION

Allen, B., Research project on the teaching of systems analysis and design of microcomputer-based library and information systems. *Program*, **18**(3), 261–262, 1984.

Armstrong, C.J., The design and implementation of a microcomputer teaching package for online bibliographic searching. *Education for Information*, **2**(1), 35–42, 1984.

Day, J.M. and Tedd, L.A., Computer software for education and training:

developments in UK schools of librarianship and information science, in *7th International Online Information Meeting*, December 1983, pp.471–481.

Large, J.A. and Armstrong, C.J., The development of a microcomputer emulation for teaching online bibliographic searching. *International Forum on Information and Documentation*, 8(2), 14–17, 1983.

Marx, B., Ghirardi, L. and Wolff-Terroine, M., A computer-aided instruction program for developing use of databases, in *6th International Online Information Meeting*, December 1982, pp.135–142.

Smith, N.R. and Roach, D.K., An interactive video disc training programme for online information retrieval, in *8th International Online Information Meeting*, December 1984, pp.493–501.

Wood, F.E., Teaching online information retrieval in United Kingdom library schools. *Journal of the American Society for Information Science*, 35(1), 53–55, 1984.

CASE STUDIES

Hare, C.E. and Winship, I.R., Using standard software for small-scale library projects: experience at Newcastle upon Tyne Polytechnic with Wordstar and dBase II. *Program*, 20(1), 62–70, 1986.

Harrison, D. and Batt, C., *Microcomputers in Public Libraries*. Public Libraries Research Group, 1983 (ISBN 0–9503801–5–6).

Holland, M.P. and Bean, M.H., The IBM Personal Computer in a large academic library, in *Online 83 Conference Proceedings*. 10–12 October 1983, pp.118–123.

Milliot, J., *Micros at Work: Case Studies of Microcomputers in Libraries*. Knowledge Industry Publications, 1985 (ISBN 0–86729–117–6).

Rowlands, J., Compsoft DMS Delta: library applications at Scunthorpe Central Library. *Vine*, (57), 27–31, 1984.

Williams, T., Microcomputer applications in a hospital library. *Bulletin of the Medical Library Association*, 73(2), 207–210, 1985.

Wray, S., Some notes on microcomputer applications in a library. *Library Micromation News*, (6), 3–5, 1984.

OTHER APPLICATIONS

Bacsanyi, K., ELL: Education Library Locator. *Education Libraries*, 9(1/2), 25, 29, 1984.

Regen, S.R. and Chen, C-c., Microcomputers: independence and information access for the physically handicapped. *Microcomputers for Information Management*, 1(4), 285–301, 1984.

Snell, M.J. and Duggua, H., Microtext — electronic blackboard, expert system or teaching package. *Library Micromation News*, (8), 9–10, 1985.

Software index

Subject index